THE PRISON

THE PRISON
Policy and Practice

Gordon Hawkins

The University of Chicago Press
Chicago and London

GORDON HAWKINS is associate professor of criminology at the University of Sydney, Australia. He has been a lecturer at the University of Leeds, a fellow of the University of Wales, and an assistant principal of the United Kingdom Prison Staff College. He is the coauthor of *The Honest Politician's Guide to Crime Control* and *Deterrence: The Legal Threat in Crime Control,* both published by the University of Chicago Press.

The University of Chicago Press, Chicago 60637
The University of Chicago Press, Ltd., London

Library of Congress Cataloging in Publication Data

Hawkins, Gordon, 1919–
  The prison.

  (Studies in crime and justice)
  Bibliography: p.
  Includes index.
  1. Prisons. 2. Imprisonment. 3. Prisoners—
Legal status, laws, etc. I. Title. II. Series.
HV8665.H39 1976 365'.6 75-20892
ISBN 0-226-31999-7

CONTENTS

PREFACE

This book is principally concerned with penology in the narrow sense of that word which refers to prisons and prison management. No attempt is made to cover the whole field of government policies and practices dealing with persons convicted of crimes, for which the term "corrections" is frequently used nowadays instead of "penology."

The adoption of this restricted frame of reference may seem to require some explanation at a time when the place of the prison in the correctional universe is widely regarded as being grossly and improperly extensive. Indeed when what one may call the Kropotkin solution to the prison problem—abolish them all—is enjoying a revival among contemporary criminologists an apology seems to be called for. As this topic is discussed at length in the text, it will be sufficient to refer to it here very briefly.

Having spent some five years as a prisoner in a variety of penal institutions, Kropotkin was at least as well qualified as most of those who have written on this subject. And he was in no doubt that prisons should be abolished. The prison system, he wrote in his *In Russian and French Prisons* was "wrong from the very foundation" (1887, p. 304). There was no point in considering meliorative measures. "Nothing easier than to build Administrative Utopias" (ibid., p. 332); but "the more one reflects about the partial improvements which might be made; the more one considers them under their real, practical aspect, the more one is convinced that the few which can be made will be of no moment, while serious improvements are impossible" (ibid., pp. 303–4).

The immediate impact of Kropotkin's work must have been diminished by the fact that agents of the Russian government attempted to buy up the entire first edition. They succeeded so well, apparently, that the author seeking a copy for himself shortly afterwards found it unobtainable. However, the book was reissued by another publisher and, according to a somewhat cryptic remark in Kropotkin's biography, "sufficient precautions were taken this time to prevent a recurrence of the previous incident" (Woodcock 1950, p. 198). Even so, the practical consequences of its publication must have been less than Kropotkin had hoped. Nearly a century later prisons are still with us. Indeed those he condemned still stand and are more than fully occupied. Their number has, in fact, been vastly augmented throughout the world. Prison-building programs continue to be approved and implemented.

Moreover "the bulky literature of prison discipline" which Kropotkin despised has also proliferated. Today our library shelves are crowded with a variety of literature on prisons: government publications, historical accounts, reformist tracts, sociological studies, committee reports, the bitter reminiscences of ex-inmates, the ghostwritten memoirs of ex-wardens. A great deal of that literature is purely descriptive, although the need for penal reform is a recurrent theme. Nevertheless, for the most part, the prison is accepted as a necessary, if not altogether desirable, social institution; "the black flower of our civilization," as Nathaniel Hawthorne described it, but still an essential feature of society.

Recently, however, the traditional reformist theme has given way to a radical type of critique, more akin to that of Kropotkin, in which there are unmistakable echoes of his description of those "'respectable people' who conceal under a Christian exterior a Pharisaic egotism"; and the "cold contempt for human nature" of "the philanthropists who have schemed our prison discipline" (Kropotkin 1887, pp. 319–26). Historians have suggested that the benevolent claims of the designers of the penitentiary really masked hostility to lower-class groups and a desire to provide a dumping ground for social undesirables. Sociologists have argued that the real social function of the prison is to repress deviation from middle-class norms, maintain the status quo, and preserve an inequitable social order.

Many penal reformers have abandoned demands for improved prison conditions and have adopted as a slogan "Break down the walls!" Imprisonment, it is said, so far from being reformative, leads far more often to the increased criminalization of those confined. Offenders are more likely to commit further offenses when released from prison than if they had been subjected to some alternative punishment. Moreover what is called "the rehabilitative ideal" or "the reformist ideology" or "the individualized treatment model" is denounced as being in practice more punitive, unjust, and inhumane than either the barbarities of earlier centuries or the straightforward pursuit of retribution and deterrence. As a result, although, as Lloyd Ohlin put it recently, "an intense and critical reappraisal of the system of correctional services is now in full stride in the United States," the prison has been largely neglected; except that on occasion it serves as an example of our hypocrisy regarding rehabilitation, our intolerance of deviants, or our refusal to deal with the root causes of crime such as poverty, discrimination, unemployment, ignorance, overcrowding, and so on.

In this book, by contrast, it is argued that the prison will, in some form, be with us for decades to come. Indeed all the evidence suggests that, for a long time ahead, some proportion of offenders will be kept in secure institutions similar to, and in many cases the same as, those in which the majority of offenders are now confined. It becomes necessary therefore to direct attention specifically to the prison as it is now, and what follows is in large part a critical reappraisal of the current theory and practice of imprisonment. It is assumed, however, that, pace Kropotkin, serious improvements are *not* impossible, and, accordingly, suggestions for reform are made.

It will be clear that many issues relating to imprisonment are not dealt with in the book. In particular there is no discussion of sentencing, the mixture of minorities in prisons, or the freeing of persons who do not reasonably belong in them. This is quite deliberate. The book is concerned with essential, intrinsic problems which will remain however much sentencing policy, the composition of the prison population, or the criminal law may change. It does not pretend to be encyclopedic. No attempt is made to provide coverage of all aspects of the organization and administration of prisons or to offer a comprehensive treatment of the whole range of problems which arise in connection with the institutional confinement of criminals.

What is attempted is a critical analysis of some key issues which arise from the use of imprisonment as a penal method, though in some cases they are issues which are being raised today in public discussions of prisons and owe their selection in part to that consideration. They have also been selected because they are matters which deserve special attention in any consideration of the subject of imprisonment. Possibly, what has been lost in breadth may be to some extent outweighed by a gain in depth.

The discussion is developed throughout by reference to the major literature and research findings in the field. I have tried to break with what has been called "the tradition of unsupported assertion which is general in literature on prisons" (Thomas 1972, p. xiv). It may not be out of place to add that the argument is also informed by my seven-year experience in the governor grades of the English prison service.

For two of those years I ran the Long-term Young Prisoners Centre at Wakefield Prison, which housed a group of about fifty youths, all under twenty-one, convicted of very serious crimes of violence and serving long and in many cases indeterminate sentences of imprisonment. It was the belief of some of those who sentenced these youths that they were being "taught a lesson." However that may be, it was certainly an educational experience for me, although I do not wish to claim any special authority on that account. I mention it not merely from vanity, but to disarm the suspicion that I might be one of those persons described by Dr. Johnson as "apt to think themselves qualified by Books to treat on Subjects which are only to be understood by Observation and Experience."

This book was written during the tenure of a research fellowship at the Center for Studies in Criminal Justice of the University of Chicago Law School. I am very grateful to that law school for giving me the opportunity to work there and to Sydney University Law School for enabling me to take the opportunity.

In writing the book I have enjoyed the help and advice of three men especially: Dean Norval Morris of the University of Chicago Law School, Professor Hans W. Mattick, director of the Center for Research in Criminal Justice, University of Illinois, Circle Campus, and Professor Franklin E. Zimring, director of the Center for Studies in Criminal Justice, University of Chicago. It is impossible to settle the proportion of gratitude due to them severally. Let me say only that the collective influence on this work of Morris's creativity, Mattick's experience and erudition, and Zimring's critical acuity has been profound.

I am grateful also for compilation of the index and very able research and editorial assistance from William Geller; and to Rick Salomon for the assiduous and successful pursuit of inaccessible data and materials.

Finally, typing and retyping a manuscript is often a thankless task . . . I thank Linda Sue Seth.

1   The Prison and Its Critics

A Victory of Mind over Matter

Historians of imprisonment used frequently to begin by regaling their readers with a feast of past atrocities. This was followed by an account of the way in which, with the growth of rationality and humanity, we had in this century at last moved into the enlightened era of contemporary corrections. It is true that it was usually admitted that progress had not been uniform in all of the prison systems in the United States. It was acknowledged that there were black spots and that there had been delays and even regressions. But in general the picture was such as to induce in readers feelings of superiority regarding the barbarities of the past and of complacent virtue in relation to the present.

Today, in the aftermath of Attica and similar disturbances, this comfortable scenario is regarded by many as a ludicrous distortion of the facts. Indeed, a curious reversal has taken place. Thus in David Rothman's *The Discovery of the Asylum* it is implied that the treatment of criminals in the colonial period was benign by contrast with subsequent developments following "the invention of the penitentiary." "By what criteria," he asks, "is a penitentiary an improvement over the stocks or a system of fines and whippings?" (1971, p. xv).

Moreover, a number of social historians have argued that the nineteenth-century penal reformers who have in the past been praised for their humanitarian concern were in reality primarily concerned with the control of lower-class groups and the maintenance of the status quo. The harsh treatment of some of these hitherto respected figures incidentally reminds one of E. M. Forster's suggestion that one of the consolations of history is that "we can recover self-confidence by snubbing the dead."

However that may be, the "new" historians have themselves met with considerable criticism including charges that their picture of seventeenth- and eighteenth-century colonial society is idealized; that they have oversimplified the motives of the early reformers; that they have wrongly assumed that the historical consequences of the actions of those reformers reflect their original intentions; and that they have misinterpreted the past in accordance with their own political or ideological affiliations.

As most of these criticisms in one form or another, in greater or less degree, apply to all historians past or present, none of this might seem to be of much interest to anyone except professional historians and students of comparative historiography. But there is one criticism which is of more general interest. Professor Gerald N. Grob, in an illuminating article which deals specifically with Rothman's book among others, suggests that such works "illustrate the firm belief of individual scholars that the function of history is didactic, that a knowledge of past 'errors' will provide a beacon light for corrective action in the present and the future.... Their basic objective, therefore, is to explain ... in order to lay the basis for a more enlightened contemporary policy" (1973, p. 44). But he says, "I seriously doubt that historians are necessarily wiser human beings because they are historians" (ibid., p. 52).

This criticism, which recalls Hegel's dictum that men have never learned anything from history, is valid only insofar as it implies that historians do not necessarily possess better judgment than other men. But they inevitably acquire greater knowledge in their own field of inquiry. And the belief that knowledge of past errors can provide guidance for the future is not a scholarly idiosyncrasy but a basic principle of rational action in any sphere.

The lessons to be learned from history are largely determined by the questions we ask about it. And the important questions from the point of view of penological theory and practice are very different from those we might ask if we were primarily interested in, for example, the theater, agriculture, public health, the culinary arts, or something like the validity of the Marxist interpretation of history.

For the penologist the fundamental question is that which Kropotkin believed preoccupied the best minds of the nineteenth century: What shall we do with those who break the law? And fortunately that is precisely the question which the nineteenth-century penal reformers asked themselves and answered in a fashion which was to be conclusive for more than a century.

Now it may be true, as Kropotkin believed, that the reformers were pharisaic egotists; or, as contemporary critics have argued, that they were conservatives whose primary interest was in controlling lower-class groups and restoring order and stability to the urban community; or, as others have suggested, that they were Christian millenarians who wanted to save souls. But the penologist's concern is with the nature of the answer they gave to his fundamental question rather than with their motivation, morality, or role in the dialectical process of historical development.

The answer they gave was, of course, the penitentiary or prison system. This is not to say that punitive imprisonment was not used in earlier periods of history. But there is no doubt that the development of large prisons or penitentiaries serving wide areas—the development of what Paul Tappan called "the movement toward mass imprisonment"—was an American innovation for which the Pennsylvania Quakers may justly be credited—or blamed. This was certainly the view of those living at the time. Moreover, in the beginning, although there was some criticism, it was largely credit that was given.

Thus Francis Lieber, who translated Beaumont and Tocqueville's *On the Penitentiary System in the United States* into English, was in no doubt about the novelty or the merits of the system. Writing from "Manhattanville, City of New York" in 1833, he said, "[I]t is a matter of pride to every American, that the

new penitentiary system has been first established and successfully practiced in his country. That community which ... per-
severed in this novel experiment, until success has crowned its
perseverance, must occupy an elevated place in the scale of
political or social civilization. The American penitentiary system
must be regarded as a new victory of mind over matter—the great
and constant task of man" (Beaumont and Tocqueville 1964,
p. 6).

Of course it is true that the various elements that went to make
up the penitentiary systems were not entirely novel. Thus the
Eastern Penitentiary in Philadelphia was built on a plan designed
by the English architect Haviland, which was in part adopted
from the San Michele House of Correction in Rome and the
House of Correction at Ghent in Belgium, on both of which the
eighteenth-century prison reformer John Howard had commented
favorably. As to the reformatory or corrective approach to
offenders, it was embodied, at least in a rudimentary form, in the
Elizabethan working houses or houses of correction from which,
Coke stated, people "come out better" than they do from the
common gaols. Indeed the idea is to be found, says Thorsten Sellin,
"in documents of ancient China and in the writings of Plato."

Yet the primacy established by the Pennsylvania Quakers is of
more than merely antiquarian interest. It is not just a historical
curiosity that their penitentiaries became models for America and
the rest of the world. For the massive buildings constructed in the
nineteenth century were in most countries to remain in use
throughout the twentieth century. And it was not only the
buildings that survived. As William Nagel puts it, "The endur-
ance of these monolithic structures is surpassed only by the
tenacity of the assumptions and attitudes on which they were
founded" (Nagel 1973, p. 10).

Today those assumptions and attitudes are being seriously
questioned. What is sometimes overlooked is that they were also
seriously questioned by contemporary observers. Not all of those
earnest European visitors who came to inspect and report on the
new model prisons and the new system were enthusiastic about
what they saw. Beaumont and Tocqueville admired much, but
they had marked reservations. Their basic attitude was skeptical,
especially in relation to the idea of reformation in the sense of
"the radical change of a wicked person into an honest man."

They were quite explicit: "[W]e would say positively, if the penitentiary system cannot propose to itself an end other than the radical reformation of which we have just spoken, the legislature perhaps should abandon this system" (Beaumont and Tocqueville 1964, pp. 87–89).

In the years which have followed there have been many who felt that they were right. What happened in 1971 at New York's Attica Correctional Facility, and both earlier and later in a number of other prisons, is seen by many as final confirmation of the failure of the experiment begun by the Philadelphia Quakers with such high hope nearly a century and a half ago. If there are any persons still celebrating this particular victory of mind over matter, they have in recent years been discreet about it. Those who have been most audible have in fact been critical, and insofar as there are lessons to be learned from history it is to the critics who have been at pains to elucidate them that we have to refer.

THE CRITICS
For purposes of exposition it is possible to define four principal lines of criticism which I shall call the abolitionist, the rigorist, the reformist, and the reductivist, and I shall deal with them in that order.

Abolitionism
There is about the polemics of the prison abolitionists something of the exhilarating character which commonly infects the writing of those who are prepared to follow an argument to its logical conclusion—and beyond. The absence of tiresome qualifications, cautious parentheses, and saving clauses seems in itself like a foretaste of the mass liberation proposed. Yet on closer examination of prison abolitionist literature it becomes clear that this initial impression is misleading. In the first place, many of those who use abolitionist language are not really abolitionists. In the second place, even in the case of those who are unequivocally committed to the abolition of prisons one finds that the fulfillment of that aim is seen as dependent upon the prior achievement of other changes in social organization, changes so universal in scope and radical in nature that by comparison the abolition of prisons seems a relatively minor adjustment.

Numerous examples of persons wrongly taken to be prison

abolitionists can be found. For instance, Jessica Mitford in *Kind and Usual Punishment* cites Frank Tannenbaum as one of "those who looked beyond palliative reform proposals to the essential character of prison, found it intrinsically evil and not susceptible to reforms, hence have advocated abolishing prisons altogether." And she quotes him as writing: "We must destroy the prison, root and branch. When I speak of the prison, I mean the mechanical structure, the instrument, the technique, the method which prison involves" (Mitford 1973, pp. 272-73).

Although this may look like an unambiguous demand for the abolition of prisons, it is clear, when one refers to Tannenbaum's *Wall Shadows*, from which the quotation was taken, that it is not. What he meant is clear in the next paragraph when he says: "The suggestion for the destruction of the prison building is not revolutionary.... Those who argue that the old prison, with its isolated cells, with its narrow windows, its high walls, its constant dampness and semi-darkness, is essential to the proper handling of the prison population are simply revealing their own incompetence, fear, lack of insight into the technique of association."

Tannenbaum was, in fact, a reformist and a great admirer of the celebrated reforming warden of Sing Sing, Thomas Mott Osborne, whose biography he wrote. In *Wall Shadows*, moreover, he follows the passages quoted with details of the kind of reforms he favored, including such things as better medical facilities, the reorganization of prison industries, a systematic educational program and "the reorganization of control and the proper grouping of the prison population" (Tannenbaum 1922, pp. 142-50).

Another writer who is sometimes taken to be an abolitionist is George Bernard Shaw. Giles Playfair and Derrick Sington, in *Crime, Punishment and Cure*, refer to him as one who saw "that the evils of imprisonment are inextricable from imprisonment itself" (1965, p. 13). Jessica Mitford also cites the passage in Shaw's *The Crime of Imprisonment* which runs, "[I]f any person is addressing himself to the perusal of this dreadful subject in the spirit of a philanthropist bent on reforming a necessary and beneficent public institution, I beg him to put it down and go about some other business" (Shaw 1946, p. 13). But those who read on discover that Shaw not only recommended compulsory euthanasia for "incorrigibly dangerous persons" but "detention and restraint" for "persons defective in the self-control needed for a free life in modern society" (ibid., p. 119).

Two other examples may be mentioned briefly. John Bartlow Martin in *Break Down the Walls* writes, "Prisons have failed as deterrents to crime. They have failed as rehabilitative institutions. What then shall we do? Let us face it: Prisons should be abolished." But reading on, one finds that what he objects to are "the mammoth brutalizing *prisons of today.*" "We shall abolish prisons *as we know them now*" he says, and goes on to say that "we need to build not a dozen new institutions but scores of them" (1954, pp. 268–73; my italics).

Similarly, Playfair and Sington write, "We believe that there can be no truly civilized solution to the problem of crime prevention so long as the prison system survives" (1965, p. 13). "We are convinced that if a constructive penal policy is ever to be developed, there must be legislative action to abolish imprisonment as a sanction of criminal justice" (ibid., pp. 53–54). But once again one finds later that this does not entail abolition but rather the "replacement of prisons ... by small nonpunitive custodial treatment centres, psychiatrically and/or sociologically based, and adapted to individual needs from the viewpoints of both treatment and security" (ibid., p. 336).

But if some "abolitionist" proposals are really demands for reform, expressed in figurative terms for rhetorical effect, this is certainly not true of all of them. It is not true, for example, of Kropotkin's advocacy of prison abolition, which was referred to in the preface to this book. Kropotkin is an example of the other kind of abolitionist I distinguished who is absolutely committed to that objective but regards large-scale reorganization of society, including in his case "a thorough transformation of the present relations between work and capital," as a necessary condition of its achievement. "Some thoroughly new departure is unavoidable," he said.

The new departure Kropotkin had in mind was expounded in the form of a political prospectus rather than a contribution to penology as traditionally conceived. "Let us organize our society," he wrote, "so as to assure to everybody the possibility of regular work for the benefit of the commonwealth—and that means, of

course, a thorough transformation of the present relations between work and capital; let us assure to every child a sound
education and instruction, both in manual labour and science, so
as to permit him to acquire, during the first twenty years of his
life, the knowledge and habits of earnest work—and we shall be
in no more need of dungeons and jails." Thus, "two-thirds of all
breaches of law being so-called 'crimes against property,' these
cases will disappear, or be limited to a quite trifling amount, when
property, which is now the privilege of the few, shall return to its
real source—the community." As for crimes against the person,
Kropotkin acknowledged that there would continue to be "a
limited number of persons whose anti-social passions—the result
of bodily diseases—may still be a danger to the community." But
to "lock them up in prisons" would be, he said, a "wicked
solution of the difficulty."

All that was required was "liberty and fraternal care" (Kropotkin 1887, pp. 365–70). "Fraternal treatment to check the development of the anti-social feeling which grows up in some of us," he
wrote, "is the only means we are authorized in applying, and can
apply, with some effect to those in whom these feelings have
developed in consequence of bodily disease or social influences"
(ibid., p. 353). Unfortunately, he did not indulge in further
elaboration of the proposed fraternal treatment. The antisocial
passions, he said simply, "can receive another direction, and most
of them can be rendered almost or quite harmless by the
combined efforts of those who surround us" (ibid., p. 367).

Another example of this approach may be found in the writings
of Clarence Darrow, who declared firmly that "there should be no
jails.... They are a blot upon any civilization." He argued that
there would be no necessity for jails, that we could "wipe them
out," if we took the appropriate steps "to do away with what we
call crime." Moreover he provided a recipe for achieving that
objective, although he acknowledged that "it is not so easy to do
it."

"I will tell you how to do it," he wrote; "it can be done by giving
the people a chance to live—by destroying special privileges....
Make fair conditions of life. Give men a chance to live. Abolish
the right of private ownership of land, abolish monopoly, make
the world partners in production, partners in the good things of

life. Nobody would steal if he could get something of his own some easier way. Nobody will commit burglary when he has a house full. No girl will go out on the streets when she has a comfortable place at home" (1902, pp. 14–15). And so on.

More recently, Samuel Jordan, writing while serving as an inmate in the Pennsylvania state prison system, asserted: "An inmate or victim is not seeking a more comfortable or more hospitable arrangement with his tormentors. He wants to be completely rid of prisons and those who control them." But it becomes clear later that he too does not see this as an immediate possibility. For he says that "in the United States today, prison is a by-product as well as an instrument of the class war" and also refers to "the use of the prison as a class weapon." And his concluding paragraph begins: "Weapons or tools of control are not voluntarily discarded by the class in power."

Yet if they are not going to be voluntarily discarded, and if Jordan's description of "the root of the prison function" as "the rule of the capitalist agents versus the working class" is correct, it must follow that prisons will not be abolished prior to the overthrow of the capitalist system. Moreover it is surely not inconceivable that even then "the abused working class people" would want to preserve a number of prisons if for no other purpose than to house some of "the bankers, the chairmen and the bosses" and "the corporate leaders of the country" or their agents, who might indulge in counterrevolutionary, or other types of delinquent, activity (Jordan 1971, pp. 780–87).

Jessica Mitford provides a final example. She argues that "prisons are intrinsically evil and should be abolished" (1973, p. 293). And she quotes approvingly the remark of Federal District Judge James Doyle of the Western District of Wisconsin who, ruling on a prison mail-censorship case, said of the institution of prison: "In many respects it is as intolerable within the United States as was the institution of slavery, equally brutalizing to all involved, equally toxic to the social system, equally subversive of the brotherhood of man, even more costly by some standards and probably less rational" (*Morales* v. *Schmidt*, 340 F. Supp. 544, 548–49 [W.D. Wis. 1972], rev. [7th Cir. 1973]; Mitford 1973, p. 273).

But, like Kropotkin, Darrow, and Jordan, Mitford does not

envisage the abolition of prisons as an isolated piece of social engineering to be immediately implemented. For she goes on to say that she agrees with the authors of *Struggle for Justice* (American Friends Service Committee 1971) about "the impossibility of achieving more than a superficial reformation of our criminal justice system without a radical change in our values and a drastic restructuring of our social and economic institutions" (Mitford 1973, p. 273).

Now if one asks from the point of view of the penologist what the practical implications of this sort of abolitionism are the answer is not immediately obvious. In this connection the distinction which Karl Popper draws between "Holistic or Utopian social engineering as opposed to piecemeal social engineering" is obviously relevant. For the abolitionists are clearly holistic in their approach in that they aim at the remodeling of the whole of society rather than "piecemeal tinkering" with particular social institutions or systems. Whereas, according to Popper, "the characteristic aproach of the piecemeal engineer is this. Even though he may perhaps cherish some ideals which concern society 'as a whole'—its general welfare perhaps—he does not believe in the method of redesigning it as a whole" (1960, pp. 58-70).

Popper distinguishes between the holistic and piecemeal appoaches in terms of the impracticability or unfeasibility of wholesale utopian projects of reform and their incompatibility with a truly scientific attitude. He admits, however, the difficulty of drawing a precise line of demarcation between the two and acknowledges the possibility of ambitious kinds of social engineering such as a whole series of piecemeal reforms inspired by one general tendency.

But from the viewpoint of the penologist the distinction is in effect absolute. For the holism of the prison abolitionist does not envisage the transformation of penal institutions but their total dissolution. For the abolitionist the lesson of history is that the invention of the penitentiary was quite simply a mistake, or rather a deliberate perversion, and that to pursue the path of amelioration or reform is merely to compound that error. Indeed it may, as Mitford puts it, "tend to confer legitimacy on the prisons and thus help to perpetuate the system" (1973, p. 291). Or, as Samuel Jordan wrote, "The prison reformer—wittingly or unwittingly—

is an agent of capitalism.... His mission is to repaint, adjust, or gloss over the flaws in one of society's potent control mechanisms" (1971, p. 786).

Not all abolitionists, in fact, take the view that attempts to improve prison conditions must inevitably retard the demise of prisons. Mitford, for example, while acknowledging that "reforms may strengthen the system in the long run by refurbishing the façade of prison and thus assuaging the public conscience," argues that it is possible to distinguish between two types of reform proposals. Thus there are "those which will result in strengthening the prison bureaucracy, designed to perpetuate and reinforce the system, and those which to one degree or another challenge the whole premise of prison and move it in the direction of its eventual abolition."

Yet it must be said that in view of the way in which all reforms are liable to have unwanted consequences only the gift of prescience would enable anyone to apply this distinction in practice with any degree of success. For it is impossible to know in advance that reforms which are not in the least degree designed to perpetuate and reinforce the system, but are intended merely to make life more tolerable for the prisoner, may not have the unintended consequence of moderating demands for abolition. Thus to take one of Mitford's examples of a reform in a second category, it is by no means certain that proposals aimed "at restoring to prisoners those constitutional rights that will enable them to organize and fight injustice within the system" (1973, pp. 291-93) would, if adopted, tend to accelerate the disintegration of the system. Indeed, it could plausibly be argued that the reverse might be the case.

Many abolitionists, however, because they believe that the prison system should be wholly done away with, are not concerned with remedial measures of any kind. Moreover, penologists are naturally inclined to view them much as those engaged in operations on living animals for experimental purposes view antivivisectionists, that is, to regard their criticisms as unhelpful or irrelevant; or to dismiss their strictures as "merely critical" and "not constructive." In this connection, of course, it may be true that to suggest that the criticism does not help in the solution of some practical problem is often merely a way of evading criticism.

Yet it is understandable that those concerned with practical problems view such benign visions of a peaceful, harmonious society not merely as misguided, romantic idealism but as an irresponsible evasion of problems which will not disappear in response to philanthropic aspirations or revolutionary enthusiasm. And in a world where violence, acquisitiveness, and the pursuit of power show no signs of diminution but rather the reverse, the utopian attitude—for it is an attitude rather than an argument—does constitute, if not a deliberate evasion, at least a fundamental change in perspective in the light of which what others see as urgent, immediate problems are substantially reduced in significance if they are not totally eclipsed.

Rigorism

At what might at first sight appear to be the opposite extreme from the abolitionists are those critics I shall call the rigorists. The term "rigor" denotes severity and strictness, and in speaking of rigorism I refer to the belief that severe treatment and strict discipline should be the basic elements of strict prison programs. Critics who adopt this viewpoint are not usually overly concerned about human rights or humanitarian values. Their dissatisfaction with the correctional treatment model stems from a different ideological basis. For them, that model is misconceived not because it involves some lack of respect for individual rights but because it is seen as representing a misguided and sentimental departure from older and sounder punitive principles.

The rigorists advocate a sternly repressive, vigorously disciplined, punitive regimen for the prisons. The pendulum, they would say, has swung wildly away from the classical traditions of punishment to the side of permissiveness; we have been too soft, too sentimental, too unrealistic, and have failed to comprehend the simple truth that the only thing that will affect criminals is severe punishment. The primary object of the treatment of prisoners should be, as Lord Chief Justice Cockburn told the Select Committee of the House of Lords on Prison Discipline, back in 1863, "deterrence, through suffering, inflicted as a punishment for crime, and the fear of the repetition of it" (Fox 1952, p. 48).

Three-quarters of a century later a similar viewpoint was forcefully expressed by the late J. Edgar Hoover, when he said that "what the criminal fears" is "unrelenting punishment." "That is what he understands, and nothing else, and that fear is the only thing which will force him into the ranks of the law-abiding. There is no royal road to law enforcement. If we wait upon the medical quacks, the parole panderers, and the misguided sympathizers with habitual criminals to protect our lives and property from the criminal horde, then we must also resign ourselves to increasing violence, robbery and sudden death" (Sutherland and Cressey 1970, p. 347).

Rigorists would agree and also say that Hoover has been proven right. They would point with conviction to increasing problems of crime as we purport to be rehabilitating criminals. Moreover, they would say that in imposing severe punishments we would be giving offenders what they deserve. It is right and proper that they should be made to suffer for their offenses. And if the penalties really hurt, they will not only prevent the offender from repeating his offense but also deter others who might be tempted to commit similar offenses.

What should be done about the troublemakers, the activists, the rioters among the prisoners, is also quite clear to those who follow this line. Such people should be weeded out from the general prison population so that they cannot infect the others with their dangerous and violent ideas. They should be held in small, "maxi-maxi" security institutions where their numbers are so small and the discipline so strict that they can be a threat to nobody. If this should cost a little more, it is worth it since it means that we shall not be troubled, as we have been, by periodic uprisings throughout the prison systems in this country.

Not all rigorists are quite so rigorous. Probably there are many who would take the view that efforts at reform or rehabilitation should not be absolutely precluded so long as they do not involve any diminution in deterrence. This was the attitude of the English penologist and prison administrator Evelyn Ruggles-Brise, who deplored "that excessive zeal for aiming at the moral or religious reform of prisoners which had inspired the Quakers of Pennsylvania." "Our constant effort," he wrote in his 1911–12 annual report on behalf of the English Prison Commission, "is to hold the balance between what is necessary as punishment ... from a penal and deterrent point of view, and *what can be conceded, consistently with this*, in the way of humanizing and reforming influences" (Annual Report 1912, p. 27; my italics). Some such views as these, although unfashionable amongst academics, would probably be regarded as simple common sense by many citizens.

In *Struggle for Justice*, a report on crime and punishment in America prepared for the American Friends Service Committee, it is recognized that these views are widely held: "There is evidence that much of the public is profoundly punitive, not only toward serious crime, but toward many acts we believe should be removed completely from criminal law, such as many unlawful sex practices, all drug use, most minor crimes of theft" (AFSC 1971, p. 155). Members of "the public" are also described as showing "a curious insensitivity" to the sufferings of prisoners, as thinking that "criminals are being treated too well," as regarding treatment-oriented prisons as "country clubs where convicts are coddled and pampered," and as thinking that the courts are "too permissive" (ibid., pp. 86–94).

In most penological works, however, this viewpoint is either caricatured or totally ignored, and the notion that penal administration should to some extent reflect what the majority of the community wants is conveniently forgotten. Even in *Struggle for Justice* "the hard-line advocates of punitive law-and-order repression" and "the perversity of adverse public opinion" are tersely dismissed with the cryptic words "such forces can be contained if adequate options are developed and promoted" (ibid., p. 47).

Yet this hard-line position cannot be dismissed out of hand. Few feel the lash on another's back, and it seems obvious to many people that condign punishments deter. Indeed, there is a sense in which this belief is incontrovertible because any failure to deter merely demonstrates the need for more severe punishments. Without a showing of effective reformative processes, a persuasive case can be made for severe penal sanctions combining security, firm discipline, and deterrence. It can be argued that such a system would be cheaper, more honest, and on the available evidence no less effective than so-called reformative regimes.

To sum up the rigorist position briefly: The objective of a pris-

on system should be a combination of secure custody and deterrence. Such a system would merely provide hard labor and firm
discipline. It would make no sentimental pretense to provide a
cure for criminality. The principal lesson to be learned from the
history of the penitentiary system is that emotional idealism is out
of place in penology.

I said earlier that the rigorist position might appear at first
sight to be the direct antithesis of that taken by the abolitionists.
Yet both positions share what can perhaps best be described as
reliance on imaginative intuition and an almost nonchalant
disregard for detail in regard to the formulation of remedies. The
rigorists, despite their air of bluff common sense, are in fact less
rigorous in their mode of reasoning than any of the other species
of critic. They conceive themselves as being cynical realists, but a
moment's consideration reveals that they are impractical ideal-
ists, oblivious both to the evidence of the past and to the political
realities of the present.

In the first place, they subscribe to a theory of universal
deterrent efficacy which is quite unsupported by such evidence as
is available. For the hard line is hardly a new idea. The history of
criminal punishment, certainly up to the nineteenth century, is a
long record of bloody brutality as a response to brutal crime. But
crime did not diminish; on the contrary, it continued to increase.

In the second place, the hard line suffers from an even more
serious defect than lack of evidential support. This is the fact that
it is totally impracticable. The attempt to revert to eighteenth-
century penological principles and practice, at this time, would
lead to explosions of violence throughout the penal institutions of
this country beside which Attica would appear as a trivial
skirmish. Twenty years ago such an attempt might just have been
achievable; it cannot be achieved now. Prisons both reflect and
exaggerate the social processes of the outside world. The old order
has changed as much within prisons as without. And it is surely
clear that, if there are lessons to be learned from history, one of
them is that repression breeds violent reaction. The clock cannot
be set back to a simple, rigidly disciplined, punitive routine.

It might be argued that, by the use of modern technological
skills, it would be possible to construct and to use prisons purely
as custodial and deterrent institutions without resorting to the

cruder brutalities of the past. Hermetically sealed, electronically inviolable, remotely controlled fortresses could be built which would be totally secure and completely impervious to inmate disruption. No doubt they could; but to pretend that this is a practicable or rational program is, quite simply, cant. For forty years the better-informed prison administrators have been suggesting that they needed maximum security conditions for about 15 percent of their population. In such a situation, it would be ludicrous to build more maximum security institutions.

Yet if the rigorists seem, like Talleyrand's Bourbons, to have "learned nothing and forgotten nothing" there is a core of cogency in their critique which should not be evaded. They are quite right in insisting on the deterrent function of imprisonment even though they exaggerate its effect. They are quite right, too, when they point out that the promises of progressive penology have not been fulfilled. Finally, they are quite right in questioning the premises of the reformist ideology.

Reformism

If we cannot revert to eighteenth-century principles of penology, the efforts of those I have called reformists to reiterate those of the nineteenth century are only a little less misguided. The historical conditions which gave rise to the reformist ideology no longer exist. And amid the realities of chaos and conflict which characterize corrections in our time the irrelevance of the unfulfilled promises of the past can no longer be dissimulated.

In speaking of the reformists I am referring to those traditional penal reformers who have for the most part taken the line that although most prison correctional or rehabilitative programs have proved unsatisfactory this is due not to any defect in the underlying theory but to failure to implement adequately or properly that theory. The implication is analogous to G. K. Chesterton's celebrated aphorism about "the Christian ideal": "it has not been tried and found wanting; it has been found difficult and left untried."

Although many reformists are members of what has been called "the American correctional establishment," they do not question that American jails and prisons are extremely imperfect. The truth is, they would say, that correctional reform has as yet not been treated as a serious enterprise in this country. It is not so much that correctional system reforms have failed; it is rather that they have been token changes, nibbling away only at the periphery of the problem, with the larger system remaining untouched. We have a few front-of-the-house reforms, a few new façades, but the result remains a Potemkin village.

The reformists would applaud the chilling sentence in the McKay Commission's report on Attica: "Attica is every prison; and every prison is Attica." They would agree with the report that, although conditions in Attica may not have been exactly like those at other prisons in New York State or elsewhere in the United States, the problems in that institution at that time were representative of the prison universe. They would acknowledge that, although over the past decade the numbers in prison have declined, corections overall has maintained its broad pattern of inefficiency, brutality, parsimony, and neglect.

We recognize, they say, that we must somehow escape from the crippling idleness, lack of training, inhumanity, and futility of the mega-prison which still characterize most state systems. We know that the prisoner must be given work to do and an opportunity to develop himself, and that if we wish to reduce his later depredations on society it is incumbent upon us to give him some opportunity of a tolerable life of conformity when he is released from our control. We know our prisons are too large and generally too remote. We know all these things, and some of them we have known for over a century. The prison riots and strikes in recent decades have merely underlined the need for renovation of our correctional system.

But it is not as though we are facing a hideously intractable problem to which no solution is known. We know perfectly well what should be done. We know that we must better discriminate those criminals who present a serious threat to the community from the nuisances who continue to clutter our correctional system. We know that we must increase community links in our treatment and control processes. We know we must expand and more effectively graduate our armamentarium of reactions to crime and to the convicted criminal.

Of course, it must be recognized that the road to correctional reform has never been a smooth one. There are many reasons for this. Politically, there has been no great incentive to invest resources of men, money, and materials in correctional reform. Until quite recently there was scant public recognition of the importance of the criminal justice system to community life in this country, and so the application of resources to corrections was rarely more than a begrudged pittance. Nor have those attitudes completely disappeared. Both hostility towards reform and apathy regarding it still exist. Until recently, correctional reform has lacked both a constituency and a sound political base. And such support as it is now attracting flows in part not so much from an enlightened recognition of social necessity as from fear of crime and alarm at the failure of traditional modes of treatment of offenders.

Of course, given further large-scale prison violence, a political backlash might well come. But the prison riots did not produce any powerful political or popular backlash. Most politicians did not react with retributive aggression to the violently expressed but in many cases entirely legitimate complaints of the prisoners. For the time being, federal and state governments and preponderant public opinion increasingly support the movement towards substantial correctional reform. There is, as the reformers see it, a large measure of agreement between those within the correctional field and those outside it who have studied the matter, on the broad path to be followed. All that remains is to carry through the plans of the Pennsylvania Quakers. An end to tokenism! On with rehabilitation!

It is sometimes suggested that the reformist ideology represents merely an emulsion of class interests and also reflects, as the authors of *Struggle for Justice* put it, "the mixture of hatred, fear and revulsion that white, middle-class Protestant reformers felt toward lower-class persons" (AFSC 1971, p. 85). According to this view the penal system is a political instrument manipulated by those with status and power against the status-poor and powerless. And, "By and large the functionaries of a criminal justice system are either members of the political and economically dominant classes of society or totally subservient to these classes" (ibid., p. 134).

Insofar as those functionaries support the "treatment-oriented prison reform movement" their attitude is seen as hypocritical and their motives as discreditable. Thus what is called "the individualized treatment model" is said to have "never commanded more than lip service from most of its more powerful adherents" (ibid., p. 39). "Prison administrators" who "embraced the rehabilitative ideal" are said to have done so because it increased their power over inmates. "It wasn't treatment that excited them. It was the prospect of having greater control over their prisons" (ibid., pp. 85–86). Prison personnel are described as "unthinking, unfeeling functionaries within institutions" (ibid., p. 120).

The trouble with this type of critique is that like all ad hominem arguments it tells us nothing about the validity of reformist principles. Even if the analysis of the provenance of those principles or the motivation of their proponents were correct it would not follow that they were therefore erroneous. Joseph Schumpeter puts the matter well in his *History of Economic Analysis*: "The temptation is great to avail oneself of the opportunity to dispose at one stroke of a whole body of propositions one does not like, by the simple device of calling it an ideology. This device is no doubt very effective, as effective as are attacks upon an opponent's personal motives. But logically it is inadmissible—explanation, however correct, of the reasons why a man says what he says tell us nothing about whether it is true or false. Similarly, statements that proceed from an ideological background are open to suspicion, but they may still be perfectly valid."

It is necessary, therefore, to ask what is wrong with the reformist approach in terms of such concepts as relevance, consistency, adequacy, and validity. As Schumpeter says: "Both Galileo and his opponents may have been swayed by ideologies. That does not prevent us from saying that he was 'right'" (1954, pp. 34–43). But what warrant have we, if any, for saying that the reformists were, or rather are now, wrong in their analysis and prescriptions?

In fact, there are good grounds for rejecting their approach to the problem. For the truth is that the treatment model which underlies modern correctional ideology as opposed to the nineteenth-century version, arises out of two quite remarkable examples of conceptual confusion. In the first place there is the confusion which has been admirably dissected by Antony Flew in *Crime or Disease*. It is the notion that all crime or delinquency should properly, and can legitimately, be viewed as a symptom of mental disease or psychological disorder. The transition from the nineteenth century to the twentieth in this context is marked by the movement from judgments about sin and moral weakness expressed in concepts like "degeneracy" and "deficiency of moral sense" to judgments about mental disease expressed in concepts like "moral insanity" and "psychopathy." The second confusion derives from assimilating psychological medicine to physical medicine in a simplistic and absolute fashion. It is made easier because, as Flew points out, although there is an abundant literature on the nature and criteria of mental health, very little attention is paid to the "dissimilarities between them and their physical analogues" (1973, p. 26).

Now the treatment model which is derived from this double exercise in logical indiscrimination is immensely attractive. The concepts of prevention, diagnosis, alleviation, and cure are lifted from the context of physical medicine and applied to the "treatment" of convicted offenders in prison. And, although exact analogues for the various aspects of medical practice have proved impossible to find, this problem has commonly been solved by the ingenious method of classifying everything that happens to the prisoner after reception into the prison as "treatment"; a solution which is rendered the more plausible because the term "treatment" is ambiguous and can legitimately be used to refer to anything the prisoner undergoes at the hands of the prison authorities.

It is, of course, utterly unsurprising that in regard to results or "cures" no significant relationship between prison "treatment" programs and behavior after release from prison has been found. But to suggest, as reformists do, that those programs have failed because of the failure to invest sufficient resources in this enterprise is like saying that necromancy might solve most of our problems if only its practitioners were adequately funded.

Nor is it unreasonable to suppose that prisoners' realization of the contrast between the rhetoric and reality of correctional "treatment" has been a powerful factor in the genesis of the resentment, frustration, and anger which has over the years exploded into violence in prisons throughout the world. Indeed, one has only to refer to the growing body of writing by ex-prisoners to recognize that the subjects of prison treatment are not so much skeptical as totally cynical about the matter. An illustration drawn from English prison literature may be found in a comparison of the account of corrective training given in the exemplary prose of Lionel Fox (1952, pp. 307–15) and that given by a former corrective trainee, Frank Norman (1958). Moreover, although there are no misstatements of fact in the former, anyone with firsthand experience of corrective training would agree that for a veridical description of the realities of the system it is to the latter that one must refer; a view with which, incidentally, Sir Lionel privately concurred.

It could, of course, be argued that ex-prisoners are necessarily subjective in their judgments. But it is not only in the works of ex-prisoners that one finds today an increased cynicism. Certainly, in relation to imprisonment, serious research workers have, in recent years, come to speak in a fashion much closer to that of ex-prisoners than to the bland pronouncements of official and unofficial prison reformers. And the results of research into the effectiveness of imprisonment underline in quantitative and objective terms the message of the more impressionistic assessments. The unavoidable conclusion is that the reformist's more-of-the-same prescription, while it might meet with the approval of social homeopathists—if such persons exist—must be regarded, in the light of experience, as a recipe for further disaster.

Reductivism

What I have called the reductivist view not only deplores the hyperbolic rhetoric of the reformists but constitutes a fundamental challenge to the traditional penal reformers' basic ideas about the path correctional reform should follow. It is best exemplified in two works published in 1971, *Struggle for Justice*, already referred to earlier, and Rupert Cross's *Punishment, Prison and the Public*. The essence of this view is that the reformist approach is defective in theory and has been disastrous in practice; and that rather than further developing correctional treatment programs we should drastically reduce their scope.

Thus, *Struggle for Justice*, which was written by a working party made up of men and women familiar with the administration of the penal system, not only through their work and visitation, but also, in many cases, by virtue of having served prison terms, condemns "the correctional treatment model," as based on assumptions that are either "unsubstantiated or in conflict with basic humanitarian values" (AFSC 1971, p. 83). And it states categorically: "This two-hundred year old experiment has failed."

In the first place, the report argues that those who currently propose reforms on traditional lines—reforms that require "more and better trained personnel at higher salaries, more programs both in and out of institutions, more money for courts and corrections all along the line"—are foolish and misguided and reveal "a whimsical touch of Utopianism." "In the light of historical experience and contemporary reality, any expectation for the political viability of far-reaching court or correctional reform is visionary.... Even if the formidable political and budgetary obstacles to these programs could somehow be surmounted, existing shortages of trained personnel would delay large-scale implementation for a decade or more."

To this evocation of realpolitik is added a further argument to the effect that even were the successful implementation of current reform programs achieved, it would not serve the public interest or alleviate the major abuses of the present system. Such programs, it is argued, are totally misconceived in that they are based on a model which is "theoretically faulty, systematically discriminatory in administration, and inconsistent with some of our most basic concepts of justice" (ibid., pp. 11–12).

The argument is not entirely new. It would be possible to interpret it as a sophisticated version of Beaumont and Tocqueville. There is a pervasive parallelism which can be seen clearly in many passages of both texts. The authors' repudiation of the "individualized treatment model" and the "liberal treatment ideology" corresponds to Tocqueville's rejection of the notion of "radical regeneration" or "the thorough reformation of a criminal" as the rationale for penal treatment.

According to Tocqueville, "Society, without power to effect this radical regeneration, is no more capable of proving it, if it exists" (Beaumont and Tocqueville 1964, pp. 88–90). The authors of

Struggle for Justice are equally skeptical about correctional treatment programs, which they assert have "no proven [or likely] relationship to criminal pathology." Just as Tocqueville maintains that all which society has the right to demand is obedience to the laws, so the authors argue that the treatment-oriented approach involves an illegitimate extension of power over individuals in order to achieve "indoctrination in white Anglo-Saxon middle-class values" (AFSC 1971, p. 43).

Rupert Cross, in *Punishment, Prison and the Public*, is no less critical of the basic assumptions of "progressive penology." He is concerned with the British rather than the American prison system, but because of their common historical origin what he says is largely applicable to both. The essence of Cross's critique is succinctly and conveniently stated by the author in his Introduction. "Doubt is cast" he says, "on the possibility of there being a real reformation in any save the most exceptional cases, and it is even suggested that the belief that prison could be reformative has had a baneful influence" (1971, p. xv).

On the question of the extent to which prisons are reformatory, Cross confesses to "profound scepticism." "The chances of deterioration in prison," he says, "are at least as great as those of reform"; and "if analogies have to be drawn, prisons are more like cold storage depots than either therapeutic communities or training institutions" (ibid., pp. 84–85). As to work, education, and vocational training he is dubious about the extent to which rehabilitation is achieved by these means.

He rejects the idea of the conversion of prisons into therapeutic communities as based on the wholly inappropriate model of the mental hospital. "We are asked to imagine such a hospital in which people are detained against their will..., in which the detention may have to continue long after a cure has been effected, and in which the vast majority of the patients are not, and never have been, either mentally ill or subject to any form of namable or treatable personality disorder" (ibid., p. 36).

While Cross is highly skeptical about the reformative potentialities of imprisonment he says that "no one would be disposed to doubt the existence of deformative risks." "There is a real danger that someone who is already a bad man when he goes into prison will come out worse: hence the crucial importance of what can best be described as 'anti-deformative action' in our prisons." In fact, he concludes that "the main aim of prison reform should be the prevention of prisoners' deterioration."

It follows also that "the period of imprisonment should be as short as it possibly can be compatibly with the aims of the sentence whether they be denunciation, deterrence, the protection of the public or all three" (ibid., pp. 85–86). In practice, however, "the baneful influence of the myth that prison is reformative" ("or could be reformative if only the authorities were given time enough") has resulted in a substantial increase in the average length of prison sentences in Britain since the 1930s and a good deal of "unnecessary suffering" (ibid., pp. 101–2).

Taken together, *Struggle for Justice* and *Punishment, Prison and the Public* present a formidable indictment. Although there are differences between the two, a fundamental identity of approach emerges, and they independently arrive at very similar conclusions. This can be seen clearly if we look at the "three salutary lessons" which Cross says are provided by "the sad history of twentieth century English attempts to cope with recidivism."

The first lesson, according to Cross, is "the extreme importance of avoiding calling the same thing by different names." He refers in this connection to Alexander Paterson's proposal to the 1932 Committee on Persistent Offenders "to abolish all prisons" and replace them with "training centres" and "places of detention," a proposal which was later reflected in the provisions of the British Criminal Justice Act of 1948. Cross condemns "this kind of gerrymandering with words" as not only dishonest and mislead- ing but productive of unnecessary suffering in that offenders are sentenced to longer periods than they might otherwise receive because of the illusion that they are not being sent to ordinary prisons (1971, pp. 163–65).

A very similar point is made in *Struggle for Justice* where it is said that "many proposals that seem to urge the abolition of prisons are really exercises in label switching. Call them 'com- munity treatment centers' or what you will, if human beings are involuntarily confined in them they are prisons. . . . It confuses analysis and obscures the moral nature of our act to pretend that we are not employing punishment. . . . Proposals that we should 'abolish prisons' or 'end the crime of imprisonment' are destructive of thought and analysis when all that is contemplated is a reshuffling of our labels or institutional arrangements for coercive restraint" (AFSC 1971, p. 23). The point is also made that the "adoption of the rehabilitative ideal" has resulted in "the length of sentences [being] steadily increased" (ibid., p. 91).

The second lesson which Cross enunciates relates to the futility of incarcerating offenders for protracted periods in order that they may be trained. "We must now face the fact," he says, "that if what is wanted is training, it had better take place out of prison. We can no longer delude ourselves into thinking that we are getting the best of both worlds by deterring the offender and others by depriving him of his liberty and, at the same time, training him to lead a useful life" (1971, pp. 165-66). As *Struggle for Justice* has it, "After more than a century of persistent failure, this reformist prescription is bankrupt" (AFSC 1971, p. 8). The authors emphasize at some length "the difficulties inherent in implementing treatment in prison" and make the point that "there is evidence that people are not being helped any more by a median stay of three years in a rehabilitatively oriented prison than they were by approximately two years in a basically punitively oriented prison" (ibid., pp. 92-97).

Cross's third lesson to be learned from twentieth century attempts to deal with the recidivist is "that we have made no progress whatsoever." In fact he says, "Judged by the standard of the number of habitual criminals in and out of our prisons, our system is no better than it was in the days of the Gladstone Report" (1971, p. 166). *Struggle for Justice*, referring to the California correctional system, "which has pushed further toward full implementation of the rehabilitative ideal than any other correctional system in the United States," reaches a similar conclusion. As an indicator of the lack of progress, they too cite the consistent recidivist rates. "Through the years approximately 40 percent of the persons released on parole in California have been returned to confinement two or three years after release" (AFSC 1971, pp. 83-92).

In addition to these three "lessons" there are many other points of agreement, one of which deserves mention here. Thus in *Struggle for Justice* criticism is directed at the fact that "as part of treatment and rehabilitation, cultural assimilation is forced upon" offenders. In other words, attempts are made "to impose a middle-class life-style" and "the increasingly outmoded Protestant work ethic" on them (ibid., pp. 119–20). Cross is equally critical of the belief in "the merits of inculcating middle-class values" in offenders. He sees it as a "pernicious manifestation of the disease of 'PLU' (people like us)." Moreover he thinks that the English penal system "has been bedevilled" by this notion "that the world would be a better place if only it were inhabited by people like us" (1971, p. 132).

The crucial difference between the reductivist critique and that of the reformist lies not so much in the nature of the specific faults found as in the nature of the practical implications which are seen to follow from the unfavorable assessment. Thus the reformists maintain that correctional treatment programs can be made to work and the rehabilitative ideal can be realized, if only adequate finance, efficient administration, and community support are forthcoming.

But the reductivist explicitly rejects this line of thought. In *Struggle for Justice* it is noted that "the experts—even the most enlightened and progressive—line up solidly in support of the system, asking only for more of the same. Most established penologists and criminologists support the treatment and individualized treatment principles.... We venture to hope that this report will inspire reconsideration by such experts" (AFSC 1971, p. 156). The authors are derisive about demands for such things as more money for corrections, "more and better trained personnel at higher salaries," "careful classification of inmates," "more 'experts' for the courts," "improved educational and therapeutic programs in penal institutions" and "small 'cottage' institutions," all of which are dismissed as "all this paraphernalia of the 'new' criminology [which] appears over and over in nineteenth-century reformist literature."

"The premise of such an approach," they say, "is that the programs are on the right track but have never been given a fair trial, that the blame for past failure is public and legislative inaction." They go on to say that in fact even if all the proposals mentioned were implemented this would not either "serve legitimate public interests or alleviate the major abuses of our present programs" (ibid., pp. 8–12). This is not just because they regard the reformist program as politically unfeasible, although they do so regard it. The reason for their opposition is much more fundamental, relating not to reformist tactics but to the overall strategic plan of the reformists.

What reductivists attack is the whole reformist ideology of imprisonment. It is not merely the fact that in practice reformist programs have been defective that is criticized. Criticism is directed at the principles underlying the contemporary system of prison treatment. It is directed at the reformist justification for the use of imprisonment as a form of punishment. And as this has been the principal rationale of imprisonment since the beginning of the penitentiary system it constitutes an attack on imprisonment itself as we know it.

This is made perfectly clear in *Struggle for Justice*: "Imprisonment with treatment is identical with traditional imprisonment in most significant aspects." Although "progressive penology" inspires internal institutional reforms, the changes involved are trivial when measured against "the basic evils of imprisonment." Those evils are defined: "[I]t denies autonomy, degrades dignity, impairs or destroys self-reliance, inculcates authoritarian values, minimizes the likelihood of beneficial interaction with one's peers, fractures family ties, destroys the family's economic stability, and prejudices the prisoner's future prospects for any improvement in his economic and social status" (ibid., pp. 25–33). The radical nature of this critique appears more striking perhaps because until very recently there has been little tendency for penal reformers to question the assumptions underlying the dominant reformist theoretical orientation.

Nevertheless, the reductivists do not go so far as to suggest that imprisonment should be totally abolished. They are in favor of "the reduction and avoidance of imprisonment," as Cross puts it. They may, as in *Struggle for Justice*, be opposed to the construction of new prisons ("If prisons are overcrowded, ways should be found to cut back the mass of criminal laws and the types of enforcement that send so many people to prison" [ibid., pp. 172–73]), but they do not envisage the dissolution of the prison system.

Do the reductivists provide better solutions for the practical problems of reordering the prison system? Is the pertinence and validity of their criticism matched with an equivalent insight into the necessary task of reconstruction? The answer is that this aspect is addressed only in a cursory fashion. Cross, for instance, makes no pretense to provide any more than what he calls "incidental suggestions." "I have not regarded my present mission as one of reform so much as of assessment," he says. As to his suggestions, he states that he is "not wedded to by any means all of them"; that he knows "that some of them are mutually inconsistent"; and that he is "aware that some of them are superlatively unimportant" (1971, p. 185). Perhaps it is sufficient to observe that in the face of so modest a disclaimer criticism is disarmed.

The authors of *Struggle for Justice* adopt a different posture although one that is little more helpful. They state candidly in their first chapter that they "approach criminal justice from a Quaker perspective," but it cannot be said that this leads them to adopt a notably indulgent view of the role played by earlier Quakers in the development of penal reform. Indeed it is one of the ironies of history that "the functionaries" of the correctional system are abused by twentieth-century Quakers for attempting to perform tasks imposed on them by the Quakers of the eighteenth and nineteenth centuries.

Yet although the criticism of current practices is trenchant and specific, the question of alternatives is dealt with in an extremely imprecise fashion. *Struggle for Justice* is said to be inspired by "the desire to transfer power from the police/courts/prisons to the people" (AFSC 1971, p. 171). The reader is told a number of times that "the construction of a just system of criminal justice in an unjust society is a contradiction in terms" and warned of the "impossibility of achieving more than a superficial reformation of our criminal justice system without a radical change in our values and a drastic restructuring of our social and economic institutions" (ibid., pp. 12–16).

But beyond being advised that we must set about restructuring the entire range of social and economic institutions within our society, we are offered only desultory suggestions. As, for example, that we must join in "demonstrating solidarity with prisoners' demands," or that we must set up "referral services" (that will be "manned mostly by young volunteers") "directing callers to resources that already exist within the community" (ibid., pp. 170-71). For the rest, the authors have a "vision of a peaceful non-coercive society," in which "our institutional and non-institutional environments encourage the creation of morally autonomous, self-disciplined people who exercise independent judgment and purposefulness from their own inner strength" (ibid., p. 45).

It is all very reminiscent of the "philosophical reveries" that Beaumont and Tocqueville encountered in the nineteenth century. And, interestingly, not only is there the same utopian hope—the pursuit of the millennium—there is also the same air of moral superiority as in the nineteenth century, albeit now redirected towards "the middle class person" or "the power structure." One misses only some reference to support from "divine Providence"; although the program adumbrated is such that divine guidance if not direct intervention might seem to be a necessary condition of its fulfillment.

ENVOI

What emerges from this survey of past and present attitudes to the prison as it has developed over the last two centuries? One thing is clear, certainly: the existence of widespread dissatisfaction. Nor is this merely a function of the fact that the review was confined to critical material. It is impossible to find in contemporary correctional literature, except, possibly, in the case of annual reports of prison administrators, anything comparable to the expressions of complacence and sanguine confidence which characterized the writings of earlier generations of penologists. Yet all criticism which goes beyond mere reprobation deserves careful attention, both as a revelation of faults or weaknesses and as an index to necessary amendment, retrenchment, or, as it may be, fundamental reconstruction. The next chapter is devoted to analysis of the implications of the critical approaches outlined above.

2   The Principal Issues

Three salient questions recur throughout the body of critical argument on the subject of the prison. They relate first to the functions of the prison, second to the need for its continued existence, and third to its reform. They could be expressed in the form: What is prison for? Are prisons necessary? What should be done about prisons?

WHAT IS PRISON FOR?

The prison, or penitentiary, is commonly described as having multiple and sometimes conflicting purposes. "Whatever prison is for it is not for one clear and single purpose," said Lionel Fox (1952, p. 15). He went on to distinguish three main purposes, which he defined at one point as custody, coercion, and correction and at another as prevention, deterrence, and reform. Others have used a variety of terms to denote what they have seen as the principal tasks or goals of the prison system. Among them, in addition to those mentioned, we encounter with varying frequency: containment, control, incapacitation, punishment, retribution, restraint, rehabilitation, reintegration, therapy, and training.

Attempts have been made to bring some order into this

confusion by drawing a distinction between primary and secondary purposes. But there has been no consensus about the way in which this distinction should be applied. Thus in a recent discussion J. E. Thomas has declared firmly that "there can only be *one primary task*.... [T]he prison system has control as its primary organizational task" (1972, pp. 4–5). Lionel Fox on the other hand wrote of "the possibility of a system of treatment in which reform would hold a *primary and concurrent* place with deterrence" (1952, p. 71). (My italics in both cases.) Others have spoken of "bifurcated goals" and "congruent goals." In one notable attempt, by O'Leary and Duffee, to devise a classification system, four separate models of correctional policies are developed according to the relative emphasis that is placed on different correctional concerns or assumptions (1971).

It is not intended here to enter into argument about the taxonomy of correctional goals. The notion of an ideal, context-free classification scheme or hierarchy of aims is a delusion. The degree to which such schemes are satisfactory depends on the purpose for which they are intended. Indeed it is in part because those who have devised them have had different perspectives, that they have produced such diverse formulations and typologies.

The basic reason for the inconclusiveness of discussion on this topic, however, is that it involves a confusion arising out of the ambiguous nature of the question. To give some examples, the question, What is prison for? can and has been answered in terms of the intentions of its originators or later administrators; its actual or supposed purpose, role, or function in society; its distinctive or "essential" nature as opposed to the accidental or contingent functions it may fulfill; its historical identity; the form in which it ought to exist and be preserved; and the moral justification for its use.

Commonly a number of these questions are confused, and answers are given in mixed historical, sociological, and jurisprudential terms. Clearly it is necessary to draw distinctions between the questions. But for the purpose of this discussion it is necessary to draw only one distinction, that between justification and function. It may be that this does not fully meet the classical requirements of exhaustiveness and exclusiveness, and I shall not attempt to demonstrate that all the questions noted above regarding the prison can be grouped under these two headings.

But it is all that is required in the context of this discussion and it has the virtue of simplicity.

The question about the justification of imprisonment is: Why is it morally good or permissible for men to imprison other men? Insofar as the prison system is part of the penal system, and a method of punishment, the debate on this question is largely a reflection of the more general debate on the ethics of punishment and is usually couched in the same terms. Not only do we find ourselves rehearsing all over again the familiar championship battles between such popular contestants as Desert, Deterrence, and Reform but we are frequently expected to accept the notion that there can be only one winner; or that at the most there may be a draw, as in the case of Lionel Fox's idea of reform holding "a primary and concurrent place with deterrence." Occasionally a new challenger like Denunciation or Reprobation enters the ring, although such new challengers are usually former contestants under new colors.

It is not intended in this work to enter into a lengthy discussion of the jurisprudence of imprisonment. It will be sufficient here to refer the reader to H. L. A. Hart's *Punishment and Responsibility* (1968), where he writes of the complexity of punishment and of the multiplicity of aims and justifications which in the case of punishment, as in that of many other social institutions, may be pursued. Yet if we acknowledge, as we must, this multiplicity of justifications in relation to the institution of punishment, we must also recognize that precisely the same may apply to some of the particular methods of punishment such as imprisonment. So that, rather than seeking for some simple formula to define the justification of imprisonment in general, we should recognize that confinement in penal institutions may be justified in different ways in relation to different categories of prisoner and different purposes of imprisonment.

Very similar considerations apply in relation to the question of the functions of imprisonment. In this case other challengers such as Custody, Control, Security, Treatment, and Training enter the ring. But here too we encounter the same pursuit of primacy. Here too occasionally a new contestant appears. Thus we find Rupert Cross in *Punishment, Prison and the Public* dismissing reform swiftly as "incidental to, not the object of, imprisonment" and asserting that the main aim should be "the prevention of prisoners' deterioration" (1971, pp. 85–86).

Yes it is surely a mistake to talk about the "primary task of the system" or "the object of imprisonment" in this way. Consider for example Thomas's candidate for primacy, which he variously calls control, custody, or containment. It is true that to sentence a person to imprisonment means to order him to be deprived of his liberty by confinement in a prison. As Thomas puts it, "Society has defined the need for removal of the criminal and the prison system, as an organization, has come into being to achieve this task" (1972, p. 5). There can be no question that viewed in historical perspective imprisonment fulfills the function of removal from society formerly achieved by a variety of different methods such as banishment, outlawry, transportation, and the death penalty. There can be no question either that one of the principal measures of the success or failure of the prison system in the eyes of the public is the degree to which it achieves simple containment.

Implicit in the custodial process, of course, is prevention. As Fox puts it, "It does not . . . require any modification of the custodial function" to achieve this objective (1952, p. 17). While the offender is in custody he cannot offend again; prevention is achieved for so long as the sentence lasts. A sentence of imprisonment for life, carried out literally, so that the prisoner is detained for the rest of his natural life, constitutes an absolute preventive. It should be noted in passing that this is a somewhat ethnocentric conception of prevention in that it ignores all offenses by inmates against other inmates or prison guards. The principle of prevention is also sometimes made explicit in sentences of "preventive detention," in "indeterminate sentences," and in "measures of security" found in some European penal systems; all of which are applied to persistent offenders who are judged to be committed to a life of crime.

However, except in the case of some persistent offenders and some who are judged to be especially dangerous, few sentences are based *exclusively* on this conception. In the great majority of cases the assumption is that the offender will be returned to the community. And, since the beginning of the penitentiary system at any rate, it has been generally accepted as one of the basic premises of corrections that the offender's treatment in prison should be such that, having undergone the experience of imprisonment, on his return to the community he will refrain from further offenses, although opinions have differed, and still do differ, as to how that may be achieved.

As a matter of fact, those who dismiss the notion of the reformation or rehabilitation of the prisoner as either irrelevant, impractical, or objectionable, and promote custody or control as the primary task or principal purpose of the prison make another mistake also. For it is no answer to the question, What is the function or task of the prison? to say that it is custody or containment or confinement. It is, in fact, an evasion of the question to respond in that way. It is no more than a tautology to say that a prison is a place of confinement or captivity. To imprison a person is to confine him. But this may be done to people for a great variety of reasons. Thus we confine enemy aliens in time of war, we confine travelers under quarantine regulations, we confine insane persons in mental hospitals.

In each case it is reasonable to ask and legitimate to expect an answer to questions about the purposes of their confinement or the functions of their places of confinement. In each case answers are forthcoming: We confine enemy aliens in wartime for reasons of national security; we quarantine some travelers because they are suspected of carrying contagious diseases; we confine some insane persons because they may be a danger to themselves and others. In no case would it be enough to say: The purpose of their confinement is custody or control or containment. And what applies to the internment camp and the quarantine station and the mental hospital applies equally to the penitentiary or prison.

The basic fallacy, however, lies in the search for some simple formula or single purpose as the overall primary task of the prison system. Thus there may be prisoners in respect to whom the primary task of the system could only be defined in terms of control or containment, although both humanity and prudence would dictate that we should also pay attention to the prevention of prisoners' deterioration. At the other extreme there is unquestionably a substantial number of offenders whose imprisonment serves no purpose that could not be better achieved outside prison. In between there will be many different categories of prisoner for whom a variety of different objectives—educational, vocational, disciplinary, remedial, or therapeutic—might feasibly be suggested as primary.

When we ask about the functions of imprisonment we are asking in effect why we imprison. One way of answering this question is to refer to Wittgenstein's reply to the question, Why do we punish criminals? "There is," he said, "the institution of punishing criminals. Different people support this for different reasons, and for different reasons in different cases and at different times. Some people support it out of a desire for revenge, some perhaps out of a desire for justice, some out of a wish to prevent a repetition of the crime, and so on. And so punishments are carried out" (1966, p. 50).

Or, as H. L. A. Hart puts it, "Men punish and always have punished for a vast number of different reasons. They have punished to secure obedience to different laws, to gratify feelings of revenge, to satisfy a public demand for severe reprisals for outrageous crimes, because they believed a deity demands punishment, to match with suffering the moral evil inherent in the perpetration of a crime, or simply out of respect for tradition" (1968, p. 73).

Why then in regard both to the institution of punishment in general and the institution of the prison in particular should one particular function be nominated as the "prime" or "essential" function? Is it because, as Hart suggests, "in our inherited ways of talking or thinking about punishment there is some persistent drive towards an oversimplification of multiple issues which require separate consideration" (ibid, p. 3)? Or is it because in all areas of discourse we prefer simple rather than complicated explanations?

One other point should be mentioned which applies to discussions both of the moral justification for imprisonment and the functions of imprisonment. Very frequently when people nominate a particular justification or aim as primary or essential it seems that what they are doing in effect is recommending that justification or aim as meriting special approval. In other words, their statements are really evaluative or normative statements which only have the appearance of being factual statements.

Consider, from a different field, the debate about a quite different type of institution—the university. Just as in the case of prisons one finds a variety of functions nominated as *the function* of universities. They have been said to be schools of professional training; factories for the production of technicians, bureaucrats, and pedagogues; places for the disinterested pursuit of truth; training schools for the established order; instruments of social control, and so on. The parallel with the debate about prisons is remarkably close.

Here too one finds contributors to the discussion nominating one particular function as primary or essential. To give a recent example, Kenneth R. Minogue in his extremely readable *The Concept of a University* argues that the "essence" of universities lies in their being places for academic inquiry and the pursuit of knowledge divorced from practical considerations. This is "what makes them distinctive, quite irrespective of their social context." Other interpretations are rejected as seeing the university "in terms of contingencies irrelevant to its explicit concerns."

Yet, although there is no doubt that universities can and do accommodate the kinds of activity referred to by Minogue, they have in the past fulfilled, and continue to fulfill, a variety of other functions which he not only acknowledges but also describes in some detail. Moreover it is surely significant that what he refers to as "teasing out the features of a historical identity which has been revealing itself, in many varied circumstances, over the last seven or eight centuries," results in a concept of the university of which he manifestly approves and which he eloquently commends (1973, pp. 3–4).

Certainly different readings of the history of universities have reached different conclusions. Just as in the case of prisons different readings of *their* history have reached different conclusions, including the judgment that they should be abolished. Moreover, the functions which any social institution fulfills are subject to change as society changes so that at a particular point in time it may be extremely difficult to arrive at a precise definition of function.

In the case of the prison it is possible to point to a variety of functions which it currently serves. Thus there is no doubt that imprisonment provides a means of banishment or compulsory removal from society. As Leslie Wilkins has put it: "It is not unreasonable for persons who have suffered from some crime to demand that the offender 'get out of here.' When 'out of here' did not mean into some similar society (such as the next state!), and when transport was slow, there were several variations of the general theme of 'out of here.' Few areas of the world can today employ such methods. The prison has to suffice" (1974, p. 246).

Again there can be no doubt that imprisonment serves a deterrent function. As to how effectively it operates as a general deterrent, the extent to which the threat of imprisonment reduces the rate of any kind of criminal behavior, we are presently ignorant. But in regard to what is called individual deterrence there is an interesting finding in Glaser's *The Effectiveness of a Prison and Parole System*. Glaser conducted a prison panel study during which some 1,200 interviews were conducted with prisoners in order to study the impact of imprisonment. One of the two concluding questions directed at obtaining the inmate's evaluation of his correctional experience was "What do you think there is about your life in prison so far that would help you the most if you wanted to go straight?" He reports as follows: "Although the prison system does not officially assert that deterrence is one of its primary means of rehabilitating offenders, the aspect of prison most often mentioned by inmates as of the greatest assistance in helping them to 'go straight' was the unpleasantness of the confinement experience" (Glaser 1964, p. 481). This finding is interesting in that prisoners may be expected to be aware of the possible consequences of their answers and thus, in their own self-interest, to be less than candid. But in this case the fact that the most likely consequence of the answers given would be for the authorities to increase the unpleasantness of the confinement experience in order to increase rehabilitation, suggests that the responses were probably candid.

In addition to inspiring apprehension because of the loss of freedom and other deprivations, the threat of imprisonment is a potent deterrent for some potential offenders because of the stigmatization, reduction in status, and exclusion from society involved. Some evidence to support this can be found in the work of Willcock and Stokes, who found that 68 percent of the youths they surveyed regarded some aspect of social disapproval as the most important deterrent consideration (1968, p. 76). Nor in this connection can one ignore the fact that such other preventive effects of punishment as "its functions as an aid to moral education, as a habit-building mechanism, as a method of achieving respect for the law, and as a rationale for obedience" (Zimring and Hawkins 1973, pp. 77–89) will presumably operate no less in relation to the threat and example of imprisonment than in regard to any other method of punishment.

It is not necessary here to rehearse all the traditional functions of punishment. It can be said that insofar as punishment is in origin a substitue for private vengeance; insofar as it satisfies the public demand for retribution ("that the evil-doer should get what he deserves" [Grünhut 1948, p. 3]); insofar as it provides a symbolic affirmation of public disapproval: in all these respects imprisonment as a method of punishment fulfills recognized social functions. In addition there are other functions that imprisonment serves which derive from its unique character. Thus it serves a preventive function in that it provides for the insulation of persons regarded as posing a threat of injury to society or to individuals; and it serves also to satisfy what Herman Mannheim called the "principle of less eligibility" and Jeremy Bentham termed the "rule of severity," which finds its reflection in imprisonment in all those other deprivations, discomforts, and inconveniences, apart from the loss of liberty, that are involved in incarceration. As to the question whether it may not also sometimes serve a rehabilitative function, that topic will be discussed later in this work.

Are Prisons Necessary?

This is the second question that I have suggested as being of salient importance in considering the prison problem. It arises because, while it may be acknowledged that imprisonment serves a number of useful functions, it is still reasonable to ask whether the same objectives might not be easily achieved by other equally effective but less costly or less harmful means. Judgments of necessity in regard to social policy are always relative to the circumstances of the case and in particular to the availability of acceptable alternatives. Moreover, even when people, as they sometimes do, speak of something as being "an absolute necessity" it is relevant to ask what the thing is needed *for*. This relativity, or reference to a particular context, applies equally of course to denials of necessity.

Thus, both those who assert and those who deny that prisons are necessary always either implicitly or explicitly refer to some set of circumstances to which the assertion or denial of need is relevant. It should have been no surprise, therefore, to find that in surveying the writings of the critics of the prison system we found no absolute abolitionists and that, even in the case of those unequivocally committed to the abolition of prisons, this goal was seen as contingent on some very substantial changes being made in the social and economic structure of society at some prior point in time. This is not to deny, of course, that there are people who sometimes talk as though they would like to see prisons abolished immediately, but as we have seen these assertions on examination always turn out to be qualified in some way.

Sometimes we find that prison abolition is seen as something which, although clearly impossible in this country, might well be achievable somewhere else. An example of this attitude can be found in an interview with New York State Senator John Dunne, chairman of the State Senate's Committee on Crime and Corrections. Senator Dunne was asked: "Many people who are interested in prison reform want to ultimately abolish them. To what extent do you agree with that?" He replied: "I don't think it has any possibility in our society." But he added, "You might achieve it in Sweden or in some homogeneous community" (Dunne 1971, p. 825).

It is interesting to note that none of the other persons interviewed with Senator Dunne regarded the abolition of prisons as at all a proximate possibility. Norman Carlson, director of the Federal Bureau of Prisons, spoke of it as "from a utopian point of view . . . a desirable objective," but added, "I certainly do not think we'll abolish prisons in my lifetime." And he went on to make that desirable objective seem even more remote, if not totally unattainable: "Society will always have to deal with people who cannot conduct themselves in that society and try to change their behavior. . . . There are some hard-core offenders who are dangerous, assaultive types, and they do have to be confined both for the protection of society and also as a means to change their behavior" (Carlson 1971, p. 832). Even Herman Schwartz (professor of law at the State University of New York at Buffalo and director of the Prisoners' Rights Litigation Project), although he spoke of the prison system as "a disaster since it was first created" and an institution which "this society has no business supporting," did not mention abolition. Rather he said that he would "be working ... to attempt to change this deep-rooted social institution" (Schwartz 1971, pp. 821–23).

The abolition of prisons, in short, always seems to be located, even by its most enthusiastic proponents, at some point in space or time removed from the distasteful realities of the world in which we live. Somewhere, sometime, the walls will come down, the morning stars will sing together and all the decarcerated sons of God will shout for joy and become "morally autonomous, self-disciplined people"; but not here, not now. Here, now and for the foreseeable future, that frequently deplored, rarely defended, but "deep-rooted" institution we call prison is seen by the majority of citizens as, in some form or other, a necessary, or at least inevitable, feature of society.

This is not to say that there will be no changes in the size of the prison population or the nature of prisons. It seems likely that we will ultimately come to use the criminal justice system as "the agency of last resort for social problems" and the prison as "the last resort for correctional problems" (National Advisory Commission on Criminal Justice Standards and Goals 1973, p. 2). Certainly the most obvious practical corollaries of past experience are, first, a substantial diminution in the use of imprisonment and further expansion of alternatives to institutionalization; and, second, the construction of much smaller, specialized custodial establishments designed to meet the diversity of our penal needs and purposes.

But only an extravagantly sanguine reading of the history of penal reform could lead anyone to anticipate rapid progress along these lines. In 1954 Thorsten Sellin wrote: "Twenty-three years ago ... riots and disturbances had revealed glaring defects in our prison system. Most of those defects still exist, for progress in penology moves on leaden feet" (1954, p. vii).

Two decades later Sellin would only need to change a few words. Less than two decades later, in 1969, Hans W. Mattick, after twenty years of work in the field of criminal justice, formulated his "pessimistic hypothesis." Periodically, he wrote, there is, in this field, "criticism, exposure and crisis. . . . When that happens the routine response of the larger society, through its political representatives, is to enact a ritual known as 'fixing the responsibility'." But the main purpose this ritual serves is "to buy the time necessary to mollify a transiently aroused public interest. . . . The tumult and shouting dies. . . . The real captains and kings do not depart. The more things seem to change the more they remain the same. . . . The stage is set for a later repetition of the same cycle" (1969, pp. 368–69).

There is no doubt that Mattick is right about the cyclical pattern he identifies. Part of the reason for its persistence is probably the fact that what Daniel Bell calls "Tocqueville's law" does not directly apply to prisoners. Tocqueville's law states that "in a society pledged to the idea of equality, what the few have today, the many will demand tomorrow." Insofar as this is true, it is possible to make certain kinds of predictions about social trends by reference to the kinds of demands that will be made by disadvantaged groups. Bell cites the history of trade unionism by way of example and the way in which privileges once held by the managerial and white-collar class—pensions and security—later became diffused throughout the blue-collar class. Thus, he says, "one can chart similar rates of diffusion for the civil rights movement, for medical care for the population, for higher education for the greater proportion of youths and so forth" (Bell 1968, p. 328).

Prisons are not wholly excluded from this process of diffusion. But powerful constraints on change operate in their case which not only impede progress in penology but render prediction in this sphere more than usually problematic. One of these constraints is the prisoners' lack of any political leverage. Another is the operation of the principle of less eligibility, to which I have already referred. In this context the principle requires that the condition of the prisoner should be inferior, or at least not superior, to that of the lowest classes of the noncriminal population in a state of liberty. There is no doubt that this principle, which underlies much of the common thinking about the treatment of criminals, has always constituted a formidable barrier to penal reform. And it is surely utterly illusory to anticipate that in this field there is any likelihood that we shall move rapidly forward. Progressive politicians and correctional administrators who assume that penal reform is widely accepted as A Good Thing which reasonable people everywhere will automatically endorse are no more realistic than those whose distaste for the twentieth century induces them to keep their gaze fixed yearningly backwards.

In 1971, after the Attica uprising, Herman Schwartz said: "I hope that people will realize, apart from the killing of hostages, that what happened at Attica was the inevitable result of the inhumanity that man perpetrates against his fellow man in the name of justice" (Schwartz 1971, p. 822). Norman Carlson, director of the Federal Bureau of Prisons, said: "I am even more convinced that the long-run effect of Attica will be a positive step forward for prison reform" (Carlson 1971, p. 832). Linda Singer, of the Center for Correctional Justice, said: "Attica has alerted people to the fact that we are running a very repressive, self-defeating correction system. More and more people are becoming aware that the system not only is inhumane, but dysfunctional from the point of view of public safety, economics, or almost any way you want to look at it" (Singer 1971, p. 841).

It may appear cynical four years later to ask how large a step forward for prison reform was accomplished at that time. It may seem captious to enquire to what extent the general public realizes that the prison system is repressive, self-defeating, inhumane, and dysfunctional. But it is surely to the point to ask how many of our great maximum-security prisons—"these big Bastilles" as Preston Sharp of the American Correctional Association called them—have been shut down in the years since Attica. The answer of course is not one.

Today roughly half of the approximately 100,000 felons in maximum security facilities in the United States are still housed in prisons built prior to 1900. Twenty-six such prisons each contain well over 1,000 inmates, the largest holding nearly 4,000; and one-third of them are overcrowded. The oldest, Virginia Penitentiary, was erected in 1797; and its ancient cellblocks, too, are currently overcrowded. At the time they were built some of them were among the most costly buildings the world had seen since the Pyramids, although intended to house the living rather than the dead. Like the Pyramids, they were built to endure, and they have endured. Despite increasingly lethal explosions of violence within and persistent and mounting critical assaults from without they still dominate the correctional landscape; not merely picturesque monuments but living institutions, seemingly almost imperishable, both impregnable to attack and immune to the ravages of time.

Yet we did not relinquish our "edifice complex" in the twentieth century, and since 1900 we have built twenty-seven new state and federal prisons with room for more than 1,000 prisoners apiece (most recently at Lucasville, Ohio, in 1972); and nearly half of them are overcrowded. The State Prison of Southern Michigan holds the distinction of heading the list with a capacity for 4,764 inmates, and in the 1950s held more than 6,000 prisoners. These institutions, as the National Advisory Commission on Criminal Justice Standards and Goals stated, "form the backbone of our present-day correctional system." Moreover there is no indication that there has been any significant change in attitude on the part of those in positions of responsibility in the correctional systems of this country. It is not merely that our present prisons are seen as necessary; plans for new prisons have been approved and are in the process of implementation. To give only one example, in May 1972 the relatively enlightened Federal Bureau of Prisons, ignoring the recommendations of several national advisory commissions (for a moratorium on prison construction), published its "Long Range Master Plan." One critic, William G. Nagel, director of The American Foundation Incorporated, Institute of Corrections, has commented on the Master Plan: "A bureaucracy which had existed with only three prisons during its first thirty years, and which had gradually increased to 24 facilities during its next four decades, suddenly now planned to add 35 new correctional institutions costing over 500 million dollars. During a decade when people all over the country were seriously questioning—even rejecting—the desirability of creating any new correctional institutions at all the Federal Bureau decided to go construction crazy" (Nagel 1974, p. 6).

Another consideration which leads to the conclusion that the use of imprisonment as a punishment will be regarded as necessary for some time to come derives from the analyses of society's use of punishment to be found in the works of Nils Christie (1968, pp. 161–72) and Alfred Blumstein and Jacqueline Cohen (1973, pp. 198–207). What emerges from both these articles, the first dealing with Scandinavian data and the second principally with U.S. data, is the constancy of the imprisonment rate over long periods of time. Thus Christie demonstrates a remarkable stability in the imprisonment rates for Norway for the period 1880 to 1964 and a very similar pattern in Denmark and Sweden. Blumstein and Cohen show that, at a much higher level, the stability of the imprisonment rate in the United States for the period 1930 to 1970 was even more striking. It is of course not possible on the basis of the evidence provided to accept unreservedly Blumstein and Cohen's "conservation theory that suggests that society tries to impose a fairly constant level of punishment" (ibid., p. 207). But there is certainly nothing to suggest that the institution of imprisonment is likely to be regarded as dispensable in the imminent future.

According to Thorsten Sellin, the origins of imprisonment are lost in antiquity. It has proved to be the most perdurable of all penal methods, despite all the premature obituary notices. It is quite possible that eventually the maximum-security prison as we know it will be replaced by Playfair and Sington's "small nonpunitive custodial treatment centres, psychiatrically and/or sociologically based, and adapted to individual needs" (1965 p. 336). But it is surely both a perverse denial of experience and totally irresponsible to abjure attempts to deal with present problems because of the prospect of an imagined futurity.

Over half a century ago Sidney and Beatrice Webb wrote, at the conclusion of their survey of English prison history, "The reflection emerges that, when all is said and done, it is probably impossible to make a good job of the deliberate incarceration of human beings in the most enlightened of dungeons.... We suspect that it passes the wit of man to contrive a prison which shall not be gravely injurious to the minds of the vast majority of the prisoners, if not also to their bodies. So far as can be seen at present, the most hopeful of 'prison reforms' is to keep people out of prison altogether." Moreover they reported progress "in this direction ... during the last two decades" (1922, pp. 247–48).

But, although they were founders of the Fabian Society, it seems likely that the interminable protraction of that progress would, were they still alive, have exceeded even their predilection for gradualness and preference for slow rather than revolutionary change. For the truth is that the incarceration rate in England and Wales is actually higher than it was a century ago (Wilkins 1974, p. 236).

Prisons have survived in part because of what Morris and Zimring once referred to as "the four horsemen of political inaction: inertia, irresponsibility, ignorance, and cost" (1969, p. 138). But other factors have also been in operation: fear, resentment, vengefulness, and even, although it is fashionable to forget or depreciate them, idealism and compassion. The roots of these factors lie deep in the nature of man and human society, and they will tenaciously resist extirpation. To recognize this is not pessimism but realism; to refuse to recognize it is an evasion which can only tend to increase the amount of human suffering and waste involved in imprisonment.

WHAT SHOULD BE DONE ABOUT PRISONS?

"It is not unfair to say," Hans W. Mattick has written, "that if men had deliberately set themselves the task of designing an institution that would systematically maladjust men, they would have invented the large, walled, maximum security prison" (1974, p. 13). Indeed, there is a large measure of agreement among those who have seriously studied the prison problem that imprisonment per se is more likely to be harmful than beneficial. There is certainly agreement among all the critics we have considered that the prison system has been a failure. A widely held view is expressed by the National Advisory Commission on Criminal Justice Standards and Goals: "The failure of major institutions to reduce crime is incontestable. Recidivism rates are notoriously high. Institutions do succeed in punishing but they do not deter. They protect the community but that protection is only temporary. . . . They change the committed offender, but the change is more likely to be negative than positive" (1973, p. 1). Moreover, the prison "has persisted partly because a civilized nation could neither turn back to the barbarism of an earlier time nor find a satisfactory alternative" (ibid., p. 343).

It is true, as we have noted, that there are also those who would argue that the failure of prisons is due to their not having been sufficiently punitive. But both past and present experience clearly indicates that the only result to be expected from the implementation of a more punitive policy in prisons would be greatly intensified unrest, turbulence, riot and revolt, and a substantial increase in death and injury for both staff and prisoners. Because, for most people, costs of that order would be regarded as prohibitive, such a strategy is quite unfeasible. But apart from that, there is no good reason to doubt that insofar as deterrence is held to be a function of imprisonment it is fulfilled by the deprivation of liberty. In view of the suffering inevitably inherent in that experience, no deliberately punitive treatment of the offender in prison is necessary.

What then should be done about prisons? What are the policy implications of the theoretical discussions we have been considering? If a purely punitive approach is rejected can it be argued in the light of all the criticisms reviewed earlier that a rehabilitative policy is any more acceptable? And if that too is rejected what alternative policy is available? Before attempting to provide answers to these questions it is necessary to make two preliminary points on the subject of the rehabilitation of prisoners. The first relates to the present state of knowledge regarding the effectiveness of rehabilitation programs in penal institutions and the second to the extent to which such programs have been implemented.

Rehabilitation Reviewed

It is of course no more than a commonplace to remark that there is a notable lack of reliable empirical evidence about the effectiveness of correctional programs of any kind. "There are," as Leslie Wilkins has said, "problems arising from incompetence, unbridled enthusiasm, economy, misunderstanding, and many other factors, not excluding plain political suppression and distortion of results, which make the interpretation of the present state of knowledge in this field extremely hazardous" (1974, p. 238).

One of the best recent attempts to review the available research literature on the subject of the success or failure of attempts to rehabilitate offenders with various treatments in various institutional and noninstitutional settings is Robert Martinson's study (1974, pp. 22–54). Martinson and his associates were hired by the New York State Governor's Special Committee on Criminal Offenders to undertake a comprehensive survey of what was known about rehabilitation. They undertook a search of the literature for any available English-language reports on attempts at rehabilitation that had been made in American corrections systems and those of other countries from 1945 through 1967. They then analyzed in detail 231 selected studies which were "acceptable" in that their design and execution met "the conventional standards of social science research."

Martinson's article is condensed from a much fuller report, and it deals only with the effects of rehabilitative treatment on recidivism, which he describes as "the phenomenon which reflects most directly how well our present treatment programs are performing the task of rehabilitation." His findngs are baldly summarized in one sentence: *"With few and isolated exceptions, the rehabilitative efforts that have been reported so far have had no appreciable effect on recidivism"* (Martinson's italics). The project was formally completed in 1970, but Martinson adds, "Studies that have been done since our survey was completed do not present any major grounds for altering that original conclusion" (ibid., pp. 24–25).

Martinson goes on to consider questions and challenges that might be posed to his summary of findings. Of these it is only necessary here to mention one, which runs: "Do all of these studies lead us irrevocably to the conclusion that nothing works, that we haven't the faintest clue abut how to rehabilitate offenders and reduce recidivism?" To this he replies: "It is just possible that some of our treatment programs are working to some extent, but that our research is so bad that it is incapable of telling. Having entered this very serious caveat, I am bound to say that these data, involving over two hundred studies and hundreds of thousands of individuals as they do, are the best available and give us very little reason to hope that we have in fact found a sure way of reducing recidivism through rehabilitation" (ibid., pp. 48–49).

It may be added that Martinson's negative conclusion is in general agreement with those of earlier reviews of the literature dealing with the outcome of correctional treatment. Thus a 1954 review concluded that "most treatment programs are based on hope and perhaps informed speculation rather than on verified information" (Kirby 1954, p. 374). More recently, an article which presents the results of a content analysis of reports of empirical evaluations of correctional treatment, mainly published between 1940 and 1960, concluded that "it seems quite clear that, on the basis of this sample of outcome reports with all its limitations, evidence supporting the efficacy of correctional treatment is slight, inconsistent, and of questionable reliability" (Bailey, 1966, p. 157). In short there is a consensus to the effect that rehabilitative treatment has not been shown to be effective.

This brings us to the second point which needs to be stated about rehabilitation. It can be made by reference to the articles by Bailey and Martinson that I have cited. Bailey, in relation to the question how to account for the fact that there has been no apparent progress in the demonstration of the validity of various types of correctional treatment, suggests that it is possible that "little of the rehabilitation work being done should be dignified by the term treatment" (ibid., p. 157). Similarly, Martinson says: "It may simply be that our programs aren't yet good enough— that the education we provide to inmates is still poor education, that the therapy we administer is not administered skillfully enough, that our intensive supervision and counseling do not yet provide enough personal support for the offenders who are subjected to them. If one wishes to believe this, then what our correctional system needs is simply a more full-hearted commitment to the strategy of treatment" (1974, p. 49).

This may sound suspiciously like the kind of rationalization, popular among correctional treatment workers faced with neg- ative-outcome studies regarding programs in which they are involved, which are subjected to devastating analysis by Donald Cressey (1958, pp. 754–71). But there is surely a valid point to be made here even by those who are not committed in any way to a reformist or rehabilitative ideology. It is simply that despite the theoretical emphasis on reform and the widespread use of the terminology of rehabilitation the actual experience of imprison- ment for most persons imprisoned in this country in this century has been simply punitive. I have earlier noted Glaser's findings that even in the relatively benign federal prisons, inmates testified that "the unpleasantness of the confinement experience" was a salient feature of the impact of imprisonment on them (Glaser 1964, p. 481). The truth is that only a small minority of offenders have ever done their time in a "pastel prison" (Kassebaum, Ward, and Wilner 1971, chap. 2).

In the year in which Martinson's study was completed Norval Morris and I published a book in which the following passage occurs:

There are twenty-five prisons in the United States over a hundred years old. Sixty-one prisons opened before 1900 are still in use. Inside these fortress structures only a small fraction of those confined are exposed to any kind of correctional service other than restraint. The President's Crime Commission report speaks of conditions which "are often a positive detriment to rehabilitation" and of life in many penal institutions as "at best barren and futile, at worst unspeakably brutal and degrading." The task force on corrections summed up its findings regarding the four hundred institutions for adult felons in this country as follows: "Some are grossly understaffed and under-equipped— conspicuous products of public indifference. Overcrowding and idleness are the salient features of some, brutality and corrup- tion of a few others. Far too few are well organized and adequately funded." As for the local jails which handle mis- demeanants, these are described by the task force as "generally the most inadequate in every way. . . . Not only are the great majority of these facilities old but many do not even meet the minimum standards in sanitation, living space, and segre- gation of different ages and types of offenders that have obtained generally in the rest of corrections for several decades" (Morris and Hawkins 1970, pp. 111–12).

We went on to describe the "correctional" system as antique, overloaded, neglected, expensive, cruel, and inefficient.

Has the situation changed since Attica? Consider the following appraisal, written in 1972:

In New York State, which has the highest concentration of psychologists and psychiatrists of any place on earth, there is not one single staff psychiatrist in the state penal system. There are just sixty psychiatrists in the entire American prison system,

federal and state included. Less than five cents of each dollar
spent for "corrections" is spent on trying to correct anybody.
That five cents has to be split among the social workers, the rare
psychologist, and work release programs (for about 5,000 of
more than 200,000 inmates), or other rehabilitative efforts.

Or this passage from the same work:

Ask a state prison administrator if there is any effective
rehabilitative effort being made in his system and he will
instantly begin talking about the shortage of money, the
problems with security, and "troublemakers." He will not
answer the question "yes" or "no." But if you should manage to
confront him with the direct question, he would have to say
"no" in at least forty-six of the fifty state prison systems in
this country.
    We do not have in America, and we never have had, any
rehabilitation program on a significant scale for a significant
length of time (Badillo and Haynes 1972, pp. 178–79).

    Of course this situation has been partly concealed by what
Cressey refers to as "labeling as 'correctional' almost anything
convicted criminals are expected to do" so that "whatever is done
with prisoners to keep them occupied and/or productive and
quiet is likely to be called a correctional measure" (1958, p. 763).
But at a time when vast numbers of prisoners are neither
occupied, productive, nor quiet, this particular device is less
impressive than it might have been in some earlier periods in
history. Moreover, except for those whose preference for "words"
rather than "things" is at the level of an addiction, the crucial
issue is the nature of what we are doing rather than what we
choose to call it.
    On this point there is no shortage of information. The report
of the Task Force on Corrections of the National Advisory
Commission on Criminal Justice Standards and Goals, the last of
a series of four nationwide studies of corrections beginning with
the Wickersham Commission report in 1931, points out that
many of the recommendations of the latter report have yet to be
implemented. One significant quotation from the 1973 report will
suffice: "During the past decade, conditions in several prison
systems have been found by the courts to constitute cruel and

unusual punishment in violation of the Constitution. In its 1971-72 term, the U.S. Supreme Court decided eight cases directly affecting offenders, and in each of them the offender's contention prevailed" (1973, p. 1).

What emerges clearly is that whatever label we may choose to apply to the treatment of the inmates of prisons the experience of imprisonment has remained essentially one of deprivation and affliction for the vast majority of prisoners (even in federal prisons, as Glaser's inquiry revealed), an unpleasant experience which is seen as primarily deterrent. To say, as John Conrad does, that "the ideology of people-changing permeates corrections. Modern prisons remain committed to treatment" (1973, p. 208), may be an accurate reflection of the discourse of correctional administrators, but it can hardly be regarded as a reliable index to correctional practice.

Policy Implications

Even in situations where the rehabilitative ideal has been embodied in correctional practice the evidence from the empirical studies that have been made in recent decades is overwhelmingly negative. Thus Conrad is clearly right when he says of rehabilitative programs that "it is not possible to continue the justification of policy decisions in corrections on the supposition that such programs achieve rehabilitative objectives" (ibid., p. 209). As a result, certain questions remain to be answered: What programs should be adopted in penal institutions? On what grounds can they be justified? In the current enthusiasm for alternatives to incarceration among scholars, administrators, and clinicians, these questions have not received very much attention; although, as has been argued here, there is every indication that for the foreseeable future large numbers of offenders will certainly be incarcerated.

One of the few scholars who has considered the questions at issue is Rupert Cross. As we have seen, Cross regards the idea that prison is reformative as a myth which has had a "baneful influence." He does not subscribe to what he calls "the reform-atory theory of punishment." He rejects the promotion of reform as the object of imprisonment and says, "[I]t seems to me that evidence is not sufficiently clear to warrant the addition of a day to a prison sentence in the name of reform" (1971, pp. 124-25). Training in prison, he says, is commonly "a euphemism for a dull and inadequate day's work" (ibid., p. 169).

At the same time he draws a distinction between two types of penal reform. There is the kind of penal reform represented by a measure aimed at the rehabilitation of the offender, and there is the kind of penal reform represented by a measure the primary aim of which is humanitarian, "i.e. the provision of whatever control of crime the penal system can achieve with the minimum of suffering to the offender and those connected with him" (ibid., p. 45). He is skeptical about the former because he has "invincible doubts about the extent to which it is possible to influence the behavior of mentally normal adults by acceptable artifically contrived means while they are in prison" (ibid., pp. 84-85). But he favors the latter and protests "against the tendency to belittle humanitarianism as a yardstick of progress in penal matters" (ibid., p. 45).

"The main aim of prison reform," he argues, "should be the prevention of prisoners' deterioration." As to what this would mean in practice he indicates that the methods to be employed would be "similar" to those which are supposed to promote reformation. As ways of counteracting possible deformative effects, he suggests only that the prisoner should be provided with education "in the broad sense," vocational training, work, and means for remaining in contact with the community outside prison. In addition, he urges regular prisoner-staff communication on something other than disciplinary problems.

Another authority who has rejected the treatment model for prisons and also has given some consideration to the provision of a more satisfactory alternative is Leslie Wilkins. He believes that "something like prisons will be needed for a long time." Like Cross, he rejects the treatment model, both because the evidence is all against its being effective and because it has provided excuses for inequitable measures and abuses of power. Like Cross, also, he favors more humane procedures but does not think that the humanization of prisons requires much more than the implementation of principles which are already commonly articulated in theory although less commonly embodied in practice.

Specifically, he says:

The methods whereby prisons are operated need not involve very different procedures from those currently in fashion. There is no reason why persons who are incarcerated (for purposes of isolation, punishment or both) should not be (a) treated humanely; (b) taught trades; (c) provided with socially useful activities in their captivity; (d) adequately rewarded for work done; (e) given group therapy or other treatment (medical or psychiatric) if they volunteer for it; (f) provided with similar protections as those given to persons on the outside insofar as is feasible; (g) permitted to spend their time in captivity in as dignified a manner as is possible. The prisoner is still to be seen as a person while the society within which he is permitted to move is constrained (1974, p. 246).

Norval Morris, in *The Future of Imprisonment*, has attempted "to define the proper role of the prison in a democratic society" and to provide "a new model of imprisonment" (1974, pp. ix–x). Morris agrees that rehabilitative programs in prisons have been "characterized more by false rhetoric than by solid achievement" and that they have been "corrupted to punitive purposes" (ibid., p. 13); but he does not accept the inference that they should be totally discarded. Rather than rejecting the idea of rehabilitation altogether in favor of "the prevention of prisoners' deterioration," as Cross suggests, he argues for "the substitution of facilitated change for coerced cure" (ibid., p. 27). Rehabilitative programs in prison must be expanded and improved, he says, "but they must be related neither to the time the prisoner serves nor to the conditions of his incarceration." We should abandon the pretense of rehabilitative purposes for many prisoners and accept retraining objectives for some on an entirely voluntary basis.

Although Morris's emphasis is on the future of imprisonment and he envisages "a profound evolutionary change in what is a 'prison'" (ibid., pp. ix–x), what he says is no less relevant to prisons as they are in our society today. The distinction he draws between punishment for rehabilitative purposes, which is condemned by those I have referred to as the reductivists, and the facilitation of rehabilitative efforts during punishments otherwise justified, is one which can be applied in practice in the "mega-prisons" of which he disapproves just as easily as in the "small multi-purpose institutions" which he envisages as ultimately taking their place. Moreover it provides a definition of a role for the prison and of an appropriate function for rehabilitative purposes within the prison which can be accepted by all save those whose solutions to the prison problem are couched in terms of impossible retrogression or millennial dreams.

Rupert Cross was right to warn against "the extreme importance of avoiding calling the same thing by different names" (1971, p. 163). The authors of *Struggle for Justice* were right, too, about label switching: "Call them 'community treatment centers' or what you will, if human beings are involuntarily confined in them, they are prisons" (AFSC 1971, p. 23). They might in fact have cited good eighteenth-century authority, for in the second volume of *Institutes of the Laws of England* Edward Coke says "every restraint of the liberty of a freeman is an imprisonment, although he be not within the walls of any common prison" (Coke 1797, p. 482).

In the past, change has too often been no more than nomenclatural. Yet it does not follow, as seems almost to be implied sometimes, that the prison must be held in a condition of permanent stasis. It is worth remembering that, as Fox wrote in 1952, "Imprisonment as a punishment of the first instance has developed, as a complete conception, almost within the time of men now living" (p. 19). In the context of the American culture, which is characterized by a remarkable capacity for adaptation to change, it is inconceivable that the prison, unlike all other social institutions, should not evolve or develop at all, but remain immutable. The note of cautious conservatism sounded in this chapter is an inference from the past but it is not intended as a prescription for the future.

Certainly those for whom the full-blooded rhetoric of rehabilitation retains its perennial appeal may find flat and uninspiring the conclusion that we should do no more than try to protect the prisoner from abuse, ensure that within the inevitable conditions of custody the experience of imprisonment should not be too oppressive, and provide "rehabilitative training" on a voluntary basis. But to take that attitude is to forget how rarely even the modest objective of providing humane and decent material conditions of life has been achieved, and how frequently in our institutionalized-custody arrangements, in many cases with benevolent intentions, we have tolerated, and still do tolerate, practices totally inconsistent with even a minimal conception of human dignity.

What is called the conscience of the nation or the conscience of mankind has proved no less elastic than the consciences of individuals. Although one of the principal functions of any prison system, if it is to be more than a system of institutionalized vengeance, should be the protection of the individual offender against oppression, prisoners traditionally have been vulnerable to abuse and without effective remedy against it. The history of prisoner treatment, in fact, has been largely a record of deviation from humanitarian theory and practice.

For many people in the community, prisoners are still seen as alien, abhorrent, and inferior. In the circumstances it is easy to forget that even under benign conditions of custody the experience of captivity is stressful and oppressive; and that the physical and psychological deprivations involved commonly induce frustration and despair. The adoption of custodial methods and procedures which genuinely reflected the belief that prisoners share a humanity common with our own would alone constitute an immense step forward along the path from barbarism to civilization.

3   The Effects of Imprisonment

"Penology," Leslie Wilkins has said, "has a level of knowledge which might place it as some kind of mythology." This is nowhere better exemplified than in the literature dealing with the effects of imprisonment. If by myth is meant an ill-founded belief embodying some popular idea that serves as an explanation, then the myth of prisonization which will be considered in this chapter might serve as a paradigm.

In its most primitive form this myth may be found in the writings of the eighteenth- and nineteenth-century penal reformers. The essence of it is the notion that prisons are schools of crime or, as John Howard put it in 1777, "seats and seminaries of idleness and every vice" (p. 8). In prison, according to Thomas Fowell Buxton, "by the greatest possible degree of misery, you produce the greatest possible degree of wickedness" (1818, p. 19). The prisoner is incarcerated because "he is too bad for society," but after he has served his sentence he is returned to the world "impaired in health, debased in intellect, and corrupted in principles." Buxton illustrated this process with an account of the corruption of a young lawyer in Newgate who was initially repulsed by the thieves, highwaymen, and murderers with whom he was imprisoned, but "by insensible degrees he began to lose his repugnance of their society, caught their flash terms and sang their songs, was admitted to their revels and acquired, in place of habits of perfect sobriety, a taste for spirits" (ibid., pp. 49–50).

Bentham formulated the idea in a characteristically vigorous passage, which anticipates almost every element of early prison sociology:

Prisons, with the exception of a small number, include every imaginable means of infecting both body and mind. Consider merely the state of forced idleness to which prisoners are reduced, and this punishment is excessively expensive. Want of exercise enervates and enfeebles their faculties, and deprives their organs of suppleness and elasticity; despoiled, at the same time, of their characters and of their habits of labor, they are no sooner out of prison than starvation drives them to commit offences. Subject to the subaltern despotism of men who for the most part are depraved by the constant spectacle of crime and the habit of tyranny, those wretches may be delivered up to a thousand unknown sufferings, which aggravate them against society, and which harden them to the sense of punishment. In a moral point of view, *an ordinary prison is a school in which wickedness is taught* by surer means than can ever be employed for the inculcation of virtue. Weariness, revenge, and want preside over *these academics of crime.* All the inmates raise themselves to the level of the worst; the most ferocious inspires the others with his ferocity; the most cunning teaches his cunning to all the rest; the most debauched inculcates his licentiousness. All possible defilements of the heart and the imagination become the solace of their despair. United by a common interest, they assist each other in throwing off the yoke of shame. Upon the ruins of social honour is built a new honour, composed of falsehood, fearlessness under disgrace, forgetfulness of the future, and hostility to mankind; and thus it is that unfortunates, who might have been restored to virtue and to happiness, reach the heroic point of wickedness, the sublimity of crime (1864, pp. 351–52; my italics).

The notion that imprisonment in the conditions of promiscuity described by the early reformers must inevitably lead to mutual contamination and corruption led, in England, to the adoption of

the Benthamite idea of "classified association" in Robert Peel's
Gaol Act of 1823. But this did not satisfy some reformers, who felt
that it would only "specialize the contamination" as the Webbs put
it. It was feared, in the words of Joshua Jebb, that "if each class
respectively be composed of burglars, or assault and battery men,
or sturdy beggars, they will acquire under it increased proficiency
only in picking locks, fighting or imposing on the tender mercies
of mankind" (Webb 1922, pp. 93–94). Ultimately this line of
reasoning led to the adoption of the principle of separate
confinement and the solitary system.

But belief in the corruptive effects of imprisonment survived all
the efforts of the reformers. A. Wood Renton in the *Law
Quarterly Review* in 1890 described the English prison system as
"simply a manufactory of lunatics and criminals" (Renton 1890,
p. 338). And Kropotkin, also writing at the end of the nineteenth
century, was quite unimpressed by the results of their work. "Our
model and modern penitentiaries," he said, are "a hundred times
more corrupting than the dungeons of the Middle Ages" (1885, p.
243); he described them as "universities of crime, maintained by
the state" (1899, p. 468). Prisons in his view remained "nurseries
of criminal education" which "have not moralized anybody but
have more or less demoralized all those who have spent a number
of years there."

Kropotkin supported these assertions with some statistics
relating to recidivism in a manner which critics of the prison
system continue to do to this day. "Figures tell us loudly enough"
he wrote, "that the supposed double influence of prisons—the
deterring and the moralizing—exist only in the imagination of
lawyers." He followed this with a selection of figures from the
*Compte Rendu général de l'Administration de la Justice Crimi-
nelle en France en 1878 et 1879* including such items as, "Nearly
one-half of all people condemned by the Courts are regularly
released prisioners" and "forty-two to forty-five percent of all
assassins condemned every year are récidivistes." In addition he
quoted with approval a passage from Lombroso's *L'Uomo
delinquente* which runs: "If those who die after liberation and
those whose *récidive* crimes are not discovered be taken into
account, it remains an open question whether the number of
récidivistes is not equal to that of liberated prisoners" (1887, pp.

305-9). The implication was, presumably, that if follow-up studies were carried out the "open question" would be likely to be answered in terms of total recidivism.

But in the absence of such follow-up studies, and in view of the great variety of variables and factors which have to be taken into account in considering such questions as the causes of recidivism and the effects of imprisonment, there is something breathtaking about the inferential leap involved in this type of argument. It is an interesting example of a post hoc explanation in which both the precedent cause (corruption in prison) and the consequent effect (total recidivism) are hypothetical. Such cogency as it possesses derives from the unexpressed, unsupported, and dubious assumption that sordid or wretched conditions must inevitably produce deplorable results.

This is not to say that this does not sometimes happen. There is little doubt that some prisoners are "corrupted" by their experiences in prison and that some recidivate as a result of this. But to elevate St. Paul's advice to the Corinthians about the corruptive effects of evil communications to the status of a universal generalization is to go a lot further than is warranted by either such objective evidence as is available or by the ordinary experience of daily life. In view of the complexity involved in evaluating or assessing the effects of imprisonment the unequivocal assumption of a uniformly deteriorative impact is extraordinary.

One final example of the "crime schools" argument deserves mention. This is Stephen Hobhouse and A. Fenner Brockway's *English Prisons Today* in which it is asserted: "In general the effects of imprisonment are of the nature of a progressive weakening of the mental powers and of a deterioration of the character in a way which renders the prisoner less fit for useful social life, more predisposed to crime, and in consequence more liable to reconviction" (1922, p. 561). It is interesting to note that they also consider the argument "that this process of deterioration among prisoners is not due directly to prison discipline, but to the practice of masturbation which has its origin in the earlier life of the prisoner." The authors take the view that "even where this is true of his earlier life, there is little doubt that imprisonment considerably aggravates the tendency to such perverted

activity. . . . The true view of the matter seems to be that the habit
of masturbation is very often acquired as one of the results of
mental deterioration . . . and when this occurs, the sexual
excesses which are involved, must as a rule, considerably increase
the mental and moral deterioration which has already set in."
One "very intelligent ex-convict," incidentally, told the authors
that "self-abuse" was "*the* worst effect of the penal servitude
system" (ibid., pp. 587–88).

PRISONIZATION

It is not necessary to review the whole of the social science
literature on the prison inmate's world from its beginning in Hans
Reimer's "participant observer" study (1937). It is convenient
here to begin with Donald Clemmer's *The Prison Community,* in
which the concept of prisonization was introduced and defined as
"the taking on in greater or less degree of the folkways, mores,
customs and general culture of the penitentiary." According to
Clemmer, every prisoner was subject to "certain influences which
we may call the universal factors of prisonization." These factors
included such things as the acceptance of an inferior role,
accumulation of facts concerning the organization of the prison,
the development of somewhat new habits of eating, dressing,
working, sleeping, the adoption of local language and the recognition that nothing is owed to the environment for the supplying of
needs. He described the process of prisonization as being such
that "even if no other factor of the prison culture touches the
personality of an inmate of many years residence, the influences
of these universal factors are sufficient to make a man characteristic of the penal community and probably so disrupt his
personality that a happy adjustment in any community becomes
next to impossible." In the course of assimilation into the culture
of the prison community the inmate became subject to "influences which breed or deepen criminality and antisociality and
make the inmate characteristic of the criminalistic ideology in the
prison community."

It is important to note that Clemmer's theory of prisonization
was a good deal more sophisticated than the primitive "schools of
crime" thesis. Moreover, while he asserted that "every man who
enters the penitentiary undergoes prisonization to some extent,"

he acknowledged that there were "inmates who are incarcerated for only short periods, such as a year or so" who "do not become integrated into the culture ... and are able when released to take up a new mode of life without much difficulty." There were, he said, "degrees of prisonization," although he took the view that "it is probable that more men approach the complete degree than the least degree of prisonization."

In general he saw prisons as "part of a decadent system of justice" and was as convinced as earlier critics had been that they were harmful to society and criminogenic. "Your writer," he wrote, "is sure, of course, that prisons are awful. He is sure that the protection they claim for society is generally exaggerated, from the long-term point of view. He is sure that the prisons work immeasurable harm on the men held in them as well as the employees that care for them" (1940, pp. 299–316). Later he wrote: "It can be stated that imprisonment even in progressive institutions with their carefully developed training programs, frequently increases the criminality of the individuals it holds" (1950–51, p. 319).

Clemmer's book was the first substantial sociological work on the prison, but in succeeding years a considerable body of literature grew up in the form of journal articles, many of which explored the ideas which Clemmer had expounded. For the most part they confirmed his thesis, and when, in late 1956, Gresham Sykes and Sheldon Messinger wrote a paper entitled "The Inmate Social System," in which they attempted to codify and interpret the published literature dealing with the "inmate culture" or the "prisoner community" up to that date, they were able to summarize the salient features of the society of prisoners as presented in that literature in terms which indicated a remarkable degree of agreement amongst "observers of the prison."

They found for example that "despite the number and diversity of prison populations observers of such groups have reported only one strikingly pervasive value system." This took the form of an inmate code which reflected inmate solidarity in opposition to the prison staff and to conventional values and goals. Moreover they were able to list the chief tenets of the inmate code in the form of maxims which, they stated, "are usually asserted with great vehemence by the inmate population," violations of which "call forth a diversity of sanctions ranging from ostracism to physical violence." (It may be observed parenthetically that some of the maxims included in the code sound as though Sir Robert Baden-Powell, the founder of the Boy Scout movement, had a hand in drafting them: "Don't lose your head," "Don't break your word," "Be tough; be a man," and "Don't whine.")

In addition they found that the prison community as a social system could be described in terms of certain roles or patterns of behavior exhibited by the inmates. These patterns, "recognized and labeled by prisoners in the pungent argot of the dispossessed" (including "rat," "gorilla," "fag" and "right guy"), were said to constitute a collection of social roles which, with their interrelationships, made up the inmate social system. These roles were said to reflect the inmate code in that they were defined in terms of deviation from or conformity to the system of inmate norms.

This social system was seen as arising to cope with the problems of adjustment confronted by inmates entering prison. In particular Sykes and Messinger identified as "pains of imprisonment," which encouraged socialization into the inmate culture by prisoners, status degradation, material deprivation, sexual deprivation, and enforced intimacy with other deviants. It was emphasized that as prisoners moved toward the solidarity demanded by the inmate code, the pains of imprisonment were mitigated. It was the fact that the development of the inmate social system was essentially a response to these "conditions of imprisonment" that explained "the remarkable similarity of the inmate social systems found in one custodial institution after another."

Now it is clear that the process of prisonization, or as Sykes and Messinger put it, "the transformation of the novitiate into a fully accredited convict," is a criminogenic process which would militate against reform or rehabilitation (1960, pp. 5–16). Sutherland and Cressey sum it up as follows: "The general effect of prisonization is the introduction, with varying degrees of efficiency, of all inmates to attitudes, codes, norms and values which are in many ways contradictory to anti-criminal norms. Because it causes prisoners to identify themselves as persons quite different from non-criminals, even contact with the 'universal factors' will render difficult any effort at clinical treatment" (1970, p. 538).

It is clear also that if the observers' findings about the pervasiveness of the inmate code and the correspondence between inmate social systems in different custodial institutions represented an accurate picture of reality, then the "training schools for crime" hypothesis could be said to have been validated in essence if not in specific terms. For although Clemmer and those who followed him in the 1950s frequently qualified their statements and made suggestions for further research, there is no doubt that Daniel Glaser and John Stratton were correct in saying that "the approach ... most strongly suggested by sociological literature is to assume that all prisoners become criminally oriented during imprisonment..., that if offenders are thrown into contact primarily with other offenders and are isolated from sources of support for anti-criminal values, one should expect them to become increasingly criminal in their attitudes" (Glaser and Stratton 1961, p. 381).

CRITIQUE OF PRISONIZATION

The prisonization hypothesis did not die as the result of the administration of a skillful coup de grace. It suffered a death by a thousand qualifications, so attenuated that even now there are those who are unaware of its demise. Indeed in the case of a myth which draws strength from a traditional belief like the "school for crime" dogma, with all the unconscious and irrational power that such beliefs have, it is probably premature to speak of it in the past tense. For that reason also it is necessary to review briefly and selectively the history of theoretical developments in this area in recent years.

It is possible to trace three principal lines of criticism which, taken together, have a cumulative impact that totally undermines the prisonization thesis both as a description and as an explanation of the social organization of the prison and of inmate attitudes, values, and behavior. The three critical approaches to be discussed view the prison from different perspectives and their conclusions are not entirely congruent. Nevertheless there is a large degree of correspondence insofar as their implications regarding prisonization are concerned.

One of the first aspects of Clemmer's theory to be critically assessed was his assumption that prisonization was directly related to time spent in the institution, in that the longer the inmate spent in the institution the greater the degree of prisonization to be expected. In his schema setting out the factors tending to produce "the highest or greatest degree of prisonization," he placed first: "A sentence of many years, thus a long subjection to the universal factors of prisonization."

Stanton Wheeler reported a study which was designed to review the processes described by Clemmer and to test some of his propositions. The most significant of Wheeler's findings for the purpose of this discussion was discrepant with Clemmer's analysis, in that inmates' attitudes, as measured by questionnaire responses, did not reflect the development of prisonization in the way suggested by Clemmer.

On the contrary Wheeler found that a U-shaped pattern of responses appeared to reflect a cyclical change from socially conformist attitudes, through antisocial attitudes, and back to conformist attitudes in the latter part of the sentence prior to release. He concluded that the inmate's response to the prison is probably adaptive, in that prisons develop subcultures specific to the problems imposed by their unique characters. Thus inmates become both prisonized and deprisonized; they are probably insulated from lasting socialization effects, and it is likely that the impact of the prison culture is short-lived.

Subsequently Peter G. Garabedian reported on an independent study carried out in a maximum-security prison (1963). The evidence he presented supported Wheeler's findings. He too found that the process of prisonization was reversed as the inmate came to the end of his prison career. Similarly Daniel Glaser presents evidence which indicates that "the prison experience is not one of progressively increasing criminalization for all or most of those involved" (1964, p. 476). Glaser also found evidence of a U-shaped curve of attitudes during imprisonment, with inmates' attitudes reflecting most prisonization towards the middle of the confinement period and showing a reverse orientation near the end of their prison terms.

Some time later a study carried out in a federal maximum-security institution by Robert Atchley and M. Patrick McCabe, using exactly the same methodology as that used by Wheeler, was designed to collect additional evidence concerning the theory of prisonization as advanced by Clemmer and modified by Wheeler. The findings of this study not only failed to confirm Clemmer's observations about the influence of time in the development of prisonization but also do not support Wheeler's modification of Clemmer's thesis in terms of the importance of the phase of the prison term in relation to prisonization. Atchley and McCabe concluded their study by asserting: "The results of our research leave existing theories concerning the social psychodynamics of prison life in shambles" (1968, p. 785). They suggested, however, that a possible reason for their failure to find support for the models of either Clemmer or Wheeler might lie in differences in institutional organization and orientation between the respective institutions studied.

More recently Gene Kassebaum, David Ward, and Daniel Wilner, referring to the finding by Wheeler and Glaser of a curvilinear relationship with highest endorsement of conventional norms at the beginning and end of the prison term, reported: "Aggregate data from our own study . . . turned up no evidence of a curvilinear relationship in the endorsement of inmate norms and the time served in prison." Like Atchley and McCabe, however, they suggest that the extent and nature of endorsement of prisoner norms may be a function of institutional organization. "We would expect to find more solidarity among inmates and more traditional prison inmate types in a correctional system with only one institution for adult felons and where that institution is characterized by more severe material and socio-psychological deprivations" (1971, p. 303).

This brings us to the second line of criticism, which holds that the prisonization thesis is unsatisfactory because it does not take into account the effect on patterns of inmate behavior of variations in the organization of the institution. As Street, Vinter, and Perrow put it: "The 'solidary opposition' account fails to give sufficient consideration to the consequences for the inmate social system of changes and variations in the larger organization, particularly through the introduction of modern treatment ideology and technology." The rationale underlying this criticism is "the general proposition that the characteristics and functions of informal groups vary with the larger organizational context" (1966, p. 223).

This particular study, which deals with youth institutions, demonstrates that inmates in those institutions responded differently to the staff and to their fellows depending on whether the formal authority system emphasized custody and discipline or individual and group treatment. In contrast to the view that the inmate group is inevitably and uniformly cohesive and oppositional, the researchers found considerable variations among institutions in the perspectives and social relations of the inmates. They found also that the variations were systematically related to organizational goals in that inmates of the obedience/conformity institutions had relatively negative attitudes toward the institution as compared with those in the treatment institutions.

Two related studies, Oscar Grusky's of a prison camp and Bernard Berk's of three minimum-security prisons, point to a similar conclusion. Grusky found that "when treatment is a dominant goal in a small prison, a pattern of cooperation between the informal leaders and the authorities may be established which promotes rather than hinders treatment. The inmate culture . . . was organized not around the most hostile, but rather around the most cooperative, offenders" (1959, p. 67). Berk's study, which was designed as a replication of Grusky's, was applied to three prisons ranked on a continuum ranging from a strong treatment orientation to a strong custodial orientation. He found that inmate attitudes were more positive in treatment institutions than in custodial ones. In particular he noted that "the goal of 'custody' with its concomitant centralized and formal authority structure and increased deprivations for inmates, contributed significantly to the development of the hostile informal organization in the custodial prison" (1966, p. 534).

An associated study by David Street dealt with four juvenile institutions, two custodial and two treatment-oriented. He found that "inmates in the treatment oriented institutions more often expressed positive attitudes toward the institution and staff, non-prisonized views of adaptation to the institution, and positive images of self-change" (1965, pp. 47–49).

Other more recent studies include those by John Wilson and Jon D. Snodgrass (1969) and Gene Kassebaum, David Ward, and

Daniel Wilner (1971). Wilson and Snodgrass analyzed the relationship between a therapeutic community organized in an adult maximum-security institution and adherence to "the prison code." They found a positive relationship between the therapeutic community and socialization and a negative relationship between the therapeutic community and the prison code. Kassebaum, Ward, and Wilner's study was carried out in a medium-security prison with "an elaborate treatment program." They state that "at the time of our study, the inmates did not seem to be a well-organized community solidified in their resistance to an oppressive prison regime." Further they say: "Our findings have prompted us to question the extent to which inmates internalize criminal norms as a result of prison confinement, and the extent to which this is a factor in recidivism" (1971, pp. 297–302).

Stanton Wheeler has reported on a comparative study carried out in collaboration with Nils Christie of "old custodial model" institutions and "individualized treatment" institutions in the Scandinavian countries (1968). There, too, it was found that the responses of the inmates reflected patterns of attitudes toward the different kinds of prison similar to those reported in the American studies. Similarly, Thomas Matthiesen, in a sociological study of inmates in a treatment-oriented, medium-security Norwegian correctional institution, found that "the population of inmates was characterized by a profound lack of solidarity," and that the "inmates seemed to a considerable extent 'unprisonized' " (1965, p. 11).

One point made by Matthiesen in this connection is of interest in that it relates to the third line of criticism to be considered. He suggests that the lack of a subcultural tradition outside of the institutions in Norway may be reflected in the correctional setting and contribute to lack of solidarity among inmates "because it operates against the institutionalization of cultural dissensus inside institutions" (ibid., p. 223). The suggestion that inmate life will to a large extent reflect broader cultural conditions is the basis of the powerful critique of almost all the earlier work on the social organization of inmate social systems written by John Irwin and Donald R. Cressey. The essential point of the Irwin-Cressey paper is stated in their opening sentences: "In the rapidly-growing literature on the social organization of correctional institutions, it has become common to discuss 'prison culture' and 'inmate culture' in terms of suggesting that the behavior systems of various types of inmates stem from the conditions of imprisonment themselves. Use of a form of structural-functional analysis in research and observation of institutions has led to emphasis of the notion that internal conditions stimulate inmate behavior of various kinds, and there has been a glossing over of the older notion that inmates may bring a culture with them into prison. Our aim is to suggest that much of the inmate behavior classified as part of the prison culture is not peculiar to prison at all" (1962, p. 142).

Irwin and Cressey recognize that others, including both Reimer and Clemmer, had noted that conformity to prison expectations depended to some degree on prior outside conditions. They also refer to the work of Clarence Schrag (1961) and Donald Garrity (1961), in which some recognition was given to the importance of preprison experiences, social identities, and cultural backgrounds of inmates. But they argue that "the 'functional' or 'indigenous origin' notion has been overemphasized and that observers have overlooked the dramatic effect that external behavior patterns have on the conduct of inmates in any given prison" (1962, p. 145). They suggest moreover that the culture of prisoners is actually an amalgam of three different subcultures—the thief, the convict, and the legitimate or conventional—membership in which is determined by the participants' own previous careers.

The most significant feature of the Irwin-Cressey thesis, however, is not their typology of prison subcultures (which has been criticized by Julian Roebuck [1963–64]) but their emphasis on the fact that the patterns of inmate culture are determined primarily not by prison conditions but by factors associated with the prisoner's background in the community. In the years since their article first appeared a number of other observers have published studies which lend support to the view that preinstitutional behavior patterns are the crucial determinants of behavior inside prison.

Thus Charles Wellford describes an attempt to analyze empirically the process of socialization in correctional communities. He concludes that what he refers to as "the level of prisonization" is "chiefly determined by the characteristics of the individual prior to his commitment, particularly with regard to his prior involvement in what is often referred to as the 'criminalistic subculture'." Moreover he also refers to "the inmate society as being not cohesive but organized around roles, which are in many respects conflicting" (1967, pp. 202–3).

Rose Giallombardo describes a sociological study of an adult prison for women. She concludes that, while the deprivations of imprisonment may provide necessary conditions for the emergence of an inmate system, her findings "clearly indicate that the deprivations of imprisonment in themselves are not sufficient to account for the form that the inmate social structure assumes in the male and female prison communities." She demonstrates convincingly that the behavior patterns of women and their inmate role systems reflect cultural definitions which are "brought into the prison setting and function to determine the direction and focus of the inmate cultural systems" (1966, p. 187).

Hugh F. Cline reports a study carried out in fifteen Scandinavian prisons designed to test the relative heuristic power, in relation to the social climate of prisons, of what he calls the *direct importation* model (values being imported into the prison from the outside world) and the *deprivation* model (values emerging as a response to the physical and psychological deprivation provided by the prison). He concludes that "the results provide clear-cut support for the effect of direct importation.... they do not support the deprivation model" (Cline 1968, p. 182).

Barry Schwartz deals with the question of the inmate's pre-prison and current prison experiences and their differential impact on his behavior. He describes an investigation carried out in a penal institution for delinquent boys in which he attempted to evaluate empirically the relative importance of indigenous or situational processes arising from the nature of imprisonment itself as opposed to influences having their origin outside the prison system. He concludes that, while situational contingencies demonstrably influence the individual prisoner's behavior, prison sociologists have tended to ignore the importance of preinstitutional effects. "By devoting itself to behavior which is more dependent on and highly variable according to situational contingencies, the sociology of the prison exaggerates the effects of social relationships within the penal institution. In neglecting behavior that is deeply rooted in the inmate's past, and therefore more correlated with pre-institutional factors, current theory underestimates the role of extra-prison experiences in shaping current prison life" (1971, p. 541).

The most recent and also the most striking study in this field is James Jacobs's "Street Gangs Behind Bars," which strongly supports the Irwin-Cressey position that much of what has been termed inmate culture is actually imported from outside the prison. Jacobs's paper reports on a participant observation study carried out at Stateville Penitentiary, a maximum-security prison in Illinois, during the summer of 1972. It describes the way in which four Chicago street gangs have brought to the prison organizations roles and norms precisely patterned on those of their parent gangs on the streets. Jacobs's study provides a dramatic example of subcultural identity not only being preserved but even being strengthened in the prison situation. This phenomenon is also discussed in the context of the California prison system in John Irwin's *The Felon* (1970).

The only studies which at first sight appear to run counter to the overwhelming mass of evidence are two which were carried out in a federal hospital for narcotics addicts: Charles Tittle and Drollene Tittle's "Social Organization of Prisoners: An Empirical Test" (1964) and Charles Tittle's "Inmate Organization: Sex Differentiation and the Influence of Criminal Subcultures" (1969). The first produces results which the authors admit are "not compelling." They conclude that "the prison code does appear at least in part an institutional product" although "for some, adherence to the prison code is merely a device for survival, and has little effect on participation in the rehabilitation program" (1964, p. 221). As for the second study, "synthetic cohort and partial panel data suggest confirmation of the institutional product theory of inmate organization and indicate minimal influence of criminal subcultures." But it should be noted that this was a population of male and female drug addicts the majority of whom were volunteers ("admitted on their own request and . . . free to leave at any time"). The most significant suggestion may be that made in the final sentence of the study: "Perhaps inmate behavior represents a subclass of subordinate behavior in general, with organizational manifestations similar in a wide range of environments" (1969, pp. 503–4).

On the whole it may be said that the cumulative impact of these three different critical approaches to the prisonization hypothesis is to reduce it from the level of a plausible universal generalization to that of a somewhat dubious particular observation. For on three different levels it is shown to be inconsistent with the evidence. Whether prisonization is viewed as a function of time served, from an institutional perspective, or in the larger cultural or social context, empirical investigation has revealed not only that confirmation of the hypothesis is lacking but also that it conflicts with reality.

THE FULL CIRCLE

At first sight it might seem that it is of little importance whether the prisonization theory is valid or not. To adapt a remark of Jeremy Bentham, one might say that, if the crime school theory was simple nonsense, prisonization was nonsense on sociological stilts; and there's an end to the matter. In fact, however, this particular theoretical dispute has important practical implications which are now seen to have been much more fundamental than was realized at first.

The first hint of what those implications might be appears in Donald L. Garrity's study, which dealt with "the purported effect of prisonization on post-release behavior." He attempted to test the extent to which the hypothesized postinstitutional effects of prisonization were reflected in parole violation rates for different types of offenders. He found that the data on parole adjustment did not support the general contention that extended exposure to the prison community decreased the chances of successful adjustment on parole. He concluded that "the unqualified claims that prisons are breeding grounds for crime and that imprisonment adversely affects all prisoners do not appear to be warranted."

But Garrity also took his analysis a step further. He classified his parolee population, using a typology of inmate roles in terms of argot labels drawn up by Clarence Schrag, and developed predictions of parole performance on the basis of membership in the different inmate groups. In this case he found that the predictions of parole performance "*were* supported by the data" (1961, pp. 366–79). And the significance of this is considerable when it is viewed in the light of the contention that the roles prisoners play are principally determined not by the conditions of imprisonment but by the fact that distinctive patterns of behavior are brought into the prison from outside. For, if the origins of prison subcultures are external to the prison and it is subculture membership which determines behavior both in prison and subsequently, then this does not merely involve rejection of the idea that the prison makes prisoners into criminals; it should also, as Irwin and Cressey point out, "change our expectations regarding the possible reformative effects of that prison" (1962, p. 155).

Irwin and Cressey also mention the possibility that prisons with programs or organizational structures different from "the ordinary custodially oriented prison" might eventually affect the recidivism rate of their inmates. But it is easy to draw a much more negative inference. Thus if one believes, as Bentham did, that "an ordinary prison is a school in which wickedness is taught," it is not difficult also to accept the view that an extraordinary prison (in Bentham's case, the Panopticon) might be employed to inculcate virtue. It should after all be principally a matter of changing the syllabus. But if one is convinced that wickedness is *not* taught in prisons and that this is due *not* to the quality of the teaching but to the fact that all the pupils are more or less impervious to instruction of any kind, then it follows that it will not be possible to turn prisons into schools where virtue is taught.

Sheldon Messinger puts the matter well when he refers to the implications of the Irwin-Cressey argument: "[M]ost of all, by suggesting that the embrace of the inmate culture may be *temporary* and *weak,* Irwin and Cressey manage to take us a full circle. Once again, the question of socialization is raised. Irwin and Cressey suggest, in effect, that modern prisons have little lasting effect on the orientations of their unwilling guests" (1969, p. 141). Yet the full circle is really rather more like a downward spiral. One starts with doubt about the reformative effects of imprisonment on the ground that in fact inmates are being prisonized and in effect criminalized. One concludes with doubt about the criminogenic effects of imprisonment on grounds which imply not merely that inmates are not being corrupted but rather that neither their attitudes nor their behavior are being affected in any significant fashion by the experience of imprisonment; and this represents a much more profound level of skepticism. Moreover it must clearly have policy implications of a fundamental character, for it suggests that the question, to use Barry Schwartz's words, "whether people-changing organizations really socialize or merely serve as arenas wherein predispositions earlier acquired are acted out" (1971, p. 534), must be answered in favor of the latter alternative.

Of course if it were true that all inmates on entering prison became indissolubly wedded to criminal values, or that they all faithfully subscribed to the "inmate codes" which prison sociologists have drafted for them, then any discussion of policy implications might be of little significance. But all the evidence indicates that the accepted picture of inmate solidarity rarely bears much relation to any real-life situation. What Don C. Gibbons has called the "exaggerated view of convicts . . . that they are an aggregate of persons all standing in opposition to the administrative regime" (1965, p. 207) seems principally to be the product of impressionistic interpretation rather than objective research.

More objective studies paint a rather different picture. Thus Stanton Wheeler's work indicates that some of the conflict between prisoners and the authorities is more apparent than real and that there is much less genuine conflict between inmates and staff than has been commonly assumed on the basis of unsystematic observation (1961, p. 230). In the same vein, but rather more positively, Glaser reports: "Our findings from several different types of inquiry indicated that inmates *have a predominant interest in adjusting to the demands of the institution and that they have strong noncriminal aspirations.* However, evidence and deductive reasoning supported the notion that inmates and others generally overestimate the extent of inmate opposition to staff-supported standards, because inmates who oppose these standards are most articulate" (1964, p. 118; my italics).

It is interesting to note that one of the best recent studies which deals with an English prison lays considerable stress on the fact that insofar as both custodial officers and inmates "come as adult men from the same society, they bring into the prison certain common values and standards [which] . . . even if they do not carry much weight in any particular instance, do have the character of persistent, impersonal psychological forces" (Emery 1970, p. 33). Emery makes the significant point that "unless there were such strongly held common values, one suspects that inmates and staff alike would be very much less sensitive to the implicit, and sometimes explicit, criticism they make of each other."

More specifically, he reports that "social values specifying the immorality of a crime seem to be commonly held both by officers and inmates. Despite the theoretical speculations about 'criminal cultures,' which divorce crime of any moral significance, there was little evidence in this case to suggest that inmates regarded their crimes as anything other than immoral." He goes on to point out that "criminal offences that are socially regarded as being most immoral, e.g., sexual offences against minors, are similarly regarded by officers and prisoners.... Other offences which carry little moral significance in the outside world, particularly among the working classes (brawling, drunkenness, motoring offences) are found to be equally free from moral condemnation among staff and prisoners."

It might be argued of course that in American prisons the existence of such common or complementary values is less common and that even where it did once exist the "radicalization" of the prison population has produced a situation in which prisoners everywhere are boldly challenging conventional bourgeois morality and are refusing to accept the personal devaluation involved in acknowledging that they have done anything wrong. But although there is clearly some truth in this assertion it is questionable, first, whether what is happening or has happened represents any very novel development and, second, to what extent it is a genuinely revolutionary movement.

As to the first question, there have always been prisoners whose defense against their rejection and devaluation has taken the form of a challenge to established morality. Even in the English situation, Emery describes inmates whose self-justification in the face of the moral charge against them "is essentially that, while they have done wrong and probably intend to go on doing wrong, this is not simply because they lack these values but because they attach greater importance to other human values. In particular, they would claim to lay great value on individual autonomy, that is, the fulfillment of individual desires in the face of a hostile and unrewarding environment" (ibid., pp. 33–35). This kind of defensive self-evaluation is not very far removed from, and is indeed frequently linked with, an offensive devaluation not only of law-abiding members of society but also of society itself.

As to the second question, a concrete example may help to put the matter in perspective. In September 1971 *Time* magazine ran a cover story on the Attica uprising which was in many ways an admirable exercise in vivid news reporting. In the story some reference was made to the demands which were formulated by the Attica prisoners. They were described as "revolutionary." *Time* was not alone in this characterization; throughout the media those demands were cited as demonstrating the prisoners' dangerous radicalism. Indeed this interpretation of the events at Attica was and still is widely supported.

Thus Angela Davis wrote: "Attica before the massacre offered us a sleeping but graphic glimpse of the monumental feats obtainable by men and women moving along a revolutionary course. . . . In a figurative sense, it evoked visions of the Paris Communes, the liberated areas of pre-revolutionary Cuba, the free territories of Mozambique" (1971, p. 43). And Russell G. Oswald, New York commissioner of corrections, has also warned that the troublesome prisoners were revolutionaries and that the attack on prisons is the first step in a broader assault on society. In his *Attica: My Story* he speaks of "leftist militants . . . who . . . seek to turn America's correctional system into a revolutionary battle ground" (1972, p. vii). And again, "On the eve of Attica, then, the disinherited and the villainous, the alienated and the pawns, the flotsam and jetsam of society, and a new generation of revolutionary leaders focused on the prisons as their point of leverage. Here was where the Establishment could be made to buckle and the class issue could be most clearly defined" (ibid., p. 12).

It is instructive by way of contrast with the rhetoric to look at the "Immediate Demands" and the "Practical Proposals" put forward by the Attica inmates. Apart from those which arose specifically out of the riot situation, such as the requests for an amnesty for inmates taking part in the rebellion, the sacking of the warden, and transportation to a nonimperialist country (which was soon dropped) the list is remarkably innocuous. Most of it could easily have been compiled by a group of white Anglo-Saxon middle-class Protestant prison reformers. They requested "realistic, effective rehabilitation programs for all inmates according to their offense and personal needs" (Badillo and Haynes 1972, p. 56). They asked for a variety of things such as a modernized inmate education system, expanded work-release programs, adequate medical treatment, the abolition of censorship of newspapers, magazines, and other publications, freedom for inmates (at their own expense) to communicate with anyone they please.

It is difficult to see why any of these items should be regarded as revolutionary. None of them constituted a rejection of, or a threat to, the system. Professor Herman Schwartz of the State University of New York at Buffalo, who took part in negotiations with the Attica prisoners, spoke of the list as a very limited set of demands leaving out "a lot of things that would be put in if you were going to have complete penal reform." Nor did Commissioner Oswald regard them, at that time, as especially subversive. In fact in *Attica: The Official Report of the New York State Special Commission*, we are told: "Schwartz recalls that Oswald responded to each proposal, and told the inmates he agreed 'in principle' with most of them" (p. 223). There can have been little difficulty for him in this since most of the proposals were things he had earlier promised to implement, given more time.

There is a derisive remark near the end of *Struggle For Justice* that has been discussed earlier and may be recalled here. "The experts," says the report, "—even the most enlightened and progressive—also line up solidly in support of the system asking only for more of the same" (AFSC 1971, p. 156). Yet if we read carefully the Attica prisoner proposals the conclusion is inescapable that that is precisely what the prisoners were doing—asking for more of the same. Their demands do not constitute a revolutionary manifesto or even an assault on the foundations of the institution of imprisonment. In fact there is little in them which does not fully accord with the spirit of the celebrated "Declaration of Principles" adopted by the first American National Prison Congress held at Cincinnati in 1870.

Nor did the prisoners behave like revolutionaries. When one looks at the riots in American prisons in recent years their most surprising feature is that the prisoners have exercised appreciable restraint in their revolts. Even those who feel no sympathy for them whatsoever must acknowledge the factual point that they have in their riots and violence stopped far short of inflicting those deaths and injuries on prison staff which it was certainly in their power to encompass. Indeed it could be said that the real tragedy of Attica is that at issue in that confrontation, in which forty-three men died (a death toll surpassed only once before in the history of American prison riots), was really only the simple request that we implement promises over a century old that have not been kept.

Thus even at Attica, as the New York State Special Commission discovered, the impression that the administration was confronted with a solid mass of implacably hostile inmates was quite false. Indeed one prisoner whose testimony has the ring of truth to it told the Commission: "Well, I think the actual expectations, what individual inmates wanted, varied. There were guys in there that all they wanted was more pink ice cream, we will say, and there were guys in there that were concerned about getting cake in the mess hall and there were guys that were deeply concerned about improving the parole system and trying to get fresh minds into the institution; to do something about rehabilitation. I got the impression myself that there wasn't any real consensus between any more than 50 people. I don't think you could have gotten 50 people that could have agreed on any one point" (*Attica: The Official Report* 1972, p. 206).

CONCLUSION

It is ironic that, at a time when authorities and experts throughout America are repudiating the rehabilitative ideal, some of the most "radical" prisoners should be in effect endorsing it so forcefully. It is a factor which has some bearing on the policy implications considered at the conclusion of chapter two. For while it is true that, in the climate of ferocious sansculottism portrayed by Angela Davis and Russell Oswald, Norval Morris's program of "facilitated change" could only appear as a quaint academic aberration, it takes on a rather different complexion when viewed in the context of prisoners' actual demands for "realistic, effective rehabilitation programs for all."

This brings us to a general point which is of some importance. The point is that both the prisonization theory and the treatment ideology share a common conceptual pattern. This can perhaps best be described in terms of what Daniel Glaser refers to as "images of human behavior." In both cases the behavioral image central to the pattern is one of inmates as, to a large degree, passive respondents to ulterior forces beyond their control. On the one hand they are seen as responding to the "pains of imprisonment" and on the other hand to the various modalities of treatment. In neither case are they seen as fully responsible agents but rather as "managed" creatures moved or pushed in certain directions by extrinsic pressures.

This parallelism derives principally from the fact that underlying both approaches are certain implicit etiological premises to which they stand as corollaries. In the case of prisonization the etiological basis of the theory is naturally in terms of sociological factors. The connection with etiology comes out very clearly in Sheldon Messinger's account of the nature of the literature dealing with inmate culture up to the late fifties: "Such theorizing as had appeared," he says, "tended to take the form of inquiring how civilians became inmates, that is, how persons committed to prisons came to take on the roles and values purported to be typical of inmates. This theoretical effort was always implicitly, and sometimes explicitly, polemical, the argument running that inmates were made, not born. As such, the effort was of a piece with other sociological work on criminals, most notably of course the work of Edwin H. Sutherland" (Messinger 1969, p. 134).

Moreover, it is notable that much of the criticism of the earlier formulations of prisonization theory which has been reviewed in this chapter rests on an analogous etiological basis. The essential difference is that whereas in earlier formulations the emphasis was on the indigenous origin of inmate culture patterns, in the later formulations the explanation of inmate social relations and culture is in terms of prior involvement in cultural or subcultural milieu and of definitions which are "brought into the prison setting and function to determine the direction and focus of the inmate cultural systems" (Giallombardo 1966, p. 187).

In the case of the treatment ideology the principal assumption as to causation is evident in the use of the term *treatment*, which derives from the analogy with medicine. The offender is seen as suffering from some disorder—varying from psychopathy at one extreme to bad work-habits or lack of skill at the other—which is responsible for his criminality and failure to achieve satisfactory life-adjustment in society. The "treatment program," which may be made up variously of psychological or psychiatric therapy or educational or vocational training, is designed to change the orientation and behavior of the inmate so that he can be restored to normal functioning in society.

In both cases the etiological explanations implied may well expose at least part of the genesis of some types of criminal behavior. And it is also to some extent inevitable that, when we attempt to consider human behavior objectively with a view to understanding, explaining, controlling, or "treating" it, we conceptualize in terms of abstract theoretical images which are, in context, both adequate and valid. However when these explanations are treated as having universal application and the behavioral images in terms of which they are formulated are treated, not as abstract theoretical conceptions or heuristic devices, but as somehow embracing all the various subjective and objective aspects of human behavior, we find that we rapidly become involved in one of those conceptual imbroglios which seem to be endemic in the behavioral sciences.

All this would be irrelevant to our present concerns if it were not for the fact that there is, as G. B. Vold pointed out, "an obvious and logical interdependence between what is done about crime (penal practice) and what is assumed to be the reason for or explanation of criminality (criminological theory)." In this case the practical corollaries of the underlying causal explanations both turn out, although in different ways, to be singularly unhelpful in relation to the formulation of penal policy. Explanations in terms of cultural, sociological, or environmental factors outside the prison (which is where current theory locates them) provide the prison administrator with no guidance whatever. As Vold puts it, "The prison cannot change the society of which it is a part; it cannot modify the forces in conflict outside the institution; but it hopes it can do something with the individuals under confinement" (1958, pp. 282–93). As to that hope, it should be clear from the evidence regarding the effectiveness of rehabilitative treatment discussed in chapter two that the theory that all crime can be explained in pathogenetic or quasi-pathogenetic terms has proved little more fruitful as a progenitor of functional programs.

Nevertheless, except perhaps for those who would prefer human beings to be somewhat more easily manipulable, there seems no reason to regard these conclusions as depressing. There is after all evidence that some offenders benefit from some of the programs provided in prisons (a point which will be dealt with more fully in chapter five). At the same time it should be some consolation that the belief that all who enter prison are ineluctably doomed to deterioration proves, on examination, to rest on no more rational basis than the antithetical idea that, if only we knew how, panacean programs could be devised which would transform all offenders into model citizens.

4   The Other Prisoners

THE INVISIBLE MEN

Gresham Sykes's classic study, *The Society of Captives,* is dedicated "to the man in prison—both the prisoner and his guard." His is one of the relatively small number of books about prisons and imprisonment which has anything at all to say about prison guards or custodial officers. But in fact he does not say very much about them that is not in the form of generalizations about their "assigned role."

He tells us a great deal about prisoners and the different social roles they play. Using the argot terms of the inmates themselves, he distinguishes and describes in some detail a variety of behavior patterns: the *real man,* the *rat,* the *center man,* the *wolf,* the *punk,* the *fag,* the *gorilla,* the *merchant,* the *ball buster,* the *tough,* and the *hipster.* But the guards, who are said to stand opposed to the inmates "across the chasm which separates the convicted felon and the law-abiding citizen or the perhaps even greater chasm which divides the ruler and the ruled" (1958, p. 33), remain a faceless, undifferentiated group, their grey homogeneity unrelieved by any colorful argot role-playing.

It is true that Sykes does not accept the popular stereotype of the guard as a brutal and insensitive incompetent corrupted by absolute power. Rather he offers a new interpretation of Lord Acton's aphorism according to which "the custodians . . . far from being converted into brutal tyrants, are under strong pressure to compromise with their captives, for it is a paradox that they can insure their dominance only by allowing it to be corrupted." For the conventional stereotypical picture of the relations between guards and their prisoners he substitutes another one in which the guards are corrupted by the captive criminals over whom they stand in theoretical dominance.

It is not power that corrupts them, he believes, but the lack of it. Guards cannot rely on force to achieve compliance with regulations; nor is there an effective system of rewards and punishments. To a large extent they are dependent on inmates for the satisfactory performance of their duties. They have to *win* compliance. Thus they fail to report infractions of rules, they warn inmates of impending raids for contraband, they neglect security precautions, and even join the prisoners in criticism of the warden and his assistants. Nevertheless Sykes recognizes that the guard is "the pivotal figure on which the custodial bureaucracy turns," and his account of the way in which many guards fulfill their "expected role" as "a complicated compound of policeman and foreman, or cadi, counsellor, and boss all rolled into one," although brief, is not wholly unsympathetic (ibid., pp. 53-58).

It is a much more sympathetic account, incidentally, than is given in that equally celebrated earlier study, Donald Clemmer's *The Prison Community*, in which a prison warden is cited as saying that, instead of a sense of duty, his guards "desire to know but three things—'When do we eat, when do we quit, and when do we get paid!'" Clemmer accepts that comment as probably accurate. He allows that "not all guards are unsympathetic or vicious" and that "even those guards who seem to be persistently on the offensive have moments of kindliness." But it is clear that he is talking about exceptions to the rule. The picture of guards that he presents is one of men who "by dominance over a helpless group, . . . are able to tackle their egos and obtain some satisfaction through the power of authority"; who are imbued with "a spirit of retaliation towards inmates"; and who believe that "the essential purpose of the prison is incapacitation" (1940, pp. 183–89).

But the most striking feature of these two books, acknowledged to be among the best and most comprehensive published studies of prisons, is that the "pivotal" figure, who has, in Sykes's words, to "supervise and control the inmate population in concrete and detailed terms" and who has to "see to the translation of the custodial regime from blueprint to reality" (1958, p. 53), emerges as merely a cipher. He is seen as a cog in the disciplinary machine, reacting uniformly, seeking in one account the satisfactions of power over the "cowed, helpless inmate" (Clemmer), or in the other only "a smoothly running tour of duty" (Sykes).

Exceptions are noted only to be dismissed. Thus Clemmer tells us that the idea of reformation is "utterly foreign to the average guard." He then quotes a prison official who said to him: "I want to break up the monotony of these men as much as possible." But this proves easy to reinterpret. "Decent as his attitude was," we are told, "it is doubtful if the officer was thinking in terms of reformation. His *probable thought* was: the less monotony the less restlessness, and the less restlessness, the less chance of attempted escapes" (1940, p. 184; my italics).

In Sykes's case it seems largely to be the result of the perspective from which he examines the prison "as an operating social system" that the members of the custodial staff are seen mainly as interchangeable elements in the prison power structure. This leads him to dismiss the suggestion that some improvement in prisons might be achieved by recruiting better personnel. He sees no reason to believe that "a different crop of guards" would make any significant difference to the situation. In his view the failure of prisons is due to "structural defects in the prison's system of power rather than individual inadequacies" (1958, p. 61).

When guards are seen as more than anonymous components in larger patterns of power they are frequently cast in the role of rigidly unyielding opponents of any change or amelioration in prison conditions. Thus Richard McCleery describes the change in a prison over a period of years from an authoritarian, traditional, maximum-security institution to one with some inmate self-government and a more "liberal" atmosphere. In this case "the custodial force" is depicted as engaging in a "custodial counterattack." The new program is said to have "challenged the moral order of the guards' universe and provoked an organized and effective revolt—based on a righteous conviction that the liberal program was a compromise with criminals and sin."

The disruptive tactics employed by the guards are said to have included literal enforcement of rules, restriction of inmate movement, harassment of inmates, prediction of failure of the treatment program, and exploitation of contacts with senior inmates in order to ensure fulfillment of that prediction. The guards are shown as being unanimous in their efforts to preserve the "authoritarian power structure." The only distinction that McCleery draws is one between those guards who aimed "simply to defeat the liberal program" and a group he calls the "old guard" which was not content with that, but "set out to regain control over prison policy" (1960, p. 70).

More recently, Donald Cressey suggested that prison guards may play a crucial role in prison riots which lead to the demotion or discharge of prison wardens or commissioners "who introduced too many changes too fast." His account of the guards' attitude is reminiscent of McCleery's "the moral order of the guards' universe." "[A] working-class prison guard," says Cressey, "who has learned what is 'right' and 'proper' in the world is likely to implement in his work a strong moral code that stresses righteous indignation about crime, hatred of robbers and rapists, intolerance of slovenliness and laziness, disdain for acquisition except by the slow process of honest labor, and 'self-discipline' rather than 'self-expression'." And he adds: "Any prison reformer who tries to implement a program at variance with such attitudes must expect resistance" (1973, p. 142).

When confronted, as one is throughout the literature, with these one-dimensional composite conceptions of the prison guard, one finds it difficult to avoid the conclusion that they are no less stereotypes than the earlier conceptions of guards as merely brutal, sadistic illiterates indulging in capricious cruelty. The existence and persistence of such stereotypes may be due, as Korn and McCorkle suggest, to the fact that "information about the prison guard usually derives from two sources: the writings of inmates and the works of criminologists and penologists, whose impressions seem to be largely colored by inmate reports" (1959, p. 495).

In this connection it is interesting to read the appendices on methodology which both Sykes and Clemmer provide at the conclusion of their books. In both cases, while there is mention of contacts with officials, the overwhelming emphasis is on relationship with inmates. Thus Clemmer speaks of building up "close rapport" with inmates and developing "positive friendly relationships" with them characterized by "social warmth" (1940, p. 323). Sykes, too, talks of "establishing close relationships" and achieving "fairly close rapport" with inmates (1958, p. 135). In neither case is there mention of any such intimacy with guards.

It is in fact remarkable how little serious attention has been paid to prison officers in the quite extensive literature on prisons and imprisonment. It is almost as though they were, like the postman in G. K. Chesterton's celebrated detective story, so commonplace and routine a feature of the scene as to be invisible. Yet their role is clearly of critical importance. Custodial personnel make up the majority of correctional manpower in the United States. Within penal institutions their influence is inevitably predominant. The *Task Force Report on Corrections* for the 1967 President's Commission on Law Enforcement and Administration of Justice said this: "They may be the most influential persons in institutions simply by virtue of their numbers and their daily intimate contact with offenders. It is a mistake to define them as persons responsible only for control and maintenance. They can, by their attitude and understanding, reinforce or destroy the effectiveness of almost any correctional program. They can act as effective intermediaries or become insurmountable barriers between the inmates' world and the institution's administrative and treatment personnel" (p. 96).

There is no doubt that this is correct. Yet what appears to amount almost to a systematic bias in perception has meant that the vast majority of studies in the sociology of prisons has overlooked this salient feature of the social structure and organization of penal institutions. This has serious consequences when inferences are drawn about the future of imprisonment because it means that a basic premise is either suppressed or distorted. In the case of Sykes for example, whose chapter on "The Pains of

Imprisonment" is in many ways one of the most perceptive analyses of the *inmates'* perspective on captivity ever written, his conclusion appears to be that "the totalitarian regime of the custodians" is, if not absolutely immutable, at least unlikely to be significantly altered by the recruitment of better-qualified persons to serve as guards.

THE ROLE AND THE MAN

It is possible that part of the reason why some sociologists, when they have not ignored them altogether, have tended to stereotype prison officers is that they are inclined to view them almost exclusively as members of a group with a common organizational role. For example, an interesting recent study by David Duffee (1974) affirms the existence of "an officer subculture," "the officer subculture values," and "the officer value complex" on the basis of such findings as that officers differed considerably from correctional managers in their perception of correctional policy. But the question of attitudinal variation within the officer group is ignored. And if prison officers are viewed from this kind of perspective in terms of the dimensions of their common role or as members of a particular "subculture" there is an inevitable tendency for them to emerge as a homogeneous group with a common value-orientation.

When a different perspective is adopted a somewhat different picture appears. Thus it is surely significant that the relatively few studies which deal specifically and in detail with the custodial staff do not report the kind of uniformity in patterns of behavior, attitude, and feeling found among guards in the more inmate-centered studies. Two examples of studies made in maximum-security penal institutions may be mentioned. First, Joseph Motivans, in a study of guards in an Illinois maximum security prison, found that "there is no evidence that the popular stereotype of a guard is applicable to even a small number of officers in this particular institution." He found "no indication that one type of individual, in terms of personality makeup, is attracted to seek employment in the penitentiary." The results of personality tests on a small number of randomly chosen guards were also at variance with the traditional conception of the guard's role. Thus, although most of their time was "spent in a domineering position over inmates the guards did not score high on 'Dominance and Aggressiveness'." Again "the guards were not markedly 'Conservative and Accepting' as could be expected from their ritualized and bureaucratic role" (1963, pp. 189-95).

The second example may be found in Terence and Pauline Morris's *Pentonville*, one of the few substantial sociological studies of a prison which deals at length with the custodial staff. The authors found little to support either "the stylized myths of cruelty and victimization which abound in prison" (1963, p. 255) or the "uncomplimentary popular image of the prison officer . . . [as] . . . a harsh disciplinarian who joins the Prison Service in order to continue the pleasure of ordering other men around which he has hitherto enjoyed as a non-commissioned officer in the armed forces" (ibid., p. 77). So far from finding homogeneity of attitude, they report that "reformist, punitive and apathetic attitudes are quite fantastically confused." Insofar as they are able to generalize about staff attitudes to inmates they note that these are characterized not by hostility or dislike but rather by despair and disappointment. "In particular," they say, "it is the fact that prisoners recidivate that the staff find intolerable" (ibid., pp. 255-56).

That last finding is of significance not only because it runs counter to the popular stereotype of the prison guard or custodial officer, but also because it reflects a type of interest which relates to a quite different standard of reference from those of discipline, custody, and security with which the guard is commonly supposed to be exclusively concerned. If guards were devoted unambiguously to securing and maintaining dominance and control, then recidivism would be either a matter of indifference to them or, conceivably, something to be welcomed as representing an extension of control over inmates.

That these findings are not peculiar to the English prison system is clear from one of the most thorough and extensive sociological studies ever made of an American prison system, Daniel Glaser's *The Effectiveness of a Prison and Parole System*, which deals with the federal system. Glaser attributes the fact that "abstract theoretical analyses by sociologists of prison social organization present an excessively melodramatic view of relationships between prison staff and inmates" to the necessity for oversimplification or overstatement when trying to explain "the varieties of human behavior in a complex organization." But at another point he explains "sociological ignorance" as due to the fact that "academic students of prison-inmate life are disproportionately in contact with 'front office politicians' who are the most articulate spokesmen of antistaff values" (1964, pp. 116–19).

Whatever the truth may be, and it would be reasonable to assume that both factors play a part, Glaser's own study indicates enormous variations both in inmate attitudes to guards and guard attitudes to inmates. Thus he found, on questioning inmates about their staff preferences and prejudices, that "custodial officers are very frequently the most liked, in addition to being more often than others the most disliked staff members." Despite the fact that Glaser's research was essentially inmate-centered, so that custodial staff attitudes can only be inferred from inmate responses, it is clear that there were very great contrasts in the different guards' treatment of prisoners. It is notable, incidentally, that "several of the successful releasees who had prior experience in some of the more backward state prisons mentioned a contrast between federal and state prison officers." The federal officers "treat you like a man."

One of the most interesting findings to emerge from Glaser's study is his conclusion that, except in one of the federal institutions, "custodial officers can be said to have the greatest total impact everywhere" as opposed to treatment staff and caseworkers, who although "predominantly disliked" were actually rarely mentioned as "either the most liked or the most disliked" (ibid., pp. 134–44). The significance of this finding is, as James V. Bennett points out in his preface to Glaser's study, that the ability and attitude of what he refers to as "line personnel" are "a major factor in determining the nature of the prison experience of most offenders." This being the case, the neglect of serious research into the attitudes and activities of prison guards or correctional officers is quite extraordinary.

OFFICER-INMATE RELATIONSHIPS
Because of the crucial nature of their role, it seems likely that the recruitment of better custodial personnel could radically transform the nature of the experience of imprisonment for the inmate.

While the maximum-security prison itself is intrinsically a somewhat inflexible institution, its staff composition is one aspect of it which is not merely susceptible to change but among the most easily manipulable features of the system. Moreover, if as appears probable the use of imprisonment as the principal sanction of the penal system is to be superseded by a system in which it is employed to deal with more restricted classes of offenders, then the problem of recruiting adequate staff should be a less daunting one than was posed by the demands of a system of mass imprisonment.

The obvious question which arises is: What is the meaning of such expressions as "better custodial personnel" or "better-qualified persons to serve as guards" in this context? For the context in which we are talking is one in which prisons are no longer seen as institutions designed to produce moral transfiguration but rather as institutions in which change is, at most, facilitated; institutions in which we attempt, to use Rupert Cross's words, "to do all that reasonably can be done to prevent the permanent moral degradation of the prisoner."

Before the question of personnel selection is dealt with it may be mentioned that in one respect the role of the custodial officer may be less complex and more straightforward than under correctional treatment regimes. Donald Cressey has noted that under that type of regime those subject to most role confusion are the custodial officers, because they are also expected to behave like treatment agents or therapists. Thus the prison guard who commonly sees his role principally in terms of control, discipline, and punishment is faced with a complex set of expectations centering around treatment operations. As Cressey puts it, they "must 'use discretion' and somehow behave both custodially and therapeutically." Yet "[i]f they enforce the rules, they risk being diagnosed as 'rigid'" whereas "if their failure to enforce rules creates a threat to institutional security, orderliness or maintenance, they are not 'doing their job'" (1960, p. 103). It is scarcely surprising that a frequent reaction is to call for a return to the "good old days."

To what extent, and for whom, the "old days" were good is no less debatable in this context than in any other. But, in that the past is customarily seen as less complex and frustrating than the present, our redefinition of the role of the custodial officer entails a degree of simplification which may recommend it. Rupert Cross, it will be remembered, in urging that the main aim of the prison authorities should be "the prevention of deterioration" rather than "the promotion of reform" added that "the methods of achieving the two objects are similar." Although it might seem difficult to be very confident about the validity of a parallel when the items compared are both undefined, the evidence suggests that Cross is right. Moreover, although it might seem an impossible task to say anything constructive about the qualities or qualifications necessary for the performance of duties which are unspecified except in very general terms, it is in fact possible to advance certain propositions.

That it is possible to say anything at all is largely due to the work of Daniel Glaser, to which I have already referred. The point at issue is a relatively simple one. What emerges, with a unanimity that is compelling, from the literature which has developed over recent decades about prison inmate social systems is that some prisoners find that a most satisfactory means of adjustment to the "pains of imprisonment" (which include the deprivation of autonomy, liberty, heterosexual relations, and a variety of goods and services) and to rejection by society is what Korn and McCorkle refer to as "rejecting the rejectors" (1954, p. 88). It has been shown that this method of coping may lead to identification with antisocial or criminal values and may prejudice rehabilitation. This process is facilitated or encouraged if the staff members' attitude to inmates is hostile, superior, and disparaging because they (the staff) thus become more suitable and appropriate targets for resentment and rejection. It is clear therefore that the attitude of the staff member toward inmates is of crucial importance.

It is in relation to this process that Glaser's findings are significant, for he not only inquired into inmates' reasons for liking and disliking staff members but also asked successful releasees, who credited staff members with being influential in their reformation, what it was about their treatment by staff members which had made their influence rehabilitative. If Glaser's findings sound like truisms it has to be said, first, that insofar as they have been recognized in the past they have rested largely upon an intuitive basis; and, second, that they are truisms that have for so long and so consistently been ignored in correctional practice that to regard them as too obvious or unimportant for mention would be a grave error. Indeed James V. Bennett is right when he says that Glaser's report points up "rather clearly the qualities to be encouraged in officers not only through recruitment standards and training but through administrative policies which affect the specific approaches they make in day-to-day work with prisoners" (Glaser 1964, p. x).

It is no surprise to find that the statements of successful releasees regarding staff who were influential in their rehabilitation were consistent with the reasons given by inmates for liking one staff member more than another. This makes it possible to deal with the question, What are desirable staff personality attributes? in a reasonably compact, summary fashion. It should be noted that the reasons inmates gave for liking or disliking staff members were recorded verbatim as responses to interviews and not in response to a structured questionnaire with all the possibilities for distortion which that method entails. Only subsequently were the reasons given classified for purposes of analysis. Another problem with opinion surveys of inmates in institutions is that the responses may be self-serving in that they are deliberately designed to influence prison policy in the direction of increased amenities and permissiveness rather than being candid avowals of opinion. In this case it is significant not only that the responses of inmates and successful releasees were consistent but also that they consistently stressed "friendliness and fairness . . . rather than permissiveness or leniency."

But if the emphasis on fairness, consistency, and predictability as opposed to laxness and flexibility is striking, even more significant is the importance assigned to friendliness. The following passage which refers to the successful releasees is relevant. "What seems to be common to all of these testimonials is that the officers whom these men credited as having been rehabilitative influences gave the inmates self-respect. This did not mean that the officers were unusually lenient, lax or permissive; it meant only that they treated the men with a personal interest and without pretension or condescension. The officers were friendly in a way that inspired confidence and respect rather than contempt; they were frank, fair and considerate." Similarly, in respect of inmates not yet released, Glaser reports that "at every one of the five prisons studied, the most frequently cited type of reason for disliking an officer was his manner of expressing himself toward inmates, rather than specific things he did."

Neither profound insight nor familiarity with psychological theory is necessary to interpret these findings. Men with a history of "failure, rejection, and ego-deflation" who have previously been "treated as though members of an untouchable caste" are peculiarly sensitive to slights both real and sometimes imaginary. A hostile, superior, contemptuous, or dismissive attitude on the part of a staff member constitutes an attack on the prisoner's self-esteem and inspires resentment both against the staff member and against the values and standards which he symbolizes. Such an approach might almost be designed to cause prisoners to identify with criminal attitudes and values. By contrast a pleasant, friendly approach which allows prisoners to preserve some self-respect, while it is unlikely to inspire instant conversion of criminals to noncriminals, is at least unlikely to be positively damaging. As Glaser puts it: "A necessary condition, if not alone sufficient, for a staff member's favorable influence upon a prisoner appears to be the capacity to treat the prisoner pleasantly. Such an attitude conveys to the prisoner the notion that he is accepted as a person even when his attitudes or actions are opposed. There is ample evidence that control can be achieved by staff without a hostile or superior attitude, and that positive leadership and influence is difficult to achieve without at least a minimum of friendliness and respect" (ibid., pp. 132–48).

It is interesting to consider the position at the Attica Correctional Facility in 1971 when the September uprising occurred. The New York State Special Commission's report on Attica is illuminating not only about inmates but also about the officers and especially in relation to officer-inmate interaction. As the report correctly states: "The relationship between officer and inmate was the central dynamic of life at Attica, as it must be in every prison." It is clear that the nature of that relationship was at Attica a crucial factor in the revolt.

There were, in 1971, 380 basic-grade custodial officers at Attica out of a total 543 staff members. They constituted 70 percent of the staff and their salaries ($9,535 to a maximum of $11,941 after fifteen years) absorbed 62 percent of the budget. About one-third of them had received no formal training whatsoever, because between World War II and the late 1950s there was no such training. Those who started after that were given two weeks of training. They were expected to enforce a set of rules which the commission described as "poorly communicated, often petty, senseless or repressive." Poor communication was common, as officers "were required to explain the reason for the rules to inmates" and yet "new officers had almost as much difficulty as new inmates in ascertaining what the rules were." As a result, a group of senior officers prepared an unofficial guide which stated: "Until you are familiar with what is allowed, tell inmates 'No' when they ask for any special permission" (*Attica* 1972, pp. 44–49).

The organization of the custodial staff shifts was such that officers were not assigned to individual groups of inmates or companies but to housing blocks as a whole, which meant that they were likely to work with a different group of inmates each day. Thus "the officers had no incentive to attempt to establish any rapport or respect with a group of inmates whom they might not see again for days or weeks. There was neither opportunity nor desire to develop any mutual understanding" (ibid., p. 127).

In addition to these two factors, the lack of training and a work schedule which might have been designed to increase alienation, the Attica officers were all white whereas nearly two-thirds of the inmates were black or Puerto Rican. As the commission report puts it, "Predominantly poor, urban, black and Spanish-speaking inmates were placed under the supervision of white officers from rural areas.... They began with little or nothing in common, and Attica was not a catalyst which made people want to learn about each other" (ibid., p. 80). Thus although it is clear from the report that some officers felt sympathy for some inmates, "the relationship between most officers and inmates was characterized by fear, hostility, and mistrust, nurtured by racism."

Finally, and this comes out clearly in the special commission's report ("one theme stood out above all others"), there is no doubt that many of the officers were, in their attitudes toward offenders, dominated by the kind of moral indignation which Svend Ranulf has remarked as characteristic of the lower middle-class (1938).

For those officers an inmate's presence at Attica was enough to inspire feelings of resentment, hostility, malice, and rancour ("These men are not here for missing Sunday School," said one). "The inmate who refused to regard himself only as a criminal simply could not relate in any meaningful, constructive manner with a prison staff that could not regard him as anything else," says the Attica report (*Attica* 1972, p. 120).

Two conclusions may be drawn from what the report has to say about the custodial officers at Attica. In the first place, quite apart from their lack of training, they were, judged in the light of Glaser's study, very largely a negative selection in respect of the qualities necessary for effective performance of their task. Second, it is utterly ludicrous that these men should be, as they were at Attica, designated "corrections officers" with the implication that they had some skill or ability which enabled them to treat inmates in such a way as to help them or induce them to return to society as useful, law-abiding citizens. It was not their fault that they were badly selected or untrained. There is no reason to doubt that, as Dr. Robert Gould, the New York Special Commission's psychiatric consultant, testified, they were "really quite decent people." But they were placed in a position so grotesquely false that it might have made a good subject for comedy had its consequences not been so bleakly tragic.

In saying that the officers at Attica were a "negative selection" it is not suggested that some peculiarly perverse system of selection was employed. Thus it may be true, as the commission report states, that "racism among Attica officers may be no greater than what is present in society at large" (ibid., p. 81). But in this connection it is interesting to contrast the findings of James Jacobs and Harold Retsky in their recent study of prison guards at various stages of their careers at Stateville Penitentiary, Joliet, Illinois. "Stateville guards do not openly indicate racist attitudes. Whatever prejudices may exist are kept to one's self. This is in sharp contrast to studies of the police which have found an abundance of openly stated racist comments . . . and to other prison studies which have stressed the blatant racism among guards. . . . Even in informal discussions, we have not heard guards refer to black inmates as 'niggers' or in other racist terms, although whites continue to be disproportionately represented in better 'up front' jobs. We suspect that much that has been explained in the literature as racist attitudes toward inmates stems from the organizationally sponsored conflict between guards and inmates" (1975, p. 26). (Mr. Retsky, it should be mentioned, is a former prison guard at Joliet.) It may also be true that in adopting a moralistic and punitive attitude toward inmates the officers were to some extent reflecting community attitudes. But it is certainly true that no better recipe for disaster could have been devised than for young, inexperienced, untrained men with these attitudes to be assigned to carry the main burden of the daily supervision of an inmate population which was composed to a large extent of bitter, angry, unintimidated, aggressive inmates many of whom regarded themselves as "political prisoners," claiming that responsibility for their actions belonged to a society which "had failed to provide adequate housing, equal educational opportunities, and an equal opportunity to compete in American life" (*Attica* 1972, pp. 117-18).

SELECTION

Very little has been published about the recruitment and selection of prison officers. This is probably in part due to the fact that manpower, recruitment, and retention problems have long been widespread in the correctional field. It is impossible to be highly selective in a situation where there is a shortage of guards, a high turnover rate, and not infrequently political interference, that is, patronage; and as a consequence selection procedures for the most part remain at a rudimentary stage of development. Ironically, however, it is probably in part due to failure to consider the question of selection objectively that the shortage exists.

The truth is that selection procedures and recruitment standards are commonly both too rigid and not restrictive enough. Thus the task of a custodial officer calls for, and always has called for, a great deal more than the minimum height, weight, vision, and hearing requirements and high school diploma demanded at Attica and in the majority of penal institutions in America. At the same time it also calls for a good deal less. Indeed a great many of the restrictions currently imposed in personnel recruitment are not only irrational and unnecessary but also prejudicial to the effective functioning of the prison system.

One thing which is quite certain is that the almost universal insistence on certain physical standards which restrict the selection of potentially qualified employees is a mistake. The fact that a man weighs 145 pounds (the Attica requirement) is no index of character or ability or indeed of anything except the extent to which he can tip the scales. In fact the emphasis on such nonmerit factors must have frequently excluded otherwise well-qualified candidates. A good case can be made not only for the abolition of such rigid exclusionary rules but also for the recruitment of physically handicapped persons. The Joint Commission on Correctional Manpower and Training put this very well: "In the present labor market, as well as in the interest of full utilization of the nation's manpower resources, there should be an understanding of the contribution the physically handicapped can make in correctional institutions. . . . A positive point can be made for their employment with a realization that in the personal adjustment of many who are physically handicapped, they carry a message through to others in visual contact and in compassionate understanding that often characterizes a very effective relationship with other people" (1970, p. 124).

The racial disparity mentioned above between the guards and inmates at Attica is common throughout the American prison system. As the National Advisory Commission on Criminal Justice Standards and Goals put it: "For too long, minority groups have been overrepresented as offenders and underrepresented as staff" (1973, p. 599). The Commission found that of the total number of correctional employees (110,000) only 8 percent were blacks, 4 percent Chicanos, and less than 1 percent American Indians, Puerto Ricans, or Orientals. All institution administrators in the adult correctional system were white. Although racial discrimination is prohibited in most civil service jurisdictions, the Joint Commission on Correctional Manpower and Training acknowledged: "Undoubtedly discrimination in some form still persists" (1970, p. 125). At a time when racial strife is a major problem in many correctional institutions a policy of active recruitment of such minority groups as blacks, Puerto Ricans, and other Spanish-speaking Americans, rather than discrimination against them, is necessary.

In most states laws or civil service policies or practices prohibit the hiring of ex-offenders, although a number of experimental correctional programs have employed them. It is clear that this is a large, underutilized manpower resource pool (Joint Commission on Correctional Manpower and Training, 1968). There are two powerful reasons why ex-offenders should be recruited as prison guards. The first is that it is reasonable to assume that some ex-offenders will have a better understanding of other offenders than staff members who have never themselves been involved in serious crime or delinquency. The other is that correctional institutions and other government agencies have a responsibility to set an example of less discriminatory employment practices in relation to ex-offenders.

Other restrictions on staff selection which are both unnecessary and unreasonable relate to age and residence. It is very common for those under twenty-one and over forty-five to be excluded from employment as prison officers as well as for a mandatory retirement age of sixty-two to be fixed. The Joint Commission found in fact that only 26 percent of all correctional employees are under thirty-four years of age (1969, p. 13) which is a curious situation in view of the fact that crime itself is so largely a function of age. In the year 1965 persons under the age of twenty-five constituted 68 percent of the arrests for robbery, 77 percent of the arrests for burglary, 72 percent of the arrests for larceny, and 88 percent of the arrests for motor vehicle theft. (The President's Commission on Law Enforcement and Administration of Justice 1967, p. 56). If the "generation gap" does constitute a problem it is likely to be exacerbated if more attempts are not made to recruit younger personnel, and one of the best ways to do this would be to recruit young persons from eighteen to twenty-one. The upper age limit for recruitment should be at least fifty-five and the mandatory retirement age should be at least sixty-five. And residence requirements ought to be abandoned: "Residence of the state as a requirement of selection on condition of continuing employment imposes a limitation on the public service that no private employer has to contend with. Such a requirement is obviously a non-merit factor in excluding a candidate. It is based primarily on political considerations" (Joint Commission 1970, p. 123).

But if some selection criteria are arbitrary and unnecessary it is equally true that some are not merely desirable but essential. Back in 1961, Clarence Schrag, who has had considerable practical experience in correctional institutions, pointed out that the idea that the custodial officer is able to control inmates because he has unlimited authority and that his orders carry the full sanction of the prison's administration is an illusion. In fact, he says, "The officer's control over an inmate depends primarily on his skills of persuasion and leadership." Schrag sees "skill in interpersonal relations" and the ability to win voluntary cooperation as being the crucial factors in securing and maintaining control (1961, p. 340).

There is no doubt that Schrag is right, but a high school diploma is no guarantee of the possession of such skills, and, in the absence of a training program designed to teach them, the fact that a number of officers are recruited with the necessary ability must be almost entirely fortuitous. There is no reason, however, why this situation should be regarded as unalterable. Personnel selection is not an arcane mystery open only to those possessed of special gifts of insight. If it was possible for the New York State Special Commission on Attica to discover, *after* the Attica uprising, by means of interviews, that many of the Attica officers had negative attitudes towards criminals and blacks, it would have been possible for others to have done the same *before* those officers were recruited. It is true that, to take racism as an example, many people would deny on questioning that they felt any racial prejudice, but skillful interrogation can, as the Attica Commission discovered, undercover underlying prejudice and reveal racist feelings of which individuals may not themselves be consciously aware. Of course more positive qualities than an absence of racial prejudice and of negative attitudes to criminals are necessary for the performance of the custodial officer's task.

Over a quarter of a century ago D. E. Lundberg wrote: "Methods of selection of the Prison Guard are generally loose and have had little experimental study of validity. Of some 13,000 guards in this country, it is safe to say that over three-fourths have been selected by unscientific methods" (1947, p. 38). A decade later Richard Downey and E. I. Signori asserted: "[S]o far as one can discover, there are no reported attempts to investigate the problem of prison guard selection in terms of interest and personality objective testing procedures" (1958, p. 234). (They had in fact missed one reported attempt by the Federal Bureau of Prisons, described by A. A. Evans [1954, pp. 70–78].)

Downey and Signori report on a study of prison guard selection in which they administered four objective ability, interest, and personality tests: the Wesman Personnel Classification Test, the Kuder Preference Record-Vocational Test, the Minnesota Multiphasic Personality Inventory, and the Manson Evaluation. They found that fourteen out of an aggregate of thirty-eight measurement variables discriminated between "good" and "poor" job-performance-rated prison officers. Subsequently, William Perdue, in two papers (1964 and 1966), reported the successful use of the Johnson Temperament Analysis, devised by Roswell Johnson and published by the California Test Bureau, in screening applicants for custodial work. As Perdue wrote, "The Johnson Temperament Analysis is certainly not the sole answer to the many and complex problems that arise in personnel work in a prison, but it might be a step toward the direction wherein the real answers might lie" (1964, p. 19). It may be that such tests are better as "eliminators" than as "selectors," but even if that is true the need for "eliminators" is clearly considerable. And there is no reason why temperament and aptitude tests should not be devised to be used in the selection of custodial officers.

More recently, in fact, Don Hardesty described an attempt to develop selection standards in order to obtain better qualified and more effective correctional officers. Hardesty found that it was possible to identify reliably good correctional officers and poor correctional officers prior to appointment and that there were measurable differences between these groups which could be used, in the process of selection, to identify more accurately potentially good correctional officers (1969, 1970). While it is true that Hardesty's proposed correction-officer testing selection battery and procedure were developed on the basis of a particular set of measures of correctional-officer performance (both objective and supervisory appraisal measures), which might not be generally regarded as acceptable, the essential point is that he demonstrates that effective and objective selection procedures for correction officers are feasible.

TRAINING

No less important than personnel selection is the training of personnel. Two of the foremost prison administrators of this century were James V. Bennett of the U.S. Bureau of Prisons and

Alexander Paterson of the British Prison Commission. They both wrote on the subject of prison staff selection and training. Although they were both convinced of the supreme importance of training, when it came to the content of a proper training program for what Paterson called "subordinate officers" they were both afflicted by a lack of precision.

Paterson speaks of "the grave responsibilities" of prison officers. Bennett tells us that correctional work is "a highly complex activity." Paterson offers: "Candidates for the prison service ought to familiarize themselves with the history of prisons, the rules which govern them, and the principles which have dictated the choice of those rules" (1951, p. 105). Bennett echoes that the new correctional employee should be taught "the background and development of modern penology, and the history, present organization, philosophy, and goals of the employing agency" (1964, p. 266). Paterson says: "So far as this exceedingly subtle art can be learnt they must learn to be leaders." Bennett says that the period of basic training should "be a time for molding desirable employee attitudes." Phrases like "breadth of vision," "sense of perspective," "well integrated," "force of character," "self-reliance" recur in both papers.

There is nothing much wrong with what they say, but to anyone with experience in prisons they sometimes seem removed from the reality of the actual prison world. Paterson asserts that we must "select and train masters who will control men by force of personality and leadership, who will by example and influence train them in decent habits of self-control and industry" (1951, p. 102). Bennett writes: "[T]he task of supervising and guiding prisoners is no job for amateurs.... It is necessary to look for skills, talents, and unusual capabilities in persons recruited for this work. This means not only the necessary skill and capacity for doing a particular job, but also the ability to instill the same skill and capacity in untrained and frequently hostile inmates.... There is no substitute for personality, genuine interest, judgment, and understanding in personal relationships between workers and inmates" (1964, pp. 262–63).

If it were possible to recruit such professional paragons as prison guards the problem of training might prove a relatively simple one. But in real life such persons are rare in any trade or calling. Moreover, although it is easy to talk, as Paterson does, about the necessity for "a rigorous course of training" or, as Bennett does, about "the progressive development of skills and knowledge essential for the rehabilitation of prisoners," it is, as no doubt they discovered, extremely difficult to go much further than that. For when we ask what body of knowledge exists, what discipline, what field of study do we look to, to provide the content of the "rigorous course of training" which will enable men to function in the required manner, we find no answer at all forthcoming from either Paterson or Bennett or indeed anyone else.

Indeed even if we retreat from the illusory pursuit of men with "special gifts of personality and character" capable of achieving the moral transformation of their fellow men merely by the exercise of "personal influence," there still remain problems. Thus the Joint Commission on Correctional Manpower and Training provides a much more modest definition of the custodial officer's role. "Line Personnel," they say, "are charged by management with maintaining the security of institutional property and assuring peace and equity among offenders." But they go on to say that even in relation to this role the officers receive little guidance. "Too often they receive little useful direction from management or professionally trained staff, and they find themselves in something of a sink-or-swim situation."

Why is this? Why are there no members of "management or professionally trained staff" prepared to teach them to swim or at least to throw them a life preserver? It is because "unfortunately, there is little scientific knowledge about handling offender populations, few principles for consistent practice, and almost no provision for assessing the value of particular measures in various situations. Custodial staff generally operate on the basis of lore which has made for continued improvements in practice in other fields and occupations. Very little has been written on group management practices with confined offenders. What there is has come mainly from social scientists and has little relevance for the line practitioner."

In the circumstances perhaps it is not surprising that the Joint Commission was unable to provide much more on the subject of training than the somewhat jejune statement that "considerable thought and attention will be required by top experts in various fields of endeavor to devise ways of training correctional workers" (Joint Commission 1969, pp. 40–43). Nevertheless, it is possible to say something more about training even without the benefit of top expert advice. Thus in a situation where, as the 1967 President's Crime Commission put it, the majority of custodial officers are "undereducated, untrained and unversed in the goals of corrections," it is a simple truism that for all custodial officers an initial period of basic training is essential. As to the form and content of such training, the adoption throughout all states of the *Correction Officer's Training Guide* (1959), prepared by the American Correctional Association's Committee on Personal Standards and Training, would in itself constitute a significant advance.

But this provides little more than the basic essentials regarding the techniques and procedures of custodial care. And it is abundantly clear that while technical proficiency in this area is necessary and will in fact vastly improve the performance of officers, of much more fundamental importance is the officer's attitude toward inmates. This is because the officer's attitude toward inmates may be to a greater or lesser degree a factor in determining the inmates' attitude not merely toward the penal institution and the experience of imprisonment but also toward society and social values generally. This has long been recognized in some European countries, and the syllabi of such establishments as the Central School of the Danish Prison Administration in Copenhagen, the Dutch Central Training School in The Hague, and the Norwegian Training School for Prison Staff in Oslo reflect this fact.

Thus the three-month course for candidates for positions as prison officers provided at the Danish school, which is designed, among other things, *"to develop the proper attitude of mind,"* includes courses of lectures not only in criminology and in penology but also in psychiatry and in "knowledge of human nature" (Council of Europe 1963, p. 37; my italics). Advanced courses are also provided for more experienced prison officers after six to eight years of service. At the Dutch Training School the aim of the course is not merely imparting of technical knowledge and functional skill but also *"bringing about a change in attitude"* (my italics). Attempts are made to achieve this by "confronting the students with situations and problems identical with those of everyday practice, in this case through single and multiple role-playing, group discussions, case-study and group experiments." It is interesting to note that in the Netherlands the retraining of more experienced prison staff is also regarded as a function of the training school. Norwegian candidates for the prison service, who are required to take a six-month course of practical training which is followed by another six-month course of theoretical training, are given instruction in nineteen subjects including criminology, psychiatry, psychology, sociology, and even moral philosophy (ibid., pp. 64–67).

The most sophisticated prison-officer training program in the U.S. is that conducted by the U.S. Bureau of Prisons at its two regional staff training centers (Atlanta, Georgia, and Dallas, Texas) and by institutional training coordinators at each of the major institutions operated by the Bureau. Thus the syllabus includes, in addition to the conventional training in, amongst other areas, disciplinary procedures, report writing, and "correctional techniques," a forty-hour introduction to interpersonal communication as well as twelve hours on improving staff relations and communication, for all employees.

One of the most interesting studies of correctional-officer training is David Duffee's. Duffee took the view that the conventional training programs, in which the courses principally "tend to be taught in the style of a several-period lecture on the freshman level in a university," were inadequate even where the goal of the educator was merely to impart information. Where attitudinal and behavioral change was required, he argued, the usual educational techniques would be unlikely to be at all effective. Accordingly, he devised an experimental in-service training project in which he employed a combination of Floyd Mann's survey feedback technique, which has been used in upper management training (Mann 1961), and participant-observer group research. A small group of correctional officers was brought together at a minimum-security prison in 1971 and given three charges. These were: first, to study the goals of the institution and the role of the officer in achieving them; second, to study the organizational structure and operations to ascertain if there were any problems in day-to-day operations; and, finally, to study the activity of two other projects in the prison, team classification groups and inmate discussion groups.

Duffee's conclusion is that, evaluated in terms of criteria formulated prior to the beginning of the project, such as the admission of inmates into the group, the program was successful. He sums up by saying that the group proved: an effective method of achieving a new, more open perception of inmates by officers; an effective method of improving officers' problem-solving skills; and a potentially sound device, if expanded, for freeing top institutional managers for policy decisions and more interaction with other agencies (Duffee 1972). Of course it is not possible on the basis of one small experimental project to make general recommendations. But what Duffee's work does is to point in the direction in which officer-training programming should be oriented.

Another method that may be used to increase the officer's understanding of inmates is the case-study method, which is used in mental hospitals. The use of this method with prison officers is well described by Dr. Hector Cavallin. The method used by Dr. Cavallin was that of small-group discussions (each group consisting of eight correctional officers, a senior correctional supervisor, and a clinical person who was either a psychiatrist or a psychologist) in which the teaching material used consisted of a psychiatric report and an autobiography prepared by the prisoner. He reports that because of the fact the cases were known to the officers "very soon they were able to make a comparison between the way they had looked at this particular prisoner in the past and the new insights that the clinical evaluation had given them. This was manifested for instance in their becoming very much involved . . . in discussing the dynamics of the prisoner's personality development and attempting to make sense of the longitudinal study of the prisoner as a whole" (1967, p. 15). Dr. Cavallin was concerned with turning prison officers into "therapists"; but the case-study method can be equally well employed with the more realistic aim of enabling officers to view inmates' behavior more objectively and with more insight and understanding.

One of the best general discussions of the problems involved in prison-officer training was written by Dr. J. E. Thomas, who has had experience in both prison administration and prison staff training. He maintains that a crucial prerequisite to successful training is a clear answer to the question: What is this training intended to achieve? A good deal of confusion has been generated in the past, he argues, because prisons have been set "entirely unrealistic reformative goals." He advances a case for a training program which in addition to providing education in essential practical and vocational material also deals with the other constituent of the prison officer's role, which is concerned with how he deals with prisoners. This part of the officer's role involves treating prisoners "with sympathy, with dignity, and with respect." He advocates the inclusion in the syllabus of what he calls "a liberal component" aimed at helping officers "to be more tolerant, more capable of accepting difference, and generally more sympathetic (in the best sense) to the prisoner's position." He also gives a salutary warning about expecting training to achieve too much: "Much disappointment and misunderstanding can be avoided if it is emphasized that training is no substitute for the remedying of organizational defects such as inferior staff, low salary scales, or weak communication systems" (1972, pp. 200-205).

CONCLUSION

In 1945 Joseph F. Fishman published an article dealing with the life of the prison guard. It is a superficial article which does little more than stimulate momentary interest by the use of lurid detail. But the author had a good idea for a title. He called his article "The Meanest Job in the World." Over a quarter of a century later the title remains apposite.

One of the most curious features of the whole history of modern imprisonment is the way in which the custodial officer, the key figure in the penal equation, the man on whom the whole edifice of the penitentiary system depends, has with astonishing consistency either been ignored or traduced or idealized but almost never considered seriously. Thus Tannenbaum, in 1922, thought that "the keynote to understanding the psychology of the prison keeper" was "the exercise of authority and the resulting enjoyment of brutality" (p. 29). In 1943 Barnes and Teeters saw prison guards as suffering from "lock psychosis" as a result of a routine made up of "numbering, counting, checking and locking." Their personalities were warped by "the unnatural life they lead" (pp. 428–29).

More recent sociologists of the prison have seen the guards, when they have seen them at all, variously as involved in corrupt "alliances" with inmates, as ignorant and prejudiced functionaries of a corrupt system, or as featureless robots performing purely mechanical functions. By contrast many penal reformers and reformist administrators have endowed them with qualities of mind and character that recall the days of chivalry or those morally improving tales which used to form the staple content of Sunday School instruction. Thus Alexander Paterson opposed any time being allocated to the study of psychology for prison officers on the ground that "It is much better to leave them to their own natural good will and common sense than to stuff their ears and memories with a few scraps of scientific jargon" (1951, p. 104).

Today we have the advantage of being able to see that an ingenuous reliance on the assumed benevolence and soundness of the unreflective opinions and attitudes of ordinary men, characteristic of both nineteenth- and twentieth-century penal reformers and administrators, has led us to a crisis in penal affairs that makes the problems which those reformers faced appear relatively diminutive both in scale and significance. Moreover there is no reason at all why instruction in elementary psychology should not be given in terms of functional skills rather than theoretical abstractions. The stress should be placed, to use the words of the U.S. Bureau of Prisons training syllabus, "on easily used and understood techniques for resolving day-to-day problems."

The truth, as it emerges from the few studies which pay attention to prison guards and view them objectively, is simply that these guards were and are for the most part ordinary human beings with ordinary human failings and virtues. They have in the past been asked to perform impossible tasks without being properly trained to perform even possible ones. It is an extraordinary feature of the history of prisons that it was not until the 1930s that the first formally organized training programs for prison guards and custodial officers appeared in America. Many institutions still provide no full-time preparatory training for them before they start work. At the same time, they are the lowest paid of all correctional employees. We shall achieve nothing—worse, we are likely to do active harm—in prisons until we carefully select, train as thoroughly as we know how, and properly recompense the prison officer of the basic grade.

5   "Neither Slavery Nor Involuntary Servitude"

INTRODUCTION

The Thirteenth Amendment to the U.S. Constitution provides that "neither slavery nor involuntary servitude" shall exist within the United States or any place subject to its jurisdiction "except as a punishment for crime." The history of prison labor in this country, from the abuses of the convict lease system, the contract-labor system and the chain gang to the Arkansas Tucker Prison Farm scandal in the late 1960s, is evidence that slavery in its penal form has been a persistent feature of American society. Thorsten Sellin has argued that when imprisonment first came to be applied to all serious offenders it was in fact "only a variant" of the system of forced or compulsory labor, or penal servitude, that had been practiced in imperial Rome (1967, p. 19).

Certainly industrial policy has, from the beginning, and in a variety of ways, greatly influenced the development of the American prison system. One of the first penitentiaries built by the Philadelphia penal reformers—the Western Penitentiary at Pittsburgh—was modelled on Jeremy Bentham's Panoptican, which was intended to be "a mill grinding rogues honest and idle men industrious." Nor is this an isolated phenomenon. "Prison labour" says Max Grünhut, "is the essence of prison discipline. Throughout history the rise and fall of penal systems coincided with changing conditions of prison work" (1948, p. 196).

The central importance of this issue is not reflected in the amount of attention given to it in penological literature. Many works on prisons and imprisonment fail to mention it at all. The 1967 President's Commission on Law Enforcement and Administration of Justice, *Task Force Report: Corrections,* devotes less than two of its two hundred twenty-two pages to "Correctional Industries." The 1973 report, *Corrections,* of the National Advisory Commission on Criminal Justice Standards and Goals devotes only two of its six hundred thirty-six pages to "Prison Labor and Industries." The 1972 report of the National Institute of Law Enforcement and Criminal Justice, report on *The Role of Correctional Industries,* noted the lack of an empirical basis for making judgments regarding the operation of prison industrial programs. "Information regarding the nature of prison industry programs and their relative effectiveness is badly needed," said the report. "Recent studies of the American correctional system have not focused on these questions in any detail" (p. 58).

It is not possible here to provide the empirical basis for making the judgments called for by the National Institute of Law Enforcement and Criminal Justice. At the same time it is not possible to ignore what Lionel Fox referred to as "this central problem of prison administration."

THE PRINCIPLES OF PRISON WORK

According to Fox "the first clear principle of work generally applied in English prisons was that of 1865—hard labour as a form of punishment over and above the punishment of deprivation of liberty" (1952, p. 177). That principle is not only an ancient one which underlay sentences *ad metalla* (labor in the mines) in imperial Rome and the use of convicts as galley slaves, but it is also the basis of sentences to hard labor and penal servitude in this century. It is a principle which still exercises a considerable appeal and can be seen in operation in a few jails and some prisons to this day. The basic idea is that of work as part of the punishment. According to those who advocated it, a deterrent effect would be achieved by what Edmund du Cane, chairman of the British Prison Commission, called "the punishment of hard, dull, useless, uninteresting, monotonous labour" (1885, p. 175).

There is a curious paradox involved in this notion of enforced labor inflicted as a punishment. On the one hand work is to be made as disagreeable, irritating, and oppressive as possible. Fox describes those who called for greater deterrence in the early nineteenth century as pressing for "the enforcement of strict hard labour, meaning the use of the treadwheel or crank not only in silence and separation, but for no useful purpose, since in this view, labour, to be fully deterrent, should be not only monotonous and severe but quite useless, this being more likely to 'plague the prisoner.' Employment in useful and interesting work, on the other hand, seemed to be positively encouraging crime" (1952, p. 36). In America, too, this particular rationale was no less popular. As Thorsten Sellin says: "When the young American states built penitentiaries for serious offenders who would formerly have been executed, mutilated, or whipped, the law provided that prisoners confined in them should perform labor of the 'most harsh and servile kind' (a phrase borrowed from John Howard)" (1967, p. 21).

On the other hand it was clearly the hope of those who advocated and administered such programs as these that, as a result of prison experience, those discharged from prison would eschew a life of crime and set about earning a living by honest toil. It seems odd to expect prisoners, who are ordinarily, as Dr. Grünhut puts it, "a negative selection with regard to ability and inclination for regular work" (1948, p. 223), after being subjected to a regime designed to render work offensive, unrewarding, and distasteful, to be motivated to adopt it as a means of obtaining a livelihood. Patients undergoing aversive therapy do not usually become addicted to emetics or electric shocks. Thomas Mott Osborne put the essential paradox well: "When men are placed at work, usually without consulting their preferences or capacities, are held at work only by dread of punishment, and receive no pay—or very inadequate pay ... [they] ... come to associate work with prison and so desire to escape it altogether.... Any one of us, after years of that sort of labor and 'discipline' would find burglary a most refreshing contrast" (1924, pp. 39–40).

It is difficult to think of a principle combining a greater degree of inutility and irrelevance to any rational purpose. Yet Fox was right in saying that "it has never been wholly exorcised" from consideration of the question of prison labor. As Sutherland and Cressey put it, not only is "the punitive element in labor still retained in many institutions" but "the idea that monotonous, hard, unpleasant work is necessary if the prison is to perform its retributive and deterrence functions" still enjoys a good deal of popular support (1970, p. 559).

A second assumption which has in the past governed and still does influence the provision of employment for prisoners might be called the "Satan's mischief" principle after the hymn "Against Idleness and Mischief" by the eighteenth-century divine Isaac Watts, which recommended "works of labour, or of skill" as an antidote to the temptations inevitable in a state of idleness. The English Quaker Elizabeth Fry seems originally to have had something of this sort in mind when she provided work for the women prisoners in Newgate and, as one account has it, "brought into this bedlam of harridans the calm and industrious order of a cloister" (Fox 1952, p. 28). It is a principle which is capable of both negative and positive interpretations. In its negative form work is seen purely as a disciplinary device or even as an incapacitatory one. Sutherland and Cressey cite the fact that "routine prison labor often is defended on the ground that it keeps inmates 'out of mischief'," as evidence that it is "considered part of the prison program of incapacitation" (1970, p. 560).

A somewhat different emphasis can be found in the statement of E. R. Cass who, as general secretary of the American Prison Association, said: "Idleness in a prison is subversive of discipline and hurtful to the moral, intellectual and physical well-being of the inmates. No greater cruelty can possibly be inflicted on prisoners than enforced idleness" (Robinson 1931, p. 2). Louis Robinson distinguishes between labor being introduced as "a punitive factor" in prisons and as "a mitigating factor." He regards it as axiomatic that a long period of idle detention involves physical and moral degeneration for the prisoner. From this viewpoint the rationale of prison industries is that, like occupational therapy in mental hospitals, they contribute to the psychological well-being of prisoners. As W. M. Wallack says, prisoners "should work in order to keep them physically and mentally fit." Sutherland and Cressey refer to this as "the 'inmate-welfare' point of view." Idleness in prison is seen as something which "contributes to the incidence of 'prison stupor'" and is "conducive to low prisoner morale." Work keeps prisoners "occupied so that they leave the prison in good psychological and physical condition" (1970, pp. 567–68). Otherwise, to use E. R. Cass's words, "Their health declines and in a large proportion of cases the mind, burdened by the monotony of the slowly passing hours in which neither hand nor brain is active, becomes affected" (Robinson 1931, p. 2).

The third conception of the purpose of prison work in penal theory is that expounded at some length by Grünhut but also put succinctly by him as follows: "The object of prison labour in a rehabilitative program is twofold: training for work and training by work" (1948, p. 209). It would probably be true to say that this principle is the one most widely accepted by penologists and prison administrators throughout the world today; although it is necessary to add that in most countries adherence to the principle is very dimly reflected in practice. Some historians have discerned the germ of this idea in the Elizabethan working houses, or houses of correction, where vagabonds, beggars and prostitutes were confined "to be corrected in their habits by laborious discipline." But the emphasis in those institutions seems to have been predominantly punitive. Indeed, as Fox points out, they "soon came to be more an arm of the penal than of the poor law" (1952, p. 24).

The concept of training involves a redefinition of the purpose of prison labor in terms of two objectives which are enunciated in the United Nations *Standard Minimum Rules for the Treatment of Prisoners*: "So far as possible the work provided shall be such as will maintain or increase the prisoners' ability to earn an honest living upon release"; and "vocational training in useful trades shall be provided for prisoners able to profit thereby and especially for young prisoners" (1956, p. 72). This represents the abandonment of the concept of prison work as a punitive device and its replacement by the view that prison work should serve the purpose of providing occupational experience and/or training to facilitate the rehabilitation of the prisoner after his release.

The basic practical implication of this approach is simply that prisoners should be permanently occupied with useful work. This is seen to be of value for two reasons. In the first place there is the point Grünhut makes: "Regular performance of useful work certainly produces valuable educational factors: the acquisition of skill and abilities, the habit of exactness and regularity, the experience of the beneficial rhythm of work and leisure, and the satisfaction that a job has been properly done" (1948, p. 216). At the same time it is hoped that the acquisition of satisfactory work-habits during the inmate's term of imprisonment will produce a change of attitude which will be reflected in ex-prisoners' careers after discharge from prison.

Unfortunately there is no necessary connection between good prison work-records and crime-free subsequent careers. Indeed such evidence as is available suggests that although the relation is positive it is not very significant. Nor does there appear to be any very significant relation between institutional training, parole employment, and recidivism. Thus Daniel Glaser's report on the 1959–60 study by the U.S. Parole Board found: "Those using prison training on one or more jobs had a 55 percent violation rate on first parole, as compared with 51 percent for those with employment not using prison training." The conclusion of Glaser's own Post-release Panel Study was as follows: "[O]ne can make the tentative generalization that in about one-tenth of inmate postrelease jobs, there are benefits from new learning acquired in prison work, in about three or four percent of these jobs there are benefits from the preservation of old skills through practice in prison, and in about five or six percent of the postrelease jobs the prison provided useful physical or psychological conditioning" (1964, pp. 252–54).

For a number of reasons, however, it would be a mistake to infer that, because recidivism has not in the past been significantly reduced by prison industrial experience or training, such experience and training should not be provided. For one thing, this failure, although doubtless partly a function of factors outside the control of the prison authorities, is almost certainly due to some extent to the nature of the prison programs themselves. One has only to read any of several studies on prison labor conducted over the last twenty years to recognize that in the

United States and in most other countries prison industrial programs are extremely defective (United Nations 1955; California State Assembly 1969; National Institute of Law Enforcement 1972). For another thing the provision of work in prisons is not justifiable solely in terms of its effect on recidivism.

This brings us to the question of what has been called "the right to work." Despite the Protestant work ethic, relatively few people are afflicted with what Kipling called "a morbid passion for work"; for most it is a necessity rather than an avocation. In the circumstances the nineteenth-century notion that penal labor might be an instrument of restoration of offenders to industrious citizenship seems to be based on an almost perverse misreading of the nature of the problem.

On the other hand it is also true that enforced idleness is not only punitive but can have deleterious effects on human beings. It is for this reason that many penologists have insisted that prisoners should enjoy the right to work. As Grünhut puts it, "[W]ork is a much-coveted remedy which helps men to endure the unnatural state of captivity. . . . Prison labour is a benefit, and to forfeit it is a severe blow to the prisoner. . . . Deprivation of work in connection with solitary confinement is a severe disciplinary punishment. Enforced labour may be oppressive, but to withhold it would mean even more hardship to the prisoner" (1948, p. 198). Moreover in a number of countries the law explicitly or implicitly guarantees prisoners the right to work. This is the case in Denmark, Norway, Sweden, and Mexico. In some others, for example, France, the Netherlands, and Switzerland, the right to work is recognized and reflected in administrative principles and practice although not guaranteed by law. Moreover the right to work is included in Article 23 of the United Nation's "Universal Declaration of Human Rights," which states: "Everyone has the right to work, to free choice of employment, to just and favorable conditions of work and to protection against unemployment." Although imprisonment will inevitably put limits on the application of this principle, there is no reason to regard the prisoner's right to work as cancelled, unless the criminal law expressly provides otherwise.

The prisoner's right to work should be clearly recognized. There is no justification whatever—neither legal, moral, economic, or penological—for imposing on the offender, in addition to the deprivation of liberty, compulsory unemployment. Grünhut is right in saying that the state "would forfeit the right to inflict punishment in the name of justice if it were to take a man from his place in society to enforced idleness within prison walls" (1948, pp. 197-98). Indeed it seems clear that an adequate justification for prison labor programs can be found in their representing a recognition of the prisoner's right to work. And the duty to provide work can equally be seen to derive from what should also be recognized as a fundamental penological principle: that the prevention of prisoners' demoralization or deterioration must be regarded as a prime duty of any prison system.

But it is possible to go further than this. It is the acknowledged aim of all prison systems that offenders should be returned to society in a condition in which they are able, and if possible willing, to play a part as constructive members of the community. A constructive member of the community is, by definition, a working member. A common characteristic of offenders is a poor work record. It is reasonable to assume that some of them took to crime in the first place for lack of the will, ability, or opportunity to earn a legal living (for an account of others whose choices were guided by different considerations, see Jackson, *A Thief's Primer*, 1969). Therefore satisfying work experiences for institutionalized offenders, including vocational training when needed, should be at the heart of the correctional process. To subject people with poor work-habits and a low work-motivation to the enforced idleness that prevails in most prisons and all but a few jails, or to the meaningless chores and humiliating working conditions that are characteristic of many prison programs, is simply to reduce further their capacity to derive satisfaction from, or even take part in, workaday community life.

The conclusion is that the provision of work and training for work in prisons should be regarded as an obligation by prison administrators and correctional authorities for two reasons. In the first place those authorities have an indefeasible duty to ensure as far as is possible that the experience of imprisonment is not a deformative or demoralizing one for the prisoner. In the second place they have no less an obligation to provide facilities whereby prisoners are able through engaging in productive work or vocational training to take part in activities which may help them to achieve their rehabilitation.

VOCATIONAL TRAINING

It is convenient to consider the practical aspect of the prison work problem under the two headings of vocational training and prison industries. Vocational training or "training for work," as Grün-hut terms it, is frequently described as having proved a failure in prisons. This is because, as was briefly mentioned above, vocational training seems to have very little effect on the level or type of work to which inmates go after release and also because its effect on the recidivism of participants seems to have been at best marginal.

Nevertheless, some reservations need to be made before this negative verdict is accepted. Although it appears that only a relatively small proportion of released prisoners find employment which utilizes prison training, this is evidently in part due to the unavailability of work for which training is provided. This was true even in the case of the relatively successful Rikers Island Project for young offenders, which was described and evaluated by Clyde E. Sullivan and Wallace Mandell. In that case prisoners were given training on IBM punched-card data processing machines. Yet only 18 percent of the group trained were hired for work specifically related to their IBM training because employers were reluctant to hire young male offenders to work alongside the women who predominate in this field of employment. Neverthe-less, comparison of the post-release experience of participants with that of a control group led to the conclusion that training had a favorable effect both on post-release employment and recidivism. Sullivan and Mandell are extremely conservative in their estimate of the project's success, but they say: "A program of vocational education and training in a jail, coupled with appropriate post-release services to manage re-entry into free society *does* make a difference in subsequent job performance and social adjustment of young offenders" (1967, p. 11).

The best and most comprehensive available evidence regarding the effectiveness of vocational training in prisons is an evaluation of vocational training provided in correctional institutions through the Manpower Development and Training Act. Twenty-five projects funded from 1968 through mid-1969 were carefully studied. In this case the evidence indicates that while the training programs' impact on employment was very slight, recidivism was 4 percent less for trainees than for controls at both three and six months after release (Abt Associates 1971, pp. 8–10).

Although it is true that the results cannot be regarded as indicating a great success, it seems likely that this may have been in part due to defective implementation. Thus the Abt report states:

We conclude that most projects offered few training courses, thereby limiting trainee choice. In the selection of these courses too much emphasis was placed on the availability of prison facilities and the local economy as opposed to the interests of inmates and the broader economy. With respect to the training courses themselves, there was a wide variation in the number of hours of training received. This was true even for the same course when provided at different projects. Very few trainees had the opportunity to receive off-site training, e.g., at local area schools. In many projects there were serious deficiencies with materials, equipment or facilities. When assessing impact we conclude that course completion, significant prison involvement with projects, and a rehabilitative rather than custodial focus had a positive influence on post-release impact (ibid., p. 17).

The fact that under those circumstances MDTA training was not highly effective does not lead to the conclusion that vocational training cannot be effective in prisons.

It is important to note also that, while the impact of vocational training may be marginal, it can in individual cases be crucial. This emerged from Glaser's study in relation to prison work and recidivism. He reports:

When, in terminating our interviews with the "success" cases, we asked them when and why they changed from interest in pursuing crime, thirty percent mentioned their improved work habits or skills as a factor in their change. A number of these mentioned trades learned in prison as a factor, especially the secure and skilled "career" trades, such as printing, electrical, and machinist trades. It was quite clear that the few whose vocational prospects in the noncriminal world had been completely metamorphosed by their acquisition of a rewarding trade in prison were extremely appreciative.

One of Glaser's principal conclusions is in fact that "at present the post-release employment of at least half the men released from prison does not involve a level of skill that requires an appreciable amount of prior training, but for the minority who gain skills in prison at which they can find a post-release vocation, prison work experience and training is a major rehabilitative influence" (1964, pp. 255–59).

Prison Industries
Glaser also found that: "(1) prison work can readily provide the most regular employment experience most prisoners have had; (2) prior work regularity is more closely related to post-release success or failure than type of work; (3) relationships with work supervisors are the most rehabilitative relationships with staff that prisoners are likely to develop." And he concludes therefore: "Not training in vocational skills, but rather, habituation of inmates to regularity in constructive and rewarding employment, and anti-criminal personal influences of work supervisors on inmates, are—at present—the major contributions of work in prison to inmate rehabilitation" (ibid., p. 259).

Reference has been made earlier to the fact that what might be called the reformative theory of prison labor has not in practice justified the promise implicit in it. Most of the reasons for the failure to develop efficient and effective systems for the utilization of prison labor in prison industries are well known. Many of them were pointed out over forty years ago in the Wickersham Commission report (1931). They were noted again in the report of the President's Commission on Law Enforcement and Administration of Justice (1967). It is not necessary therefore to provide a detailed analysis here. A summary statement of the principal problems will suffice.

There are in this country five principal problems which arise in connection with the organization of prison industries. The first relates to the question of the payment of prisoners. As Freedman and Pappas say, "The wages paid to prisoners define to them the value of the work they are doing" (1967, p. 5). In practice the wages paid to prisoners might be designed to ensure that work should *not* be meaningful to the prisoner. When labor is unrewarded or inadequately rewarded, it runs counter to all reason to expect prisoners to be motivated to work diligently. If we ignore what Grünhut calls "the common human experience, that adequate earnings are a stimulus to work and a visible expression of its successful performance" (1948, p. 211), then we must expect the inmate work force to be indolent and inefficient.

Wages paid in American prisons range from no payment at all in a number of states to a maximum of eighty-five cents per hour in one state (where the minimum, incidentally, was four cents per hour). To take people who are, to borrow Sir Norwood East's description of the prison labor force, "seldom efficient. . . , often indifferent and sometimes useless" and to ignore normal economic self-interest and pay them derisory wages is to invite industrial disaster. As a result where, as in California, some attempts have been made to evaluate inmate institutional job performance, it has been found that measured in terms of absenteeism, productivity, and hours of work per person the standards of prison industries are far below those obtaining in private industry.

The second major problem concerns the fact that there is a substantial body of both state and federal law (including the Hawes-Cooper Act passed by Congress in 1929 and the Ashurst-Sumners Act passed in 1935) which with few exceptions restricts prisoner employment (apart from maintenance work in institutions) to manufacturing goods for use by government agencies or to engaging in state public works. This type of legislation, which proliferated during the depression of the 1930s, has effectively restricted the development of prison industries ever since.

The third major problem is that even state-use markets have, because of political pressure by private industry and by labor organizations, been largely closed to the products of prison industries. "Numerous instances could be cited of expensive plants being constructed in prisons, operating for a few years, then becoming idle because of campaigns by private business lobbies to persuade state officials to purchase from them, often at much more than the cost of the prison-made goods. Instances also could be cited of construction firms and labor organizations successfully preventing inmate labor from being used in construction and maintenance work on prison buildings, and even in the destruction of old prison buildings" (President's Commission on Law Enforcement and Administration of Justice, *Task Force Report: Corrections*, 1967, p. 55). Many examples of the harrassment and obstruction of prison industries by private industry and labor are in fact given in the Freedman and Pappas report.

The fourth obstacle to prison industrial development is that the operations of prison industries are notoriously inefficient. Outdated equipment, obsolete machinery, poorly organized activities, and antiquated work methods have resulted in a situation where, it is reported, "In many cases the prison-made goods are inferior in design and workmanship to those available from private firms; their delivery has been unreliable; and despite the availability of cheap prison labor, the state still may charge more than the price of the products on the open market" (ibid.). A major factor here is that, as the California Assembly Office of Research report on correctional industries noted, prison industries are characterized by *"the planned unreality of working conditions inside an industrial system that must deliberately aim at inefficiency"* (1969, p. 7; my italics). The problem is that prison administrators, faced with the need to avoid idleness and provide employment for as many prisoners as possible, are reluctant to take advantage of technological advances which would reduce employment, and at the same time almost all prison industrial enterprises tend to become inflated "busywork" programs, overmanned and wastefully organized.

The fifth problem is one which is not really an independent problem but rather an inevitable consequence of all those matters I have already mentioned. One of the recognized objectives of prison industrial programs is to provide training in work habits, attitudes, and skills that will assist inmates to obtain employment after release. In fact most prisoners, even when they are employed, are underemployed. Ralph England has described the situation as follows: "The public image of state prisons as beehives of productive activity, with 'cons' working long hours manufacturing auto tags, road signs, brooms, and clothing is largely erroneous. Even the few so employed seldom work more than six hours a day. The rest are subjected to the demoralizing and wasteful assignment of trying to appear busy at housekeeping tasks, most of which can be completed easily in the first hour or two of the work period" (1961, p. 21). The likelihood of the development of any valuable work habits, skills, or attitudes in these circumstances is clearly very remote. As Freedman and Pappas assert, "Meaningful work experience can only take place under conditions approximating those of real work settings with respect to production methods, work expectations and super-vision" (1967, p. 11). In fact, for the most part prisoners work in conditions as remote from the real world of competitive business as it is possible to conceive. Such "work" can be of little help in training offenders for later employment and may well constitute a serious obstacle to it.

There is a final point which must be made in this context. It relates to the potential labor productivity of inmates. Economist Neil M. Singer puts forward estimates of the value and use of adult institutionalized offenders' manpower. His estimates are based on the National Prisoner Statistics compiled by the Law Enforcement Assistance Administration, the U.S. Census Bureau data relating to the educational level and occupational back-ground of prison inmates, and statistics on income and earnings compiled by the Labor Department's Census Bureau and the Commerce Department's Bureau of Economic Analysis.

After calculating on this basis the gross potential earnings of those incarcerated in adult penal institutions, Singer estimates what proportion of inmate productivity is actually being utilized in work-release, prison industries, vocational/remedial programs, and institutional maintenance activities, and what proportion is being lost to society. He arrives at "an estimate of over 700 million dollars as the cost of wasted manpower in adult prisons, or roughly the institutions' current budgetary cost." In addition, "the manpower wasted in jails is worth as much again, or $1.1 billion minus maintenance work valued at $250 million and whatever work or training programs jails may offer. Thus, the total loss from wasted adult inmate labor is conservatively $1 billion and probably nearer $1.5 billion per year" (Singer 1973b, p. 17).

Singer does not underestimate the barriers to using inmate

labor power effectively, which include restrictive legislation, declining average sentences, and, particularly in jails, the high turnover rate. But his economic analysis, based on reasonable and clearly explained assumptions, demonstrates the extent to which the prison system falls short of full utilization of the productive capacity of inmates in confinement. The enormous magnitude of unutilized inmate labor power represents a loss not merely to inmates but to the whole of society.

WHAT SHOULD BE DONE
It is clear that in order to deal with problems as longstanding and deep-seated as those described some sort of federal initiative will be necessary. This is one of the principal themes of the report of the President's Task Force on Prisoner Rehabilitation. The essence of the report's recommendations on this subject is that the only way to make prison work and to make work-training programs effective is by means of close collaboration between the prisons and industry and labor. The Federal Bureau of Prisons has in fact pioneered such relationships in, for example, the training program for electronic welders operated by Dictograph in the Danbury, Connecticut, prison and a similar program for aircraft sheetmetal workers run by Lockheed in the prison in Lompoc, California. The report's principal recommendation is the establishment of a national agency whose function would be to stimulate the adoption of similar programs in the states.

What is required, the report says, "is a mechanism that could expand such efforts, coordinate them, bring additional expertise to both economic and correctional planning, disseminate information about programs to correctional authorities throughout the country and to the public, stimulate with ideas and money innovations and experiments, and evaluate ongoing programs." "One form such an agency might take would be a public corporation with a presidentially appointed chairman and half a dozen directors representing industry, labor, voluntary agencies and the public."

The agency would have the function of taking part in the contractual negotiations between the industry and the prison authorities; making sure that the standards of instruction and working conditions were equivalent to those of outside industry;

and evaluating each program. It should also "review jointly with labor and management all laws, regulations and practices concerning the purchase of prison-made products and beyond that look into the possibility of the sale of such products to government agencies and through voluntary non-profit channels for domestic and foreign use."

The task force further recommended that the agency should initiate and support experimentation with a variety of industrial programs in prisons. In particular it suggested that the time had come—one might say that it is overdue—for an experiment with what is called a "prevailing wages" or "factory" prison in which the prisoner would be paid at full market rates for his labor and would meet the costs of his board and keep and contribute to the support of his dependents, if any.

As to the cost of agency operations two suggestions are made. The first is that private industry would probably be willing to pay all or part of the cost of training programs, which might well be less than they would have to pay for training programs elsewhere. The second suggestion is that a possible source of funding might be the annual dividend that Federal Prison Industries, Inc., currently pays to the United States Treasury. It is pointed out that in 1969 this amounted to five million dollars, which "would be more than enough . . . to fund the agency" (President's Task Force 1970, pp. 11–13).

The necessity for a federal initiative is cogently argued in an article by Neal Miller and Walter Jensen, which commends the task force recommendation that a public corporation or agency be established that would have as its function the adoption of programs for the employment of prisoners. The authors also favor a legislative proposal designed to reform existing prison industries introduced into Congress by Senator Charles Percy as the Offender Employment and Training Act.

Designed to modernize and reorganize existing prison industries and coordinate federal and state efforts, this legislation is based on the premise that the success of prison industry programs depends on the cooperation and expertise of private industry and labor. It would authorize Federal Prison Industries to contract with businesses, corporations, or other private groups to establish factories or projects within federal prison walls for the purpose of employing or training offenders. It would also authorize Federal Prison Industries to make loans, at an interest rate not to exceed 6 percent annually, to any corporation, association, labor organization, private nonprofit organization, or federal agency associated with penal or correctional institutions for the purpose of employment and training of inmates.

Under this scheme prisoners would be trained in the manufacture of products which could be sold in competition with goods made by private industry using free-market labor. Federal restrictions on the sale and distribution of prison-made goods and on the employment of inmate labor in direct competition with free-market labor would be repealed or modified. Participation both by employers and offender-employees would be voluntary, but both would have to agree to certain conditions. The employer would have to agree to pay the free-market wage for the job, and the offender would have to agree to pay costs incidental to his confinement and support for his dependents together with federal and state taxes and social security charges. The offender would also be required to contribute to a fund to compensate victims of crime.

State participation in the program would be dependent upon prison-made goods being allowed to enter from other states. In many states this would require legislation to permit interstate and intrastate sales of prison-made goods. The proposed Offender Employment and Training Act also authorizes the attorney general of the United States to make contracts and agreements designed to assist financially state authorities in establishing programs for the training and employment of offenders in state penal or correctional institutions. In order to finance the program the federal government would appropriate not less than $10 million for fiscal year 1974 and for each year thereafter. In addition a federal employment and training fund would be set up, and all proceeds received from the sale of any products or goods manufactured pursuant to this plan as well as rentals in connection with leases made with private industry would be paid into this fund.

Common to both the task force recommendations and Senator Percy's scheme is the utilization of the expertise and experience of private enterprise in order to expand and reform prison industries. Two considerations indicate the wisdom of this approach. In the first place the kind of managerial skills required might well not be readily obtainable in any other way. In the second place, as Miller and Jensen observe, "Rather than have the government make direct payments to improve today's outmoded prison industries system, a subtle program of tax credits or grants to the private sector on a contract fee basis would be more politically acceptable to the voters" (1974, p. 21).

It is not proposed here to compare the merits of the two schemes. In fact they can best be viewed as complementary rather than as competing proposals. What seems clear is that it will only be by means of a systematic approach on a national basis that prison industries can be transformed into effective economic operations. This could probably be best achieved by the adoption of a program which embodied elements from both of the two plans referred to above.

Despite the broad support for private-sector involvement in prison industries, there are commentators, like economist Neil Singer, who oppose the expansion of prison industries through the introduction of private firms. Singer agrees that "the only feasible route for expanding prison industries probably lies in inviting private businesses to establish branches within correctional institutions." Moreover he fully acknowledges the advantages of expanding prison industries, admitting even that "some impact on post-release employment and even recidivism rates might be observed." Nevertheless, he does not think that such expansion is desirable.

His argument against this development runs essentially as follows: "There are only two ways to improve the use of prison manpower": to upgrade prison industries or to provide expanded work-release programs. Of the two alternatives, expansion of prison industries seems less likely to benefit inmates, prison administrators, or society at large than would an expanded reliance on work-release. This conclusion, he says, "rests on a comparison of the primarily economic costs and benefits of the two programs." For he points out that, whereas "society as a whole is best off when producers are able to arrive at the most efficient combination of factors of production," which will produce a good at the lowest unit cost, the development of prison industries will generally occur under constraints that prevent the attainment of the most efficient mix of factors. Consequently, society as a whole will suffer. On the other hand work-release would result in an improvement of the overall allocation of society's resources, an increase in society's effective labor force, and an increase in productivity. Singer also adds another noneconomic argument in favor of work-release, to the effect that it might create "a sense of social accountability for prisons and the correctional process by exposing society to inmates and showing that inmates can respond to the same incentives as everyone else."

Unfortunately, Dr. Singer's argument has two crucial weaknesses. In the first place, assuming it to be true that there are only two ways to improve the use of prison manpower, it does not follow that these "two alternatives to the current system" are mutually exclusive. Thus an expanded work-release system could perfectly well coexist with more efficient industrial organization within prisons or, for that matter, with a rapidly deteriorating prison industrial system. In the second place, as Singer explicitly recognizes when he puts forward his final argument about the creation of a sense of social accountability for prisons and the correctional process, the issue involved is not solely an economic one involving only the most efficient use of prison manpower. If it were, its solution would be much simpler and might well be along the lines which he suggests.

The fact has to be recognized, however, that the expansion of work-release to accommodate Singer's estimated number of 375,000 inmates (out of an estimated 500,000 in custodial institutions), even if it would represent an increase in the labor force of only 0.4 percent, would represent a revolutionary change in prison policy. And although it might attract more than 0.4 percent public support, such a policy would be a singularly precarious plank in anyone's political platform. Curiously, Singer seems to forget that at an earlier stage in his argument he has described "the attitude of the general public, which regards prison as a place whose primary purpose is punishment," as one of the principal obstacles to "the productive use of inmate labor" (1973a, pp. 200–211).

This is not to say that Singer is mistaken in advocating expanded reliance on work-release. Moreover those who advocate expanded and improved prison industries rarely confine their recommendations to programs within institutions. Thus the report of the President's Task Force on Prisoner Rehabilitation specifically recommends that the proposed national agency would not merely develop prison programs, "but would seek to encourage training and employment programs for prisoners granted work-release from institutions" (1970, p. 12). Miller and Jensen concur: "An overhaul of the nation's prison industries cannot realistically be considered apart from other aspects of correctional reform such as . . . halfway houses and work-release plans designed to ease the offenders' transition to the free world" (1974, p. 19). There is no good reason why both types of development should not proceed simultaneously.

Prison Inmates as Research Subjects

Finally, we come to an issue regarding the employment of prisoners that raises serious ethical problems. Prisoners have for many years been used as research subjects in the testing of a variety of cosmetics, food additives, and drugs. As Norval Morris and Michael Mills put it, "Prisoners make splendid laboratory animals. Healthy, relatively free of alcohol and drugs, with regulated diets they are captives unlikely to wander off and be lost to both treatment and control groups, and they are under sufficient pressure of adversity to 'volunteer'" (1974, p. 60). There is also a better assurance of patient safety in a prison setting because prisoners are available for constant observation and treatment in a controlled situation.

It is not known how many prisoners are involved as subjects in this kind of research, but it is estimated that half the nation's prisons have some research involving prisoners in progress. The use of human beings as experimental subjects raises problems in regard both to the nature of that research (witness the case of the Nazi doctors who conducted experiments on concentration camp prisoners) and the consent of the subjects. The question regarding what research using human subjects is justified will not be discussed here because that problem is of a general nature and not peculiar to the prison context.

It is sufficient to note that the present practice in research on humans is controlled by the Department of Health, Education and Welfare through the Food and Drug Administration and the National Institutes of Health. The National Institutes of Health operates a system whereby a review committee of scientific and medical peers of researchers is charged both with assessing the scientific quality of any experiment and with ensuring that "the rights and welfare of the subjects involved are adequately protected, that the risks to the individual are outweighed by the potential benefits to him or by the importance of the knowledge to be gained, and that informed consent is to be obtained by methods that are adequate and appropriate." That this sort of control is necessary is amply demonstrated in *Research on Human Subjects*, where Bernard Barber and his coauthors have shown that the research world has a significant minority of hyper-competitives and incompetents who are prepared to expose human subjects to unjustified risks. But on the whole the peer review system seems to be a reasonably effective control.

It is with regard to the question of consent, however, that peculiar difficulties arise in relation to prisoners because their freedom to consent is questionable. It was because of doubts on this point, and in reaction to the Nazi use of prisoners in medical experiments, that the World Medical Association's initial draft of the Declaration of Helsinki banned the use of all prisoners in medical research. Although the ban was subsequently modified to prohibit only the use of "administrative and political prisoners," some prison administrators in Europe and America have refused to accept the modification on the ground that prisoners are not in a position to give a genuinely "free" consent.

An example at this point will illustrate the nature of the problem and some of the main issues and interests involved. At Stateville Penitentiary in Illinois, under the sponsorship of the U.S. Army, Navy, and the State Department, a malaria research project employs prisoners as subjects to test antimalaria drugs. One of only three human testing centers in the United States, the program at Stateville has over the past twenty-nine years employed some four thousand inmate participants. There have been no deaths related to the project and no lasting side effects from either the drugs or the induced disease. Twenty-five inmates have become certified medical technologists, through working in the project's laboratory.

It is estimated that two hundred million persons, mostly in the developing nations, annually suffer from malaria and that two million per year die from it. According to the sponsors, the research program has directly resulted in the development of several highly effective antimalaria drugs. Recently they have been preparing to test what may become the first vaccine to prevent the disease in humans. There can be no doubt that the project is of great actual and potential benefit to society. There is no substitute for testing on humans after a certain stage in animal tests has been reached.

The Illinois Department of Corrections has recently ordered that this project be phased out and ultimately ended. Allyn R. Sielaff, the director of the department, has stated: "Our stand is based on the question of whether an inmate can truly volunteer his services and we do not believe he can." His view is that prisoners are in an inherently coercive situation and that there are pressures on them to volunteer "even in the best-run project" which are unavoidable, not least the fact that volunteers are paid for their services $30 to $50 monthly in a situation where there are few alternative ways of earning that much money.

The ban is not popular with prisoners. As in other states where decisions have been made to stop all medical experiments on prisoners, they have protested both to the state governor and the director of the Department of Corrections, urging the continuation of the project. They have called it "a vital force in our rehabilitation." They have also said that the project is "the only program here in which we can make a contribution to society" (Stone 1974). No doubt their motivation is often more complex than that; a variety of factors in addition to the altruism of community service may play a part, such as the pleasure of risk taking, the desire for expiation, the hope of earlier release, the desire for temporary escape from the squalor and violence of the prison itself, the reward of payment, and in some cases perhaps psychopathic elements are involved.

In the light of this example it is possible to examine briefly the crucial issue involved in the employment of prisoners as research subjects, the issue of consent. Four of the suggested types of motivation raise difficulties in relation to the ethics of consent although they are not of equal magnitude. Nevertheless, all of them appear to involve constraints which can properly be regarded as diminishing the inmate's freedom of choice. The question is whether they are of sufficient weight to compel the conclusion that prisoner participation should be prohibited or whether they are of such a character that they can either be ignored or provided for by safeguards protecting the prisoner.

Let us consider first the possibility that some prisoners cannot, because of psychological disorder or neurotic compulsion, be regarded as really exercising a free choice when they volunteer to participate in experiments. This problem is not peculiar to the prison situation except perhaps insofar as the conditions of imprisonment may themselves be psychopathogenic. It does not, however, seem to present an insuperable objection. There is no reason why provision should not be made, as is in fact done in some prison research projects, for all volunteers to be subjected to psychological examination and testing to ensure as far as possible that their desire to participate is not the product of psychosis or neurosis of any kind.

Second, there is the question of the hope of earlier release from prison. It could be argued that this possibility constitutes undue pressure on the inmate. It is probable that some prisoners do volunteer in the hope that their participation will win them earlier release on parole and a shortened prison term. Nathan Leopold, who as a participant in the Stateville program, says: "There was no assurance whatever that the volunteers would be rewarded by having their time cut. Of that fact each group was solemnly and emphatically reminded before they were allowed to sign their contracts. But the possibility did exist that there would be time cuts. And that was a chance I could not afford to miss" (1958, pp. 331–32). In practice, however, this particular motive does not appear to be of major significance. Few prisoners seriously believe that they will obtain earlier release as a result of participation in the research.

Next there is the question whether the squalor and violence of the conditions of imprisonment from which the inmate seeks escape in the experimental haven should not be regarded as a factor reducing his freedom of choice. This is a more serious objection although its cogency is relative rather than absolute, for the truth is that no human choices are totally free of any constraints of circumstance. It is true that we are under a moral obligation to ensure that prison conditions are made more tolerable and decent so that the prisoner is not subjected to the rigors of fortuitous and arbitrary suffering. But in the meantime to deprive him of an opportunity for temporary escape from that suffering would in fact be a restriction on his freedom.

Finally there is the question of the economic incentive. This raises more difficult problems. Indeed we face a dilemma—a situation involving a choice between two alternatives both of which involve exploitation of the prisoner. The usual payment to the prisoner research subjects at Stateville is, as stated above, $30 to $50 monthly. This is above the average prison wage, but at the same time it is clear that the researchers are obtaining the prisoners' services at far less than the free-market rate and in effect are exploiting them. On the other hand, were the project sponsors to pay the ordinary market rate this would in the prison situation represent so massive an incentive as to almost constitute compulsion.

There is of course an ideal solution to this difficulty. Earlier in this chapter the establishment of a full-wages prison was discussed. If such a program were to be adopted generally throughout the prison system the prisoner's involvement in medical research would present no problem on economic grounds. He would receive the full market rate for his services as would all other prisoners. In the present situation, however, this solution is not available.

Morris and Mills suggest an alternative solution that appears to be both presently practicable and equitable. They note that the payment to the prisoner of "what would be necessary to attract the next less vulnerable group, say the free unemployed" would "in the prison marketplace be unacceptably coercive." They suggest therefore that "prisoners must be paid what would be required to attract a free volunteer to the same research project. So long as internal prison wages are low, the difference between the low prison wage and a free volunteer's reward must be paid into a fund for the general welfare of prisoners." They suggest also that in order to protect the prisoners' economic interests, "Prisoners must be compensated for all lasting injury or loss of earnings suffered as a result of participation in a research project." They make one further recommendation which they regard as, taken together with those already mentioned, representing the minimum safeguards necessary as a precondition to the use of prisoners as subjects in research: "Any prison permitting research must establish, in addition to a scientific review group, a subject advisory group, a majority of whose members are prisoners" (1974, p. 66).

It seems that if such protections as these were provided, the principal objections to the employment of prisoners in this way would be met. It is true that they constitute a peculiarly vulnerable group. At the same time, given adequate safeguards, there is no reason why they should not be allowed to perform services which can contribute both to their own welfare and that of society. This is especially true in a situation where providing satisfactory employment opportunities for prisoners is a major problem.

6   The Rights of the Prisoner

INTRODUCTION

The United States is a country with a tradition of adherence to the rule of law; a commitment to government by law rather than by man or men. In the criminal justice system this regard for the rule of law has in the past found extensive application up to and including the stage of a conviction. But beyond conviction, until relatively recently, nearly arbitrary and largely unsupervised discretion held sway.

This was true of sentencing, for which guiding criteria were absent and from which appeals were both rare and difficult. It was true of the discretion exercised by the institutional administrator concerning prison conditions and disciplinary sanctions. It also applied to the exercise by the parole board of releasing and revoking discretions.

Within the last decade, however, the movement to bring the law, judges, and lawyers into relationship with the correctional system has grown apace. The judiciary and the legal profession have begun to play a significant part in the movement for penal reform by ensuring increasing substantive and procedural due process in the authoritative exercise of correctional discretions.

Modern legal initiative in the criminal justice field was taken by the work of the American Law Institute in drafting the Model Penal Code, which has stimulated widespread recodifications of the substantive criminal law, or the refashioning of parts of it, at the federal and state levels. A subsequent step was the extension of legal aid to the indigent accused, a development achieved by a series of Supreme Court decisions and by the Criminal Justice Act of 1964 and similar state legislation. This step brought more lawyers of skill and social sensitivity into contact with the criminal justice system. Then, the remarkable project on Minimum Standards for Criminal Justice, pursued to completion over many years by the American Bar Association, together with the model acts sponsored by the American Correctional Association and the National Council on Crime and Delinquency, began to have a similar influence.

In addition, the Supreme Court and the Chief Justice have lately manifested their concern that correctional processes eschew the infliction of needless suffering and achieve standards of decency and efficiency of which the community need not be ashamed and by which it will be better protected. Stimulated by the Chief Justice's initiative, the American Bar Association has embarked on an ambitious series of programs to involve lawyers in correctional processes, both institutional and in the community.

At the same time federal and state legislatures have increasingly concerned themselves with correctional legislation. One state, Illinois, has promulgated a complete set of correctional regulations, trying to make its institutions settings for the exercise of precisely defined, legally controlled decisions, rather than forums of free-flowing discretion. And the National Council on Crime and Delinquency has drafted a Model Act for the Protection of Rights of Prisoners (1972).

But more important than all these, lawyers and prisoners are bringing—and courts are hearing and determining—constitutional and Civil-Rights-Act cases alleging the unequal protection of the law, the imposition of cruel and unusual punishments, and the abuse of administrative discretions. A series of cases have begun to hold correctional administrators accountable for their decision-making, especially where such decisions affect First

Amendment rights (religion, speech, communication), the means of enforcing other rights (access to counsel or legal advice, access to legal materials), cruel and unusual punishments, the denial of civil rights, and the equal protection of the law.

The emerging view, steadily gaining support since it was enunciated in *Coffin* v. *Reichard* (143 F. 2d 443 [6th Cir. 1944]; *cert. denied*, 325 U.S. 887 [1945]), is that the convicted offender retains all rights which citizens in general have, except such as must be limited or forfeited to make it possible to administer a correctional institution or agency—and no generous sweep will be given to pleas of administrative inconvenience. The pace and range of such litigation has recently increased sharply; the "hands-off doctrine," insulating the correctional administrator from juridical accountability, no longer provides effective protection for arbitrary decisions or unduly restrictive regulations. For the correctional system, historically wracked by riot and rebellion, the abandonment of this doctrine has in some cases had a dramatic impact.

Naturally, this litigation is seen by some correctional administrators as a wasteful consumption of their time and energy, as an expression merely of the lawyer's capacity for officious interference. Some correctional officials regard the courts' decisions as written by judges lacking correctional expertise who have no appreciation of administrative exigencies or of the inadequacy of resources. In sum, it is argued that this whole development is counterproductive. Sometimes, of course, some of these criticisms are legitimate.

Nor have all lawyers regarded this development with enthusiasm. Thus Charles Friend has written: "It is doubtful that the goals of modern penology will be served in a prison where the administration is handcuffed by judicial controls, and the prisoners (armed with habeas corpus, mandamus, the Civil Rights Act, the Federal Tort Claims Act, and the First and Eighth Amendments) run the institution. In a country where the skyrocketing crime rate has become a national issue and law enforcement is having its own problems with judicially imposed restrictions, a breakdown of the prison system hardly seems desirable" (1967, p. 192).

The issue is in fact a contentious one. On the one hand it is argued that it is entirely proper that the judiciary and the legal profession should in this way play a part in the reform of the correctional system and that this development constitutes a politically and practically important lever of change for improved prison conditions. On the other hand it is said that the nature of prison society calls for special rules and restrictions not applicable in a free society. And, to quote an Australian minister of justice, "The setting up of juridical processes mirroring those which prevail in the courts, or giving access or recourse to the courts as of right, would create a monster which would undoubtedly destroy any system of corrections as presently structured" (Maddison 1972, p. 13).

This movement is not only novel and controversial but has also been regarded by some commentators as revolutionary. In this chapter an attempt is made to provide an assessment of the significance of this development and of its implications for the future of prison administration.

THE HANDS-OFF DOCTRINE

The prisoner, a Virginia court declared just over a century ago in *Ruffin* v. *Commonwealth* (62 Va.[21 Gratt] 790 [1871]), "has, as a consequence of his crime, not only forfeited his liberty, but all his personal rights except those which the law in its humanity accords to him. He is for the time being the slave of the State." And until well into the 1960s, with a few exceptions, such as the case of *Coffin* v. *Reichard* cited above, the prisoner found that the law, to use Gerhard Mueller's phrase, "left him at the prison entrance."

In more recent years, however, the denial of due process of law and the abrogation of criminal procedural legality in the handling of prisoners has been justified on somewhat different grounds. What has been called both "judicial restraint" or "judicial abstention" and, by those less enamoured of it, "judicial abdication," has found a rationale not in the concept of a prisoner as a person without rights but rather in the "hands-off doctrine," which states that "courts are without power to supervise prison administration or to interfere with ordinary prison rules or regulations" (*Banning* v. *Looney*, 213 F. 2d 771 [10th Cir.], *cert. denied*, 348 U.S. 859 [1954]).

In support of what Mueller has called this "virtual 'Monroe

Doctrine' of American criminal law toward penology" (1966, p. 86) a variety of arguments have been deployed. These have included the separation of powers argument (the administration of prisons being viewed as an executive function); the financial feasibility argument (the recognition of rights is expensive, and courts cannot appropriate funds or interfere with resource allocation); and the subversion of discipline argument (unfettered administrative discretion is essential to prison discipline).

In fact it seems clear that the major influence on the courts in a long series of federal and state judgments refusing to grant relief to prisoners was what has been referred to as "the dogma of the independence of prison authorities" (*University of Pennsylvania Law Review*, Comment, 1962, p. 986).

The courts' failure to grant relief . . . appears to stem from a conviction held with virtual unanimity by the courts that it is beyond their power to review the internal management of the prison system. The reason underlying refusal to review the administrative decisions of prison officials is the unquestioning acceptance by courts of the assertion repeatedly made that judicial review of such administrative decisions will subvert the authority of prison officials, the discipline of prisons, and the efforts of prison administrators to accomplish the objectives of the system which is entrusted to their care and management (*Yale Law Journal*, Note, 1963, pp. 508–9).

What adherence to this doctrine by the courts meant for prisoners has been described in a number of books and articles published in the last decade, most notably in Philip Hirschkop and Michael Millemann's *Virginia Law Review* article, "The Unconstitutionality of Prison Life" (1969) and in Ronald Goldfarb and Linda Singer's book, *After Conviction* (1973). Goldfarb and Singer, in particular, document their assertions by citing a number of recent federal court judgments in which prison conditions are condemned in quite unambiguous terms.

Thus in 1966 a federal district judge in California declared: "Requiring man or beast to live, eat and sleep under the degrading conditions pointed out in the testimony creates a condition that inevitably does violence to elemental concepts of decency." A year later, in 1967, the United States Court of

Appeals for the Second Circuit declared in regard to a New York State prison: "[Such] subhuman conditions . . . could only serve to destroy completely the spirit and undermine the sanity of the prisoner. The Eighth Amendment forbids treatment so foul, so inhuman and so violative of basic concepts of decency." And in the same year the Supreme Court in the case of a Florida prisoner asserted: "The record in this case documents a shocking display of barbarism which should not escape the remedial action of this Court" (Goldfarb and Singer 1973, pp. 380–82).

The change from "judicial abdication" to what some have called "judicial activism" in this field has led to the discovery of an abundance of evidential material regarding the practical implications of the hands-off doctrine and the significance of judicial intervention. It would be impossible to summarize that evidence here in any meaningful fashion. But rather than offer what would be little more than a catalogue of squalor, neglect, abuse, and atrocity one case from the United States District Court for the Southern District of New York will be referred to for illustrative purposes.

In *Sostre* v. *Rockefeller* (312 F. Supp. 863 [S.D.N.Y. 1970]) a prisoner sued under the Civil Rights Act of 1871 for damages for deprivations inflicted on him by prison officials. Martin Sostre, a black militant, by litigation during a previous term of imprisonment, had secured certain religious liberties for Black Muslim inmates. On being sentenced to prison again, he quickly found himself in trouble.

What happened to him has been succinctly stated by Robert Kutak, a practicing attorney with an active interest in prison matters. "Sostre immediately was transferred from one institution to another based on what an official termed 'the best interests of the state and the inmate'. He was placed in solitary for trying to mail a certificate of reasonable doubt to a state court. He was again placed in solitary for trying to mail some handwritten notices to the court and for the further reason that he refused to tell the warden what the letters 'RNA' meant in a letter he wrote to his sister. The inmate spent thirteen months in solitary with only one other prisoner housed in the same group of cells. He remained in the cell around the clock. He was allowed one hour per day of recreation in a small, completely enclosed yard, but refused this 'privilege' because it was conditioned upon a mandatory 'strip frisk' including a rectal examination. He was not permitted to use the prison library, read newspapers, see movies, or attend school or training programs" (1970, p. 42).

Why was Martin Sostre treated in this fashion? According to the court, "Sostre was sent to punitive segregation and kept there until released by court order not because of any serious infraction of the rules of prison discipline, or even for any minor infraction, but because Sostre was being punished specially by the Warden because of his legal and Black Muslim activities during his 1952–1964 incarceration, because of his threat to file a law suit against the Warden to secure his right to unrestricted correspondence with his attorney and to aid his codefendant, and because he is, unquestionably, a black militant who persists in writing and expressing his militant and radical ideas in prison." The court also said that his incarceration was "physically harsh, destructive of morale, dehumanizing in the sense that it was needlessly degrading, and dangerous to the maintenance of sanity."

The *Sostre* case was not an isolated instance. Goldfarb and Singer offer numerous similar examples of what happens when prison administrators have absolute, unreviewed discretion (1973). And it is that which is the crucial issue. Hirschkop and Millemann make the point: "Prisoners often have their privileges revoked, are denied right of access to counsel, sit in solitary or maximum security or lose accrued 'good time' on the basis of a single, unreviewed report of a guard. When the courts defer to administrative discretion, it is this guard to whom they delegate the final word on reasonable prison practices. *This is the central evil in prison.* It is not homosexuality, nor inadequate salaries, nor the cruelty and physical brutality of some of the guards. The central evil is the unreviewed administrative discretion granted to the poorly trained personnel who deal directly with prisoners. The existence of this evil necessarily leads to denial of communication, denial of right to counsel and denial of access to the courts. Prison becomes a closed society in which the cruelest inhumanities exist unexposed" (1969, pp. 811–12; my italics).

PRISONERS' RIGHTS
It would not be true to say that the hands-off doctrine is

moribund. The federal courts, even when they have strongly condemned correctional practices, have invariably affirmed that judges should not ordinarily interfere with the administration of prisons. And state courts have been much less receptive to claims involving prisoners' grievances, frequently taking the view, for example, that prison discipline relates to the internal affairs of a penal institution and is within the sole discretion of prison officials. While the courts are said to have developed "the doctrine of retained rights" (that prisoners retain all rights not specifically taken from them by law) the Supreme Court has not expressly recognized this principle.

Nevertheless, although all courts have not concurred in this trend, prisoners have through litigation obtained varying degrees of recognition for a large number of rights which in the past have habitually been denied them. But it is important to realize that for many prisoners many of these rights exist only in that no-man's-land across which those who challenge and those who defend authority wage continuous warfare. Even if the status of these rights is sometimes equivocal, however, they represent a line of development which is both significant and irreversible.

I shall not attempt to review the whole range of rights that prisoners have attempted to establish or have succeeded in establishing. Nor would it serve a useful purpose to rehearse the history of the part played by litigation in prison reform in recent years. It is sufficient to note briefly some of the more important achievements. Generally it seems to be acknowledged that prisoners must be guaranteed reasonable access to the courts both to challenge their convictions and to seek remedies for their treatment. The right to be kept free from harm and to the minimal conditions necessary to sustain healthy life has been judicially recognized, as has the right to be free of cruel and unusual punishments. The courts have established that a prison inmate has the right to freedom from racial discrimination and a qualified right to engage in religious practices.

It has to be said, however, that all of these statements about prisoners' rights are subject to considerable qualification. Fred Cohen notes that the right of access to the courts is curtailed because of "severely limited opportunities for legal assistance and access to legal materials" (1969, p. 72). In fact it may be much more severely curtailed than that, as I shall indicate. Goldfarb and Singer remark that the right to physical security and to conditions necessary to sustain life is "still insufficiently protected by the courts." And the nature of the right to practice religious beliefs "subject to reasonable regulations" is itself subject to widely varying interpretations of what may constitute "reasonable regulations" in the prison context.

There are other rights about which it is not possible to speak with even the modified degree of assurance displayed above. Rights to freedom of speech and assembly, to enjoy privacy, to vote, and to communicate freely, which have been held elsewhere to be protected by the Constitution, have not in the prison setting been recognized as among the "fundamental, humane and necessary rights" whose breach violates the Constitution. Within narrowly described areas judicial rulings have resulted in increased freedom for inmates, but for the most part the discretion of correction and prison authorities has not been seriously limited or subjected to regulation.

Indeed, whatever may be the situation regarding the particular rights mentioned above, it seems that the really crucial question in this context is that of regulating the discretion of prison administrators. Hirschkop and Millemann are right in their assertion that "unreviewed administrative discretion" is "the central evil in prison." This is because the pursuit, recognition, enforcement, and enjoyment of all other rights are ultimately dependent upon the prison authorities' exercise of that broad discretion which they claim is necessary for the preservation of order and discipline and which, despite some inroads, they still to a very large degree possess unimpaired.

"Potter Familus"

The operation of administrative discretion can perhaps best be illustrated by reference to internal prison disciplinary proceedings. Until very recently the courts declined to interfere with such proceedings despite the fact that they frequently involved serious disciplinary punishments like solitary confinement, the forfeiture of "good time," or transfer to maximum-security custody. Even when the courts have been concerned about the application of due process to correctional decisions, with a few recent exceptions, they have not defined the procedural protections required. As Goldfarb and Singer point out, "[T]hey have neither defined the nature and extent of the procedures required nor supplied any reliable criteria for determining when the protections apply" (1973, p. 491).

An illuminating illustration of what this means in practice is offered by attorney William Turner. It is taken from the deposition of a New York deputy prison warden in a case where, charged with sole responsibility for discipline, he ordered the forfeiture of one hundred days of an inmate's good time:

Q. At the disciplinary hearings, are inmates entitled to call witnesses in their behalf?
A. No.
Q. Are they entitled to cross-examine guards?
A. They are not.
Q. Are they entitled to representation by anyone?
A. No.
Q. What record is made of the proceedings at a disciplinary hearing?
A. As you see here, on the disciplinary report, the punishment is noted. This disciplinary hearing is not a judicial hearing, it corresponds to, I believe, a *potter familus* [sic]. I could be wrong on the *potter familus*.
Q. *Potter familus*?
A. It is probably known as the authority figure, as meting out what is family punishment, or family discipline. This is not a judicial thing in the sense of a court of record, and there is no provision for it as a court of record, and there is no provision for it being held, yes, but not as a matter of a court of record, and this is an internal disciplinary thing, very much as a father and mother in the home who say, "Johnny, you have done so and so, and you are forbidden to do it, and therefore you will stay in your room" (1971, p. 500).

Turner cites this example as illustrating "the strange notion of due process held by many prison administrators." But what it illustrates is an attitude toward inmates which pervades every aspect of prison administration and is by no means restricted to prison disciplinary proceedings. What one might call the pater-familiary concept of authority in prisons is as old as the prison system itself. Prisoners are seen as being in a state of pupillage and are expected to accept a dominance-submission pattern of relationships. Their status is inferior and dependent, and their access to rewards—and for that matter to necessities— is subject to their total obedience to the rules of the institution.

This does not mean, incidentally, that their superiors also have to obey the rules. In this connection it is interesting to read the judgment of Lord Chief Justice Goddard in a case where some English prisoners instituted proceedings against the home secretary and the governors of certain prisons, claiming that they had been treated as prisoners of a different classification from that which should properly have been applied to them under the prison regulations. "It would be fatal to all discipline in prisons," Lord Goddard said, "if governors and warders had to perform their duty always with the fear of an action before their eyes if they in any way deviated from the rules" (*Arbon* v. *Anderson* [1943] 1.K.B. 255).

In England, of course, there do not exist the constitutional guarantees which can be invoked in the U.S. But just as it would have been a mistake prior to the 1960s to assume that those guarantees, being in some way self-executing, provide effective protection for the inmates of American prisons, so today it would be equally mistaken to assume that all those resounding courtroom triumphs are instantly translated into operational reality within prisons. As Cohen puts it: "No one who is familiar with correctional administrators believes that a courtroom victory for an inmate is followed by a staff meeting on how best to implement the letter and the spirit of the decision. Indeed it is far more likely that the meeting will involve the problem of how to avoid the ruling or achieve minimal compliance" (1972, p. 857).

Clutchette v. *Procunier* (328 F. Supp. 767 [N.D. Cal. 1971]) is a case in point. The court required, in the case of hearings where serious punishments may be involved, that inmates be given notice, the right to call witnesses, confrontation and cross-examination, the right to counsel or counsel-substitute if the case will be referred for prosecution, and a decision based on the evidence by an impartial tribunal. But there is no doubt whatever that in the vast majority, if not all, of the penal institutions in this country procedural realities will still conform to "potter familus"

far more closely than to anything U.S. District Judge Alphonzo
Zirpoli had in mind in *Clutchette* v. *Procunier.*

Those who assert, as I have done, that there is an enormous
gulf between theory and practice, between judicial decision and
administrative implementation, commonly have little more than
anecdotal evidence to offer in support. Discussion is carried on in
an ambience which, while not entirely fact-free, is at least
relatively unencumbered by empirical data. Fortunately in this
instance there are available results of some research undertaken
by the Center for Criminal Justice of Harvard Law School into
prison disciplinary practices.

The occasion of this particular study was a consent decree
issued on March 11, 1970, by Federal Judge Raymond J. Pettine.
In *Morris* v. *Travisono* (310 F. Supp. 857 [D.R.I. 1970]) Judge
Pettine established comprehensive procedural regulations for
handling disciplinary matters in the Rhode Island Adult Correctional Institution. The decree was aimed at ensuring fairness in
the prison's disciplinary proceedings by establishing a variety of
procedural safeguards. The order laid down certain mandatory
steps to be followed in prison disciplinary proceedings. It required
that for the initiation of disciplinary proceedings an inmate
violation report should be completed, with details of the alleged
violation, and that the inmate should be given notice informing
him fully of the charge or charges. It required that prehearing
detention be limited to cases in which there was present a threat
to institutional order or the physical safety of inmates or personnel.
It required that in every case a superior officer should conduct a
preliminary investigation and submit a written summary of it to
the deputy warden. It required that the inmate being charged
should have the right to be assisted by a classification officer at
the disciplinary board hearing. It required that a determination
by the disciplinary board "must be based on substantial evidence." It specified actions which might be taken by the disciplinary board and placed a limit on the duration of any particular
punishment. It provided that the warden should review the record
of any proceeding which would result in an unfavorable decision
for the inmate.

The Harvard Center for Criminal Justice set out to study the
impact of the *Morris* decision within the prison. The study

included observation of disciplinary hearings, interviews with both staff and inmates, and examination of disciplinary records covering periods both before and after the entry of the *Morris* decree. The decree also included provisions relating to classification procedures at the Rhode Island Correctional Institution, and the Harvard study also covered the implementation of those provisions. For my purpose, however, it is sufficient to refer simply to a summary of the findings as they relate to the disciplinary provisions I have noted above:

Disciplinary . . . procedures at the ACI, observed by the Center's researchers after the imposition of the *Morris* decree, did not meet the expectations of the court. While notice was often given, its adequacy was questionable; indeed, a substantial number of the inmates interviewed claimed that they never received any notice. Prehearing detention was as prevalent after the decree as before, and the reasons for such detentions were nowhere recorded. The superior officer's investigation was little more than a restatement of the charge and a cursory report of the inmate's attitude. Classification counselors were torn between conflicting role requirements and consequently were unable to afford the inmates the vigorous advocacy which was anticipated by the representation provision of the regulations. The Disciplinary Board hearings were substantially dispositional in nature, with little effort at fact-finding and a great deal of deference given to the testimony of the charging officer and to the views of the Board chairman. While the extremes of the Board's dispositions were ostensibly eliminated, there were one or two cases in which the maximum punishment limits appeared to have been exceeded. . . . And finally, the review process was inadequate (Harvard Center for Criminal Justice 1972, p. 222).

HABEAS CORPUS
Another area in which there are available empirical studies which throw some light on important aspects of the prisoners' rights problem is that of habeas corpus. Two of the most significant studies, which shall be discussed below, concern California prisoners' petitions for writs of habeas corpus (Bergeson 1972; UCLA Program in Corrections Law 1973).

Writs of habeas corpus have traditionally been used by prisoners to challenge the legality of their imprisonment. Since the

California Supreme Court handed down *In re Chessman* (44 Cal. 2d 1, 279 P. 2d 24 [1955]) and a series of more recent cases, it has become possible, at least in theory, to challenge unlawful or unconstitutional *conditions* of confinement. William Turner describes habeas corpus as one of "the two principal means of seeking federal judicial review of internal state prison practices" (the other being a civil suit under 42 U.S.C. section 1983), and adds: "[T]he scope of habeas corpus under California state law is extremely broad; habeas lies to vindicate any statutory or constitutional right of a prisoner while in prison" (1971, pp. 504–5). A UCLA study on the impact of the courts on the California Department of Corrections refers to the filing of petitions for writs of habeas corpus as "the primary means of inmate-court communication."

The findings of the UCLA study on this subject are briefly reported and may conveniently be dealt with first. According to the report, the most common judicial response to an inmate's petition was "rejection of the petition on its face." Only a minority of judges made any inquiry into an inmate's complaint. When an inquiry was made it "typically involved a telephone call by the judge to the institution asking the superintendent to look into the matter. Again, typically, if the superintendent convinced the judge that the problem did not exist, or that there was sufficient justification for the conditions complained of, or that administrative action would be taken to correct the matter, the judge would deny the petition." There was one judge who stated that, if there were any complaint worth investigating, it should be investigated formally. But the report adds that this judge "has never found any complaint about prison conditions to be worthy of such investigation" (1973, pp. 461–64).

It does sometimes happen, however, that a judge decides that a formal investigation of the inmate's complaint is required. At one time this was accomplished by referring the matter to the office of the district attorney or the attorney general. However in *Reeves* v. *Superior Court* (22 Cal. App. 3d 587, 97 Cal. Rptr 866 [3d Dist. 1971]) the California Court of Appeals declared that this process, which had been followed in San Joaquin County, was unlawful as a violation of the separation of powers doctrine. As a result the San Joaquin County superior court discontinued utilizing the district attorney as its investigator and instead adopted a "form letter" procedure.

This procedure involves four steps, and its operation is described by B. E. Bergesen III in his study as follows:

First, a deputy clerk, upon receipt of a prisoner's petition, sends to the institution a form letter which summarizes the prisoner's allegations and requests a sworn response or investigative report by a certain date. Second, the institution, on its own form, submits to the court its version of the claims raised by the prisoner-petitioner. Third, the deputy clerk fills out and submits to the judge a form entitled "Report on Investigation," which summarizes the respective claims of petitioner and respondent. Fourth, an order is prepared which in virtually every case denies the petition based upon the facts alleged by the respondent.

The final result of this procedure is not altogether surprising. As Bergesen puts it, "[A]ll prisoners' petitions complaining of the conditions of their confinement are routinely denied solely upon the factual allegations of one or more prison officials." Thus he found that "for calendar years 1971 and 1972 (through the month of August), approximately 159 such petitions have been processed by the court, yet no hearing has ever been held, and no relief has ever been granted" (1972, pp. 19–20).

Bergesen's study deals specifically with San Joaquin County, but he argues, on the basis of such statistics as are available and the absence of reported cases affording relief to California prisoners challenging their conditions of confinement (or even denying relief after a full hearing), that "other superior and appellate courts throughout the state which act on prisoners' habeas petitions treat them in essentially the same way" (ibid., p. 26). His conclusion is that "although California prisoners possess many constitutional and statutory rights which they may theo-retically enforce by habeas corpus, there is in fact no judicial forum in which such claims will be heard and determined fairly. Instead, state courts either deny such claims summarily, or else decide them against the prisoner-petitioner by routinely giving conclusive effect to the factual allegations of the respondent prison officials. In the process, state courts [in California, as well as other states] deny to such prisoners—usually sub silentio—the

right to engage in discovery, to invoke basic rules of evidence, and
to have their claims adjudicated according to the normal standards of proof" (ibid., p. 49).

"PLUS ÇA CHANGE ... "?

Such findings as we have noted above suggest that the degree of
alarm expressed by some writers over the possible consequences
of what Daniel Skoler has called the "case law explosion"
resulting from abandonment of the hands-off doctrine was not
altogether justified. Thus Friend's predictions (in 1967) about the
danger of "a progressive decay of authority," "a breakdown of
the prison system," and "pandemonium not only in the prison
itself but throughout the entire legal system" (pp. 189–92) seem,
in the light of experience, to have been at least premature.

It is of course true that since 1967 there have been a large
number of inmate strikes, protests, and rebellions, of which
Attica was the most publicized. But this really does not represent
a novel development. There was after all a wave of serious prison
disturbances in the late 1920s. When John Bartlow Martin
published *Break Down the Walls* in 1953 he wrote that the
1951–53 riots "clearly proved" that "the American prison system
has broken down." And when Donald Clemmer's classic study,
The Prison Community, was reissued in 1958 the author pointed
out, in the preface to that edition, that "there have been 105 riots
or serious disturbances in American prisons since 1950."

It is arguable, and indeed it is argued by Goldfarb and Singer,
that the prison riots of recent years are due more than anything
else to the fact that prisoners lack "effective, legitimate means to
communicate their grievances" (1973, p. 359). David Greenberg
and Fay Stender argue that, for the most part, administrative
decisions within the prison, including punitive measures such as
transfer and solitary confinement, are "still not subject to due
process procedures and are ordinarily immune from judicial
review" (1972, p. 806).

Back in 1968 Edward Kimball and Donald Newman declared:
"A single successful prisoner petition may have far-reaching
implications, for it takes only one such court decision to alter the
system. A definitive decision by a court will require reconsideration of the whole practice or procedure involved, not merely
redress to the individual petitioner. Judicial intervention in

correctional matters thus assumes critical importance far beyond
that indicated by the raw number of cases, successful or not"
(1968, p. 3). But Greenberg and Stender, writing four years later,
maintain that "the prison system is almost totally non-responsive
to 'due process of law' or 'law' itself" and speak of "the massive
ability of administrators to circumvent court-imposed limitations" (1972, pp. 808–10). The UCLA study concurred, reporting:
"Most administrators agreed that it is usually possible to circumvent court orders" (UCLA Program in Corrections Law 1973, p.
531).

Yet to say that nothing has changed as a result of prisoner
litigation and judicial intervention runs counter to the available
evidence. For even those critical studies demonstrating limitations on the effectiveness of prisoners' rights litigation, which I
have cited above, do also show that something has been achieved.
Thus the Harvard study of the application of the *Morris* decree to
the Rhode Island Adult Correctional Institution was not entirely
negative in its conclusions.

For it was found not only that there was a favorable inmate
response to the effects of the new disciplinary procedures but also
that there were some objective manifestations of institutional
change. "Cases were dismissed where there were technical violations of the regulations, inmate witnesses were allowed in some
cases, delays between charge and final hearing were minimized,
and the extreme forms of punishment which instigated the
imposition of the order were largely eliminated. Further, there
was a growing recognition by administrative and custodial staff
that inmates did have rights, rights that would be contested and
enforced" (1972, p. 222).

Similarly the UCLA study of judicial intervention in corrections in California, while noting a variety of limitations on judicial
effectiveness in bringing about changes in corrections, also found
that that court action *had* stimulated changes both directly and
indirectly.

Courts have acted as promoters of change in correctional
administration in several ways. They have directly brought about
change by decisions which either require specific alterations in
practices or invalidate present practices and leave correctional
authorities the responsibility of developing alternatives. More

indirectly, courts have promoted change in at least two basic ways. First, by the exposure of poor prison conditions and questionable correctional practices to the public, court review has aroused public concern. This in turn has stimulated public involvement in the area of "prison reform" and encouraged legislative action. Second, as the increase in judicial involvement has become apparent to the correctional personnel, the mere prospect of judicial review has had the effect of inducing considerable change by motivating prison officials to alter procedures or refrain from certain practices before court orders are issued. In some cases, changes are induced even before law suits are actually brought (1973, p. 528).

Nevertheless, the evidence suggests that in many cases forensic victories are not followed by any substantial alteration. Fred Cohen is clearly right when he urges that "enthusiasm for doctrinal enlargement should be tempered by an effort to assess actual results." He may also be right when he suggests that some of the ostensible gains of litigation have been more symbolic than real and, like the advances made by the Warren Court in the so-called due process revolution, have done "more to create the possibility and appearance of rights than actual rights" (1972, pp. 863–67). Insofar as this is the case it may well be that judicial intervention in penal institutions will lead to disorder and turmoil. For symbolic victories arouse expectations of access to that which they symbolize. And in the prison situation it is only to a limited extent, and for a limited period of time, that they can operate as a substitute for that access. Yet if inmates' expectations *are* disappointed, it would surely be a mistake to attribute any disorders which follow to judicial encroachment on the powers of correctional administrators. The real cause would lie in the failure of judicial intervention to compel correctional administrators to introduce substantive and procedural fairness into the prison system.

The Correctional Ombudsman
A conclusion which many commentators have drawn from observation of the limited success of judicial efforts to achieve changes in prison practices is that a greater potential for reform may lie in the development of nonjudicial remedies, particularly in the

introduction of administrative machinery for resolving prisoners' grievances. It has been noted, for example, that prisoners in Sweden have the right of all Swedish citizens to bring complaints about prison officials, or for that matter about any other government agency or official, to the national ombudsman. All prisoners have the right of uncensored communication with the ombudsman. In Denmark also prisoners enjoy this right, and the ombudsman there regularly visits penal institutions and is able to investigate complaints on the spot. In Finland the ombudsman is said to spend almost as much time behind bars, dealing with complaints from prisoners, as behind his desk.

The arguments for the adoption of a similar approach in this country and for the development of nonjudicial mechanisms for dealing with prisoners' grievances can be briefly reviewed. Perhaps the most authoritative advocate of the employment of the ombudsman in the correctional setting is Walter Gellhorn, whose *Ombudsmen and Others* (1966) deals, among much else, with the handling of prisoners' complaints by ombudsmen or their equivalents (for example, procurators in the USSR) in Norway, Denmark, Finland, Russia, New Zealand, and Japan.

Gellhorn's view is further elaborated in another book.

The likelihood of success in a suit against prison officials is small. . . . The judges tread gingerly in the ill-defined area where claims of individual right compete with assertions of institutional need. Unwilling to ignore rights, yet fearful of destroying good order, judges have thus far developed no sure tests for accepting or rejecting prisoners' complaints about their treatment behind bars. But why, in any event, should the courts be the sole or even the chief reliance in these matters? Here is an inmate whose only surviving relative, his only correspondent in the world, is his Hungarian sister; her letters never reach her brother because the prison officials, unable to read Hungarian, cannot censor them; and so the prisoner, linguistically and financially handicapped though he may be, must commence a formal action in court to gain the correspondence privileges his fellow prisoners already enjoy. Here is a prisoner who says that money orders sent to him by his relatives have not been handed over to him nor returned to the senders; when the prison authorities give him no explanation, he sues to protect his property. Here is a man who contends that he has been arbitrarily penalized by prison officials; as a consequence of their allegedly improper acts he has lost the "good time credit" that would have shortened his incarceration; and now he goes to court to seek help in overcoming the claimed injustice. Superintendence of prison superintendents should not be a task for judges in the first instance. Nor should a lawsuit be the only recourse of friendless men in straitened circumstances who think themselves wronged. . . . If a state ombudsman existed, he would be a pre-eminently suitable person to inquire into conflicts between convicts and their keepers. Foreign ombudsmen have successfully reconciled disciplinary demands and inmates' interests. Their work in this respect has been a social service of high order. An American counterpart is badly needed (1966, pp. 147–51).

It is true that some judges have trod less gingerly, if not always to more effect, in the years since 1966, but this does not invalidate Gellhorn's argument. The examples he cites are all drawn from actual cases. Courts themselves have indicated that they are dismayed by the prospect of "judicial supervision of penal institutions in such minute detail as to encompass even the selection and make up of daily menus and the direction of the service of coffee three times a day" (*Barnett* v. *Rodgers*, 410 F. 2d 995, 1004 [D.C. Cir. 1969]). Gellhorn's point that prison inmates should not be obliged to initiate lawsuits in order to obtain remedies for all their grievances indicates that prisoners, too, have an interest in avoiding litigation. Certainly there will be many kinds of mistreatment in prison which, although they deserve attention, may not involve violations of constitutional rights. As Singer and Keating put it, "The legal needs of inmates are not confined to the settlement of institutional confrontations of constitutional dimensions" (1973, p. 343). And Bergesen makes the point that lawsuits constitute "a time-consuming, expensive and inefficient way in which to handle most problems which originate in the state penal institutions" (1972, p. 9).

Another argument in favor of developing procedures or mechanisms, such as the ombudsman, which do not involve the courts, is based on the general incompetence of courts in this area. The UCLA study summarizes the courts' difficulties:

Courts are primarily designed for resolving factual disputes, and are not structured to effectively resolve complex administrative problems. They are also limited in their capacity to provide relief from conditions or treatment which violate constitutional requirements. Additionally, most judges lack the background and expertise which is necessary to understand all of the ramifications of prison problems which are put before them for resolution. Finally, court action is essentially negative and, with the exception of a few innovative decisions, most action takes the form of invalidating practices or procedures deemed unconstitutional or illegal. . . . Courts have difficulty finding remedies which bring about desired and novel changes, while at the same time avoiding undesirable effects (1973, p. 554 n. 426).

(It might be noted in passing that the fact that a judge lacks a background in penology should no more preclude him from rendering helpful judgments in prison cases than an unfamiliarity with the intricacies of the Internal Revenue Code and economics precludes equitable judicial disposition of complex tax and antitrust cases.) The creation of a specialist correctional ombudsman in each state empowered not only to hear and investigate prisoner complaints but also to take remedial action, impose sanctions for abuse, and make recommendations for change would relieve judges of the necessity for intervention except in a minority of cases which might be appealed.

A third argument for a correctional ombudsman may be derived from considerations relating to the question of administrative discretion. In some of the literature dealing with prisoners' rights it seems almost to be implied that administrative discretion is intrinsically bad, a threat to freedom and a negation of the rule of law. The problem is seen as one of reducing discretion to a minimum or even of eliminating it altogether. As Charles Breitel has put it, "The Anglo-American is accustomed to think of discretion as a power exercised by men, as indeed it is, and therefore a departure from the doctrine that ours should be a government of laws and not of men" (1960, p. 427). Roscoe Pound points out not only that "all discretion is liable to abuse" but also that the dangers involved in discretion are particularly great in the field of criminal justice.

Yet Pound stated the argument for discretion as well perhaps as it has ever been put. Attempts to exclude all individualization and confine administration "to strict observance of minute and detailed precepts or to a mechanical process of application of law" have always failed, he said: "[T]he most constant and most universal cause of dissatisfaction with law grows out of the mechanical operation of legal rules." One passage is particularly relevant to the situation in penal institutions at the present time: "Whenever there are strong conflicting interests or divergent ideals of justice and whenever groups or classes are asserting claims which do not admit of easy reconciliation, there is likely to be vigorous complaint of the want of accord of law with individual moral sense" (1930, pp. 38–42).

The truth is that the elimination of administrative discretion in penal institutions would render the life of inmates infinitely more rigidly controlled, circumscribed, and oppressive than it currently is in any American prison. Therefore, discretion should not be and cannot be wholly eliminated; what is required is some mechanism for ensuring that it is properly exercised. "The question," says Breitel, "is not how to eliminate or reduce discretion, but how to control it so as to avoid the unequal, the arbitrary, the discriminatory, and the oppressive" (1960, p. 427). Because this is precisely the function which the institution of the ombudsman is designed to fulfill in many countries, it is not surprising that the notion of a correctional ombudsman should have been seriously considered in this country.

As generally conceived, the ombudsman's role is to supplement the conflict-resolving procedures already present in a given correctional system. The pursuit of this activity can take a variety of forms. The ombudsman may defer taking action on a complaint until he has been assured that the appropriate procedural remedies have been exhausted, or he may decide to initiate his own investigation, not awaiting institutional resolution to determine a matter's status. In addition to this internal troubleshooter function, the ombudsman's role is seen by some as that of an external critic, seeking to expose problems which prevent the humane and effective operation of the correctional system.

Of course the nature of the ombudsman's role is, to a great extent, dependent upon the discretion conferred on him. The scope of his authority (as well as the nature of his accountability), the qualifications and tenure of his office, all present issues which critically affect the character of the task he is to perform. Another question increasingly raised is whether the thrust of the ombuds-man's role should be primarily oriented toward problem-solving or toward institutional reform.

Since the advent of the 1970s various state ombudsman posts, or their equivalent, have been established in the United States, involving a wide variety of responsibilities and controls. In fact as early as 1967 Hawaii set up ombudsman programs to monitor various state agencies, later extending these services to include corrections. The Hawaiian model is characterized by a fairly narrow focus, with most investigations stemming from submitted complaints. Extending beyond the Hawaiian plan, Iowa enacted legislation creating an office of "Citizens' Aide" (1969–70)— providing for broad investigatory power, even into the area of parole grievances. An important feature of both the Hawaii and Iowa systems is the nonaccountability of the appointed officials to the agencies under study.

In 1971 the state of Maryland set up an Inmate Grievance Commission as a separate agency within the Department of Public Safety and Correctional Services. In the same year a penitentiary ombudsman was appointed in the Oregon State Penitentiary with provision for appeal by inmates to the statewide executive ombudsman. In 1972 Minnesota initiated a special corrections ombudsman program under gubernatorial super-vision. Late that year the Ohio Department of Rehabilitation and Correction appointed a corrections ombudsman and followed that closely by appointing two deputy ombudsmen. As of mid-1974 corrections ombudsman programs of one kind or another were in operation in New Jersey, Connecticut, Wisconsin, Indi-ana, Texas, Florida, Missouri, and South Carolina. There have also been attempts to create a correctional ombudsman post in California (where a bill passed by the legislature in 1971 was vetoed by the governor and subsequent efforts also proved unsuccessful) and experimental ombudsman projects in Buffalo, New York, and Philadelphia. Finally, numerous bills have been referred to the House Judiciary Committee of the U.S. Congress to secure the appointment of correctional ombudsmen in all states participating in federal grants under the 1968 Omnibus Crime Control and Safe Streets Act, but none have yet been passed.

One general point which emerges from the growing literature

on correctional ombudsman systems can be made by reference to the Ohio model, which has been adopted in other states, including South Carolina, New Jersey, and Oregon. After the appointment of the chief ombudsman in Ohio it was found that there was some difficulty in maintaining satisfactory contact and communication with inmates. Accordingly two deputy ombudsmen, both ex-offenders (who had spent a total of twenty-five years in prison), were appointed to act as liaison officers at the state prison facilities. This kind of appointment at the institutional level is a necessary link in the grievance procedure, providing inmates with direct "on-the-spot" access to an official whose responsibility it is to help resolve grievances. In fact, as was noted by J. W. Lewis and G. Rand Smith, "Most grievances are resolved at this stage of the procedure" (1974, p. 88).

The ombudsman model is of course not the only possible one. Some years ago Robert Seewald, in an article entitled "The Italian Surveillance Judge," suggested the possibility of transplanting a similar judicial-administrative institution into the American system. The *giudice di sorveglianza* is an investigative, determinative, and advisory authority who, among other duties, has to visit prisons in his jurisdiction regularly and "protect the rights and interests of prisoners." The French have also created a similar office: the *juge de l'application des peines*.

Other possibilities include an Office of Review to investigate institutional complaints similar to that in the Federal Bureau of Prisons. One of the more interesting developments in recent years is the Center for Correctional Justice in the District of Columbia. A private, nonprofit corporation, originally funded by OEO's Office of Legal Services, it both provided legal services to prisoners and parolees and attempted to resolve grievances within prison, both by acting for complaining inmates and by means of a committee of prison personnel which negotiated with inmates over changes in institutional rules. Presently it is performing technical assistance services to various states; for example, in California it is under contract to set up grievance procedures for the state's correctional divisions. In the article cited earlier by Linda Singer and Michael Keating, who are, respectively, executive director and assistant to the director of the Center for Correctional Justice, it is argued that such nonjudicial methods as we have been considering represent "the best hope of bringing the rule of law into the administration of the correctional system." The authors also argue persuasively that any mechanism for the resolution of inmate grievances "must be independent of the system it seeks to modify if it is to succeed" (1973, pp. 337-47). About the advantages of some degree of independence there can be little doubt.

EX-PRISONERS RIGHTS

The declaration in *Coffin* v. *Reichard* (143 F. 2d 443, 445 [6th Cir. 1944], *cert. denied*, 325 U.S. 887 [1945]) that a "prisoner retains all the rights of an ordinary citizen except those expressly, or by necessary implication, taken from him by law" can scarcely have caused much rejoicing among prisoners in California where, under the penal code, a "sentence of imprisonment in a state prison for any term suspends all the civil rights of the person so sentenced." But although California is more thorough than some other states, in all states some civil disabilities are imposed on offenders. No complete list of these statutory deprivations has been compiled although almost all writers on this subject compile summary lists of rights forfeited or denied, indicating in each case how many states are involved. These lists all differ from one another, and it would serve no useful purpose to add to the confusion by providing yet another variant.

It is sufficient to say that among the rights lost on conviction of a felony (or, in some states, on being sentenced to prison) are: the right to vote, the right to hold public office, the right to serve on a jury, the right to enter into contracts, the right to purchase firearms, the right or capacity to testify, the right to obtain certain licenses, and the right to bring a civil suit. In addition, in many states a felony conviction is a ground for divorce, and in some the spouse may be permitted to remarry without securing a divorce. Furthermore, in the case of a great many professions or occupations (A. R. Gough [1966] lists fifty-nine) a former offender may be excluded from reemployment.

Gough maintains that the failure "to provide accessible or effective means of fully restoring the social status to the reformed offender" (p. 148) constitutes a basic flaw in our system of criminal justice. One might go further and say that the wholesale deprivation of civil rights, which for the most part only affects the offender on his release from prison, might have been designed to prevent the reformation of offenders. In many cases the rationale for the deprivation is purely punitive, and the discharged prisoner finds that as one form of punishment ceases another begins.

If this situation has any defenders a diligent search of the literature has failed to uncover them. Commentators differ only in the degree of exasperation expressed. Jessica Mitford speaks of the "legal status (if one may call it that)" of the ex-prisoner as resting on "a mishmash of common-sense-defying legal fictions" (1973, p. 218). Fred Cohen says: "This area of the law is replete with anachronisms and injustices. . . . Most people agree that the present law on civil disabilities is irrational and dysfunctional" (1969, p. 86). The President's Commission on Law Enforcement and Administration of Justice speaks of the law in this area as "inordinately complex and confusing" as well as characterized by "inhumanity and irrationality" (1967, pp. 88–89). The National Probation and Parole Association has declared that "the present law on deprivation of civil rights of offenders is in most jurisdictions an archaic hold-over from early times. . . . There should be no loss of rights except where the protection of the public is involved" (1957, p. 136).

There is no point in lengthy discussion about a matter which is so little in dispute. It is clear that many of the civil disabilities imposed on offenders have their historical roots in ancient penalties such as "infamy" and "civil death" designed to encompass the social degradation of the criminal. Insofar as that is no longer regarded as one of the necessary purposes of punishment, the practice is no longer justified. The proper approach to this problem has been well stated by Fred Cohen, whose discussion of this subject is a model of lucidity and good sense. "The solution proposed here," says Cohen, "requires that the various legislatures adopt concise legislation following the principle that *no civil or political right is to be lost unless the right is reasonably related to the nature of the offense and the function to be performed, or is required in the execution of the sentence*" (1969, p. 84; author's italics). It is only necessary to add that except where automatic restoration at the end of a sentence is appropriate there should be proper, judicially supervised expungement procedures to handle the restoration of rights and the removal of disabilities after a reasonable period, depending on the nature of the case.

CONCLUSION

The foregoing discussion of the significance of the prisoners' rights movement and of the achievements of prisoners' litigation and of judicial intervention in prisons has been critical. For this reason it may have suggested that little value is seen in these developments. Insofar as that is the case, it is important to correct that impression.

In fact there is no doubt that such judicial intervention as has taken place has been almost wholly beneficial. At the same time it is clearly expedient that there should be further development of nonjudicial remedial devices which will reduce the necessity for courts to intervene. However, while such intervention may in the future become less frequent the courts will continue to have ultimate responsibility for protecting the constitutional rights of prisoners, as of all citizens. Had their recognition of that duty been less belated, much avoidable human suffering might have been prevented.

But it is not merely a matter of preventing needless harm. Another fundamental matter is at issue. Hans W. Mattick puts it in one sentence in his admirable paper on "The Prosaic Sources of Prison Violence": "It is perhaps gratuitous to assert that those who have been convicted of breaking the law are most in need of having respect for the law demonstrated to them" (1972, p. 1). What it comes to is this: Convicted offenders must remain within the constitutional and legislative protection of the legal system. It is foolish to treat those who have broken the law other than by processes which themselves sedulously adhere to the law.

7   Impediments to Change

At the conclusion of his history of modern America, Daniel Boorstin wrote: "Fewer decisions of social policy seemed to be Whether-or-Not as more became decisions of How-Fast-and-When. Was it possible even to slow the pace, to hold back the momentum—of packaging, of automobile production, of communications, of image-making, of university expansion, of highway construction, of population growth?" (1973, p. 598).

One area of social policy where the velocity of change has not yet induced a transition to how-fast-and-when decisions is the field of corrections. This is a point already touched on briefly in chapter 2. It would present no great problem to slow the pace or to hold back the momentum of penal reform, for there are powerful inertial forces in operation which automatically arrest any tendency to precipitate growth or development. This final chapter is devoted to an examination of some of those forces and an assessment of their strength.

In works of this nature, which deal with both prediction and prescription for the future, there is always a danger that in the anticipatory perspective, obstacles dwindle, obstructions diminish, and realism is replaced by a kind of secular chiliasm. Indeed it may seem to some readers that some of the discussion of possible developments in preceding chapters displays an ingenuous inclination to overlook impediments to change that is totally unjustified in the light of objective appraisal.

This chapter, then, may be seen as an attempt to redress the balance by considering some of the principal barriers to reform in the penal system. I do not in fact entertain extravagant hopes for the future. But at a time when, on any given day, some four hundred thousand Americans are confined in penal institutions, most of which constitute a manifest disgrace to our civilization, it can hardly be regarded as unreasonable optimism to suggest that the promise of equality, which Daniel Bell has referred to as "one of the most powerful engines [of change] in American society," will not be permanently halted at the gates of the prison. Nevertheless, there is a sense in which this attitude clearly is unreasonable. As Bernard Shaw put it in his "Maxims for Revolutionists": "The reasonable man adapts himself to the world: the unreasonable one persists in trying to adapt the world to himself. Therefore, all progress depends on the unreasonable man."

THE MANY-HEADED MONSTER

It would probably be generally agreed by penologists that one of the principal obstacles to penal reform has always been, and remains, public opinion. Indeed some would say that it is the greatest obstacle. This view was eloquently expressed over twenty years ago by the English penal reformer Margery Fry.

... [O]ne has only to propose some change in our penal laws to become aware at once that ages of traditional emotion, of obscure thinking, of desire for vengeance, of terror of "bad men," of distrust of authority, of religious doctrine, of sadism, and of love of power have woven around the subject a complex tangle of motives and beliefs. . . . At the present moment it is no exaggeration to say that the greatest obstacle to the revision of our penal administration is this mass of confused thought and emotion in the public mind. Old rules, old buildings, old cruelties are protected by this thicket of unanalyzed fears and prejudices (1951, p. 21).

This classical view of the public as a hydra-headed beast, found in innumerable literary works from Horace to Shakespeare, continually recurs in discussions of penal reform. Lionel Fox says: "As to whatever he may understand by the phrase 'prison reform,' the man-in-the-street is at best apathetic, commonly cynical, and at worst frankly hostile." He follows tradition also in saying that prison administration "cannot afford to get out of touch with the common sense of the community as a whole" (1952, p. 130). Commonly, as in Fox's case, this assertion is made without any evidence being offered in support, although sometimes it is suggested that if harsh punishments are not imposed then either self-redress, vigilante justice, or lynch law will supervene.

This kind of estimate of the importance of public opinion and its significance as an obstacle to reform seems to rest on two beliefs about the nature of popular thought and feeling regarding punishment. On the one hand it is suggested that punishment, being in origin a substitute for private vengeance, still fulfills the function of providing some kind of vicarious satisfaction for the general demand for vengeance. On the other hand it is urged that the idea that criminals deserve to be subjected to some suffering, irrespective of its consequences either for the offender or for society, is an intuitive notion which is accepted, approved, and strongly held by the great majority of members of the community.

It is questionable, however, whether this collective desire for vengeance and for the meting out of deserved suffering is anywhere near as powerful a force as it is sometimes assumed to be. This is not to say that particularly heinous or horrifying offenses may not precipitate demands for vengeance in certain circumstances. But, as Sutherland and Cressey put it, "most crimes—probably more than 75 percent—arouse the resentment of no particular individual. And even when resentment is aroused, it is generally confined to a very small number of persons, whose resentment is likely to be counteracted by a non-punitive reaction on the part of other members of the society" (1970, p. 352).

Of course, what we have here is an empirical question requiring factual evidence for its resolution. But before coming to that there is a logical point which has been well stated by Gresham Sykes:

There is a great temptation to treat society as if it were a person—to speak of society doing this or that, the reactions of society, the morals of society, and so on. The usage is convenient, for it avoids a cumbersome phrasing; but it carries the danger of viewing society as much more homogeneous than it is in actuality. Society is a diversity, a collection of individuals with varied patterns of sentiments and behavior. And this variation is particularly marked in the area of crime and punishment. How and why the criminal should be penalized is subject to sharp dispute (1956, p. 81).

It is particularly important therefore to bear this in mind when evaluating statements about what "the public feels" or what general attitudes are, in relation to the correctional system. Nevertheless, although there is no general agreement about the precise definition of "public opinion" (Harwood Childs [1965] offers some fifty different definitions), quantitative data derived from polling representative samples of populations are today generally accepted as providing measures of "public opinion" in relation to matters of public interest. And in relation to corrections there are available the findings of a survey conducted by Louis Harris and Associates for the Joint Commission on Correctional Manpower and Training in 1967 (Harris, February 1968).

That survey sought among other things to examine "general attitudes of the public toward corrections and the rehabilitation of the offender." The most striking feature of the findings of that survey is the fact that in response to the question whether the main emphasis in prisons should be on "punishing," "protecting society," or "rehabilitation" 72 percent of adults chose "rehabilitation." Among teenagers this tendency is even more marked, 83 percent favoring "rehabilitation" as the proper emphasis. It is also interesting to note that less than half of the adults (48 percent) thought that the main emphasis in most prisons was, in fact, on "rehabilitation."

A number of other findings also conflict with the common negative stereotype of the public as predominantly punitive, vengeful, or retributive. Thus the report notes a "general feeling (expressed by two-to-one margins in some cases) that not enough help is given to people who get out of prison in getting psychological help, finding a place to live, keeping out of trouble, getting training for useful work, or getting decent jobs." The notion "that the public is in a vindictive frame of mind and takes a tough view" is rejected. On the contrary, "It believes not enough is being done in prisons or in the community to help rehabilitate criminals."

It is true that on some topics the ratio of positive, rehabilitation-oriented responses to negative, punishment-oriented responses was less marked. For example, when asked whether they felt more should be spent on prisons and rehabilitation programs, 43 percent responded in favor, 40 percent in opposition, and 17 percent were not sure. With regard to feelings about contacts with convicted offenders on their return to the free community, the responses were summarized as showing "a distinct undertone of hesitation and uneasiness" (ibid, pp. 1-10). Thus it is interesting to note that 77 percent support for the idea of halfway houses drops to 50 percent when the question is put in terms of "a Halfway House in your neighborhood" (ibid., p. 16).

On balance, however, the evidence suggests that the view that public opinion constitutes a major obstacle to penal reform is mistaken. A number of other considerations reinforce this conclusion. In the first place, in terms of the distinction drawn by public opinion specialists between the "general public," the "attentive public," and the "informed public," it is probable that those falling within the two latter categories form an extremely small minority of the population. Only a few people are seriously concerned about corrections and most do not see it as a matter directly affecting them. There is no large body of people actively interested and anxiously observing developments in this field.

In fact it is probably true that in relation to penal reform much the same is true as has been found in relation to criminal-law reform in general. In that context an extremely thoroughgoing study by Heinz, Gettleman, and Seeskin carried out in Illinois reached the following conclusion:

... [A]t the level of sophistication, subtlety, or specificity at which the crucial legislative decisions about criminal law are made public opinion is unlikely to be sufficiently informed or perceptive to have real influence. If the public cannot or does not understand these issues, a legislator need have no fear that he will be called to account; he will always be able to justify his vote.... The legislators whom we interviewed felt that specific criminal law issues were likely to have little real effect on their chances for reelection, and we found little or no evidence of partisanship (1969, pp. 349–50).

Arthur Sherry confirms this view:

Influential as the Model Penal Code and other major criminal law revision projects have been and continue to be, however, this influence is almost completely confined to a narrow professional area. It is expressed in the work of academicians, the activities of small groups working under the aegis of bar associations and the efforts of interested legislators who have played a major part in obtaining legislative authorization and financing for criminal law reform projects. *General public interest is almost non-existent* (1973, p. 206, my italics).

Heinz, Gettleman, and Seeskin found that neither political parties nor elections were important determinants of the criminal law and that there were few organizations primarily concerned with it. Such groups as were interested were those having "some official, governmental role in the criminal process such as police departments or state's attorneys" (1969, p. 280). If this is also true of the narrower field of penal reform, it suggests that the opinions of those actually engaged in correctional work would be likely to be of more significance and importance than those of the "general public."

In this connection it is interesting to note the findings of another survey conducted by Louis Harris and Associates for the Joint Commission on Correctional Manpower and Training. In this companion study the Harris organization made a survey of a significantly large and representative nationwide sample of individuals working in the field of corrections at all levels, from top management to line workers. Among other areas for which information was sought, an attempt was made to determine attitudes toward the correctional system and its agencies.

Louis Harris personally summed up the implications of the study for the future of corrections by saying that this field has "a magnificent opportunity in having personnel, by and large, who are looking for a change, who are willing to accept change, who want progress" (Harris, August 1968, p. 40). It is interesting to find that while "there is a fairly general agreement on the low level of correctional accomplishments," this feeling that not enough has been accomplished in the past has not generated apathy or cynicism so much as, to quote the summary of the findings, "an expectation and readiness to accept change and new programs." Sixty-nine percent at all levels felt that rehabilitation should have the primary emphasis in correctional agencies (ibid., pp. 9–15). Only a very small percentage at any level considered that punishment should be regarded as a primary or even a secondary goal.

One final point is worth making regarding public opinion and community attitudes. In the area of criminal law and penal reform the absence of any general public interest or clear guidance from constituents means that legislators are more or less forced into behaving in accordance with the conception of the proper role of the representative set out in Burke's classic "Speech to the Electors of Bristol" in 1774: in essence, they have to vote according to their own judgment and informed consideration of the facts. Moreover, there has in recent years developed increasing recognition that reform in these areas is the responsibility of legislators and the government. (See, for example, the Spring 1973 issue of *The American Journal of Comparative Law*.)

When legislators accept that responsibility they may by their own actions produce a change in popular opinion. Thus R. J. Buxton has noted that in England, "even where, as in the case of capital punishment, legislators still lead from the front, the tone of the debate has moved on to a markedly more rational level" (1973, p. 244). As a result, even in the few instances where there is strong emotional opposition to change, reform need not be precluded. For the public commonly tends to adjust to the changed situation even when it has initially resisted reform. One of the most striking examples of this may be found in Hyman and Sheatsley's study of attitudes toward racial desegregation in America. They found that public opinion in affected areas tended to be more favorable toward racial integration of schools *after* the action of school authorities to admit blacks to formerly all-white schools than before.

There is a clear lesson for legislators and correctional planners and administrators in all of this. It has already been noted that, when asked, a clear majority of the community declares support for halfway houses. Yet let the house next door be proposed as the halfway house, and popular support drops from 77 to 50 percent. We must recognize that the criminal offender, adult and juvenile, is accorded a low level of local community tolerance when he is no longer confined but is a real presence in society. Nevertheless this attitude does not, as the Harris findings demonstrate, imply opposition to reform within penal institutions.

Nor does it in any way preclude the active involvement of wide segments of the community in prison programs. It is universal experience in this field that with imagination and willingness to take some risks, community groups, minority groups, ex-offender groups, and responsible and interested individual citizens can be stimulated to play an effective supporting role in all correctional programs, including prison programs.

Correctional administrators have tended to isolate corrections not only from the general public, by high walls and locked doors, but also from other elements of the criminal justice system from which they could gain understanding and support. But in the light of the community's ambivalence toward corrections, the scant effort of administrators at collaboration with community groups and individual citizens is particularly unfortunate. Involving the community more persistently and extensively will also stimulate the recruitment of correctional personnel, particularly if increased efforts are made to draw into collaboration, and then to employ in the correctional service, members of minority groups, women, and ex-offenders.

THE BLUE FLU
James Vorenberg has written:

City dwellers have learned recently about the "blue flu" that often afflicts police officers who are suspicious of proposed changes. Commissioner Russel Oswald's apparent sense that he had to cater to the views of the guards at Attica—even at the risk of scores of deaths—suggests how powerfully existing values now hold those working in the system. Strong and militant police and correctional officers' unions in the past few years have provided an organization which can mobilize this opposition to change (1972, p. 67).

Brief reference has already been made in chapter 4 to the way in which correctional officers or prison guards are, in the literature on prisons, frequently cast in the role of rigid opponents of change. At that point Richard McCleery and Donald Cressey were cited as exponents of the view that guards may be expected to put up strong resistance to innovation in prison programs. Clearly, insofar as this characterization is accurate, then because the guard is a pivotal figure in penal institutions, his opposition will constitute a formidable barrier to modification or development. And as I did no more than mention this topic as one aspect of a popular stereotyped image of the prison guard, it will be necessary to consider here the degree to which the stereotype, in this aspect at least, is an accurate representation of reality and the extent to which prison officers as a social group do in fact constitute an obstacle to change.

As with most stereotypes, there is an element of truth underlying this one. Hans W. Mattick, writing with a background of experience both in a large, maximum-security, state prison and in a large, maximum-security, urban jail, maintains that the single most decisive factor in inhibiting change in most American prisons and jails is what he calls "custodial convenience." New programs, he says, require a great deal of work. In underfinanced and understaffed institutions such programs and the consequent additions to the work load will inevitably be resisted. Thus "it is an unusual prison that can or will inaugurate them, and then seek to maintain them over a period of time, against the enormous drag of 'custodial convenience'."

It is important to note that Mattick does not attribute this phenomenon to the character of the custodial staff. He says explicitly: "It is not a matter of mere laziness or that prison staffs do not do any work." It is rather, he maintains, "the characteristic mode of adjustment" to program innovation of understaffed and underfinanced institutions (1974, p. 20). Resistance to change is a function of the institutional situation rather than of any ideological commitment on the part of the guard force.

A different view of the role of the custodial force in resisting change may be found in Richard McCleery's study of a prison management in transition from repressive authoritarian control to relatively liberal governing procedures. According to McCleery, when such changes take place "the first group caught in the conflicts of institutional change is the guard force" (1960, p. 76). The reason for their resistance to change emerges very clearly from his study. The new developments in that case included the publication of a statement of policy and rules, the establishment of an inmate council, and regular consultation and counseling with inmates by members of the treatment staff. These developments involved a critical redefinition of roles and powers within the institution. In particular they "served to undermine the status and authority of the guards and the control they had exercised over the inmates."

Two features of McCleery's study throw doubt on an interpretation of the "custodial counterattack" as being in any sense a defence of "existing values" rather than a reflex response to an attack on the guards' position in the prison society. In the first place little or no attempt was made by the administration to secure the guards' cooperation or to consult them about the reconstruction process. Changes were introduced in a way that "frequently left watch officers less well-informed than the inmates they guarded, and so removed the legitimate basis of the authority of the guards" (ibid., pp. 68–69). It is scarcely surprising in the circumstances that they were disgruntled, and hostile to the new policies. McCleery in fact recognizes that, if the disruptive effects of new programs are to be minimized, then "any change must be accompanied by heavy emphasis on informing and training the guards or on reinforcing the legitimacy of their status by other means." Criticism of the guards for responding defensively, or even offensively, when their authority is undercut and subverted is on a level with *"Cet animal est très méchant, quand on l'attaque il se défend."*

The second notable fact about the case which McCleery describes is that, despite the guards' initial opposition, the transition from an authoritarian to a more liberal penal orientation was accomplished. "The prison changed in character from a military dictatorship to an institution in which armed force was subordinate to the objective of rehabilitative treatment" (ibid., pp. 71–76). When it is realized that this "institutional revolution" was carried out by five new staff members "without previous penal experience" (a new warden and deputy warden, a new industrial superintendent, a new director of education, and a new superintendent), who set out simply to transform the formal power structure and policy of the prison and succeeded, it is evident that the guards' resistance cannot have presented a really serious obstruction to change. Obdurate opposition by the custodial staff, if properly organized, could effectively prevent the execution of any plan for radical reorganization in a prison.

The question which arises then is that which is suggested by my quotation from James Vorenberg. To what extent may the formation of strong and militant correctional officers' unions be expected to mobilize opposition to change? This is a hard question to answer in the American context because unionism among prison officers is at a very rudimentary stage of development here. It is, however, possible to look at the situation in Britain, where a National Union of Police and Prison Officers was formed in 1913 and a *Prison Officers' Magazine*, which was called "the red 'un" because of its radical views, started publication three years earlier. Since 1938 an independent Prison Officers' Association has been in operation. The development of unionization in the English prison service has been described both by Harley Cronin (who spent thirty-six years in the prison service, mainly as full-time general secretary of the Prison Officers' Association) (1967) and by J. E. Thomas, also a former member of the prison service (1972).

It is quite clear from both of these accounts that there has in fact been over the years considerable opposition to "reformative pressures" on the part of prison officers, but it is equally clear that this was largely due, as Thomas puts it, to "a desire to arrest the process of status erosion which the officer, correctly, felt was the most significant development in his situation." While "the familiar clichés about how crucial their part was in the new reformative measures were sustained," one of the principal effects of the reform movement was "to narrow the role of the officer, to heighten its coercive overtones and to contribute to its definition as starkly custodial," as a variety of specialists were introduced into the prison service to carry out the tasks of training and treatment (1972, pp. 199–208). One of the most striking features of the officers' response to this situation was publication by the Prison Officers' Association (and its unanimous adoption at their annual conference in 1963) of a three-page document entitled

"The Role of the Modern Prison Officer." This declaration stated that prison officers were in fact for the most part engaged in work which was essentially the same as it had been in the nineteenth century, and it went on to make specific proposals for increasing the involvement of the officers in training and treatment programs.

Insofar as prison officers resisted change, the significance of their opposition is convincingly explained by Thomas:

The resistance of officers to reformative measures has traditionally been reduced to pseudo-psychological discussion about "punitive personalities" and so on. While there may be aberrant people in the prison service as there are in other occupations, I have tried to show that this is not an adequate reason. The introduction of reformative measures created colossal, *real* problems for the prison officer, which were never faced. As the years went on it would have been remarkable if he had not become increasingly anxious. Nor was he very distorted in his perception of the situation as one where scarce organisational resources were being deployed to improve the inmates' situation, while his own very real material needs were being ignored.

Prison officers, he says, "will resist change" but that "is only to say that they will behave as other men do in other organizations" (ibid., pp. 220–21). It does not represent an insuperable obstacle to reform even when they are organized, as in the English situation, in an extremely militant and active trade union.

It cannot of course be assumed that developments in this area in America will necessarily mirror the English experience. Nevertheless the Louis Harris study of correctional personnel attitudes mentioned earlier did not reflect opposition to change but the reverse. Moreover, the fact that in the analysis of opinions the responses of "line workers" were grouped separately makes it possible to compare their attitudes with those of other correctional personnel. In this context it is interesting to note that in responding to the question, Which of four goals—punishment, rehabilitation, protection of society, changing community attitudes—*should* be given primary emphasis in corrections? 79 percent of line workers voted for rehabilitation. This was a higher percentage than for any of the other groups, which included top and middle management (68 percent), first-line supervisors (70 percent) and functional specialists (72 percent) (Harris, August 1968).

This kind of response to an opinion or attitude questionnaire, of course, does not necessarily tell us much about actual behavior. People's expressions of sentiment do not necessarily imply analogous tendencies to act. Yet the most recent American study, by David Duffee, suggests that prison officers here have in fact generally accepted the changes in correctional policy or ideology which have characterized prison administration in the past half century. Thus, he says:

> While fifty years ago he guarded subhumans and misbehavior against them was inexcusable, whenever it was even recognized, today a correctional officer is responsible for the management of human beings, whose word clinically and legally may stand up against his own. More importantly most correctional officers openly agree that the change in policy is for the better. There may be some regrets about the clear cut roles of yesterday, and there are certainly many complaints about the lack of power and respect today, but most correctional officers do not and would not care to deny that inmates are fellow human beings who should be "getting a better shake."

What seems to emerge from Duffee's study is that insofar as correctional officers are infected with the "blue flu" it is because they find themselves in a situation of role conflict or role ambiguity which is immensely frustrating.

> As one officer expressed it: "I'm not sure what I'm here for, I know it is not security. Let's face it—the joint's secure. No, I must be good for something different." In part, much of the officer value complex may be built on this flight from ambiguity: that officers have discarded the goal of punishment and find in its place only the competing claims of professors, researchers, politicians, and inmates none of which they are willing to accept. They are in the anomic position of working for a goal which is negatively defined as the absence of punishment and is manifested by no acceptably measured result and is mediated by no reliably correlated means (1974, p. 156).

That custodial officers have for many years found themselves in a situation of role conflict has already been noted in chapter 4 and is not a new insight. It has been pointed out by many writers, including, most notably, Donald Cressey (1958, 1959, 1960). Yet almost no attempt has been made to deal with this problem, and much has happened, as the English example makes plain, to exacerbate it. In the absence either of a clear definition of their role, or of training to enable them to fulfill it, it is to be expected that correctional officers' attitudes may be negative or obstructive. But that is not to say that they present an insurmountable obstacle to reform, nor is there any evidence to support such a view.

BALKANIZATION

According to the National Advisory Commission on Criminal Justice Standards and Goals, one of the leading obstacles to reform of any part of the criminal justice system is the range and variety of governmental authorities—federal, state, and local— that are responsible for it. "This balkanization" says the *Report on Corrections*, "complicates police planning, impedes development of expeditious court processes, and divides responsibility for convicted offenders among a multiplicity of overlapping but barely intercommunicating agencies. The organizational structure of the criminal justice system was well suited to the frontier society in which it was implanted. It has survived in a complex, mobile, urban society for which it is grossly unsuited" (1973, p. 11).

This balkanization reaches its limit in the multiplicity of municipal and county jails and juvenile detention facilities, scattered in every state. Certainly, for all convicted offenders serving sentences as misdemeanants or offenders against local ordinances, it would be better that they should serve their terms in state-run facilities. They should not be the responsibility of the local jail or juvenile detention facility. For others, those who must be detained pending trial or appeal, there should ideally be a statewide supervisory mechanism, preferably moving toward the establishment of regional detention facilities in lieu of the present swarm of local facilities.

Yet it is doubtful whether this fragmentation of administrative organization constitutes, in itself, a major obstacle to prison reform. Certainly there would be some advantages in organizational restructuring that would take the form of the establishment of an integrated state correctional system. Thus if prison, probation, and parole for adult and juvenile offenders were brought under one departmental structure, there is no doubt that the bargaining position of that department in the competition, within cabinet and legislature, for resources would be vastly improved. Moreover, other flexibilities would appear; career lines for more promising staff would be expanded, to say nothing of interdepartmental in-service training possibilities. Above all, such a structure would match the developing realities of correctional processes in terms of the developing interdependence between institution and community-based programs.

Yet not all persons of experience in this field would advocate such a total, unified administrative solution to the problem of balkanization of correctional services. Other less heroic solutions are available and may be preferred. For example, the probation subsidy program, as developed in California, has much to recommend it, notwithstanding the fact that recent criticism has suggested that it is less effective, less economic, and less beneficial than has been claimed. That program provides financial incentives to localities to supervise their own convicted offenders on probation, if acceptable standards of supervision are maintained. It has proved to be an effective mechanism for keeping offenders, adult and juvenile, out of institutions, and it would appear to have done so without having an adverse effect on recidivism or crime rates, though the latter consequence is hard to measure with any precision.

Thus there is something to be said for the suggestion made in the *Report on Corrections* that a possible solution might be to accept the present balkanization of agencies, recognizing its strong political support in systems of local patronage, and at the same time to prescribe defined standards, buttressed by statewide inspectoral machineries, to achieve attainment of those standards. In the case of local jails it is suggested that "they must be subject to State controlled inspection processes, to ensure the attainment of minimum standards of decency and efficiency. A further control and support which might be added is State subsidy to facilitate attainment of defined standards and goals by the local jails, the carrot of subsidy being added to the stick of threatened condemnation and closure" (ibid.).

As far as prisons are concerned the obvious parallel lies in the relation between the federal and state systems. Clearly substantial reforms will not be achieved without the allocation of substantially increased governmental funds to the criminal justice system and, within those funds, the allocation of a larger proportion to corrections. Fortunately, the federal government, followed by some states, is already giving budgetary recognition to the significance of crime and, in particular, to the fear of crime in society, requiring that a prescribed and substantial proportion of governmental funds be devoted to the corrections segment of the crime-control system and setting standards and goals for corrections. It is clearly a proper role for the federal government to assist states by funds and by direct services to help break down existing organizational inefficiencies in corrections.

In sum, it does not seem that balkanization need prevent effective prison reforms. Federal initiatives, if coupled with the allocation of funds, are likely to prove solvent of most of what the *Report on Corrections* calls "partisan, parochial and patronage interests." There do not appear to be major organizational obstacles to the attainment of more effective and humane systems of imprisonment, and such impediments as there are are neither inherent in the nature of things nor absolutely intractable.

LACK OF KNOWLEDGE

The Need for Research

The *Report on Corrections* identifies as another factor liable to frustrate progress the lack of a knowledge base for planning.

Lack of adequate data about crime and delinquency, the consequences of sentencing practices, and of the outcome of correctional programs, is a major obstacle to planning for better community protection. It is a sad commentary on our social priorities that every conceivable statistic concerning sports is collected and available to all who are interested. One can readily find out how many left-handers hit triples in the 1927 World Series. Yet if we wish to know how many one-to-life sentences were handed out to the 1927 crop of burglars—or the 1972 crop, for that matter—the facts are nowhere to be found (ibid., p. 14).

It would be generally agreed that critical evaluation of penal measures is an essential precondition to rational and effective policy formulation and planning. To know what policies to pursue and what plans to make, it is necessary to know what penal practices have worked in what way and to what extent, in relation to the different types of crime delinquency and with different categories of adult and young offenders. But although there is universal agreement on the need for evaluative research, this agreement often stops short of action. There is depressingly little methodologically rigorous evaluative research available to guide our efforts.

It would be inappropriate to attempt here the kind of account of our state of knowledge or overall perspective on evaluative research that can be found in the Council of Europe's report on *The Effectiveness of Punishment and Other Measures of Treatment* (1967), in Leslie Wilkins's *Evaluation on Penal Measures* (1969), and in the *Report on Corrections* of the National Advisory Commission on Criminal Justice Standards and Goals (1973). But because research is the indispensable tool by which future needs are measured and met, it is important to explore some of the fundamental distinctions of purpose, ethical and methodological difficulties, and key planning issues in evaluative research. Inevitably this will involve going outside the frame of reference within which most of the discussion has so far been confined, for research into the effectiveness of one penal method cannot be conducted *in vacuo*.

Two Caveats

Before we enter into specific issues two general caveats concerning research in the field of corrections must be entered. In the first place the evaluation of correctional programs is often rendered peculiarly difficult because of the multiplicity of purposes, and sometimes the ambiguity of purposes, being served by such programs. This preliminary point can be illustrated by an example drawn from another field—that of public health. The effectiveness of a malaria prevention program can be measured by ascertaining the mortality and morbidity rates in the region or population served by the program before and after its introduction, in comparison with other regions and other populations having similar death and illness rates from malaria.

The benefit can be quantified; so can the cost in terms of

personnel, facilities, and drugs for the program. A cost/benefit ratio can be assessed. The policymaker or the planner can then balance the short-term and long-term advantages of allocating scarce funds and personnel in this type of public health program as distinct from others which compete for these resources. I have oversimplified the problem; there are other complicating considerations here too, but broadly that is the frame of reference.

By contrast, consider the more complex competing considerations in a correctional program—say, a new community-based program in lieu of institutional placement for defined categories of offenders. The costs of such a new program in terms of personnel and resources can be calculated as they were for the new malaria project, but the offsetting benefits are much more difficult to assess. Even if it can be rigorously demonstrated that those handled in the new program commit less crime or less serious crime than those sent to the institution; even if we are satisfied that the two groups (community-treated and institutionalized) are randomly selected and their later conduct equally critically evaluated; the question of social benefit from the new program remains uncertain.

The uncertainty is multifaceted: Has there been a diminution of general deterrence of certain categories of criminals by the introduction of this new program? Has there been an increase of fear in the community because of the earlier placement of these criminals in the community? Have the particular areas where the community-based programs have been concentrated been adversely affected? Crime and the fear of crime may not be directly connected phenomena—a few crimes concentrated in a small area may have much more damaging social effects than many more crimes dispersed more widely in the community.

The legal sanction is multipurposive, looking to community cohesion and stability, to social values, and to a sense of security at the same time as it looks to the effects of the sanction on the individual criminal and on other potential criminals. Only the thoughtless planner will overlook this complexity of purposes in crime control. But that does not mean that evaluative research is irrelevant to policy and planning; quite the contrary. Because of the very complexity of the cost/benefit ratio in this field, precise evaluation to render known what can be known is of particular importance. The speculative and the known can then be more intelligently related to the costs, for planning purposes, than if all is speculation.

There is a second general caveat. Much has been passed off as evaluative research in the field of corrections which does not merit such a classification. An imprecise and eulogistic description, embellished with sprinkling of success stories, is still too often offered as an evaluation of a program. There are many reasons for this. If the continuation of funding of a new program depends on a satisfactory report to the funding agency, those running the program will be tempted to submit a blend of description and praise as an evaluation. Another pressure bears heavily on all correctional administrators. They inevitably tend to look kindly, with a generous eye, on their own. When one plans and launches a program, one is not in the best position to evaluate it. There is everything to be said for substantial independence of evaluators from the administrators and organizers of programs.

Stages in Evaluation

It may help to sketch a somewhat simplified outline of the stages or levels of "evaluation." The concept may cover:

1. a careful description of what was done;
2. the financial controls of the program, the controls of personnel, and the overall costs of the program;
3. the number of subjects dealt with and what was done for each;
4. a description of the ways in which the new program fitted into the administrative structure; and
5. the later careers of the subjects of the program after it was completed.

Many so-called evaluations stop short at that stage, adding praise for the diligence and sincerity of those working in the program, and pointing to the advantages provided by level 5 as contrasted with the low costs in level 2 as proof of the value of the project.

Such "evaluation" falls short of that which is necessary for effective correctional planning. We need to know more. We need to know in what respects the effects of this program, both on its workers and on its subjects, would not have occurred if no such program had been run or if the practices obtaining before the new program was introduced had been followed. We need to move from historical description—which is all that is involved in 1 to 5 above—to the measurement of systems change.

This point merits further stress. Benjamin Paul, in discussing the use of social science in relation to public health, has distinguished three stages of evaluation:

1. assessment of effort—the input of energy;
2. assessment of effect—the results of the input;
3. assessment of process—why and how the results are achieved (1956).

Another scholar, Edward Suchman, also writing on the subject of evaluative research, has made the same point in more detail, distinguishing five stages:

1. effort
2. performance
3. adequacy of performance
4. efficiency
5. process (1967).

What is important about these stages is the stress placed on the movement from description to analysis.

The point may be expanded by means of a hypothetical example. Suppose we are to evaluate a new program for finding jobs for certain categories of discharged offenders. We carefully describe who fell within the group to be helped, what staff we had, what we did, what it cost, how many jobs we found for the ex-offenders, how stable they were in the jobs. Have we moved to the stage of "assessment of effect" of our program (in Benjamin Paul's system) or of "efficiency" (in Edward Suchman's system)? Clearly we have not moved to process evaluation—why it worked.

Nor have we moved to efficiency evaluation—did it work? And the point is both important and frequently overlooked. First, we do not know how many would have had jobs and with what employment stability, apart from our new program. So we need either a control group or reliable base line data against which to measure our program. But more important, even with a control group or with reliable base line data, we do not know the effects of our program on others not within the area of correctional planning. For every new job we found for one of our ex-offenders, unless we have expanded the total number of jobs in the community, there is someone we do not know about who has been denied an employment opportunity. That, too, would have to be taken into account in any full evaluation of the effects of the program.

It is not suggested, however, that evaluation is worthless if it stops short of such larger inquiries. Given a control group or adequate base line data controls, evaluations that thrust beyond description into the area of critical assessment of "effect" or "efficiency" will often be the most that we can hope for. Of course if the last step in the evaluative operation—the assessment of the processes involved in the achievement of program results—can be taken, correctional planning will be greatly strengthened. But the essential point is that description of the program with its administrative, fiscal, and operational elements carefully narrated is not enough. Evaluation should always go beyond that to the stage of the measurement of effects.

Some Problems

A variety of problems arise in relation to evaluative research in this field. Some of them have been regarded as barriers to assessing the value of correctional programs. Three of the more crucial issues are: the ethics of experimentation; the nature of treatment; the controlled trial.

The ethics of experimentation. Should we use others, even criminals, as test subjects? Much has been written on the ethical problems raised by this question, particularly in relation to medical research, part of which has already been discussed in chapter 5. Where there is genuine doubt as to the choice between two or more treatments for a given illness, efficient experimentation requires that the competing treatments be tested on matched groups of patients. Of course, the analogy between the doctors' "treatment" and the courts' or correctional administrators' "treatment" is both imperfect and, as has been argued earlier, potentially misleading. Both the subjects of medical diagnosis and the criteria of successful medical treatment are better defined, and the patient can consent to treatment while the criminal rarely does so. We are forced, therefore, to pose the issue: Is it justifiable to impose a criminal sanction guided by the necessities of research and not the felt necessities of the case?

There is a respectable and reasonable ethical argument against clinical trials of correctional treatment methods which must not be evaded in our enthusiasm for the acquisition of knowledge. It runs like this: Man is an end in himself; he must never be sacrificed on the grounds that knowledge about man's behavior is of greater value than his individual human rights. This is particularly true if the sacrifice is made without his uncoerced and fully informed choice. The explorer may, choosing freely, risk his life in the pursuit of knowledge. The citizen may, under certain controlled conditions, risk his life and physical well-being in furtherance of medical experiments. But when coercion or restraint or unduly influencing pressures appear, it is unethical and socially inexpedient to permit such sacrifice of the individual to the supposed collective good.

Put in less pretentious terms, the proposition is: Given that our knowledge is exiguous, we must, nevertheless, at all times act in the way and within the knowledge that is thought best for the individual we are treating. When the problem of his treatment raises (as it generally does in relation to criminal sanctions) the issue of the proper balance between the community's need for protection from the criminal and his needs if he is to be reestablished as a conforming member of society, the same principle holds true. We are never justified in ignoring the offender's interests for the sake of experimentation.

It is my view that this particular ethical argument against clinical trials is not entirely convincing and that, given certain safeguards, it is entirely appropriate, indeed essential, for evaluative research projects of this type to be built into new correctional developments. The principle which would govern these safeguards might be called the principle of "less severity." By this I mean that the sanction being studied should not be one that is regarded in the mind of the criminal subjected to it, or of the people imposing it, or of the community at large, as more severe than the traditional sanction with which it is being compared.

To take a group of criminals who otherwise would be put on probation and to select some at random for institutional treatment would be unjust. Conversely, to select at random a group who would otherwise be incarcerated and to treat them on probation or in a probation hostel would seem to involve no abuse of human rights. Applying this principle, it should be possible to pursue many decades of valuable evaluative research, without infringing the rights of the offenders.

The nature of the program. A central problem in the evaluation of a new program in corrections is to define precisely enough for research purposes exactly what are the characteristics of that program. The point can be made by means of an example. Assume a parole system where the supervision case load of each parole officer exceeds one hundred. We wish to test a new program of intensive community supervision of, and assistance to, certain defined categories of releasees from prison. So, we randomly select our test group and provide counseling, job placement, educational assistance, generally closer support and supervision.

Whatever the results, however assessed, we are little further advanced in knowledge. What amongst all the actions we have taken, all the services we have provided, works well and for which categories of offenders? It is as if the doctor were to prescribe six or seven drugs, packed in a single huge pill. It is swallowed; some patients recover, some die. And he still has no idea of the specific effectiveness of any of the drugs administered.

Unfortunately many correctional programs are of this composite nature and are applied randomly to all types of offenders. In planning a program the problem of defining the precise technique being employed should be carefully addressed. At the same time the program's focus—what it is intended to achieve—should be precisely defined. Unfortunately, in the field of corrections we do not have anything resembling what is called nosology in medical science; we are as yet unable to classify offenders in terms of their deficiencies or their needs.

The controlled trial. The analogy with medical treatment is seductive; that probably explains why so many penologists and criminologists see the controlled clinical trial as the model for evaluating research in corrections. It has certainly proved of overwhelming value to medical research. The randomization of a test group and a control group, the "double blind" where appropriate and feasible, and the careful measurement of outcome has great attraction as a research design. It is not surprising that the controlled trial should have been seen as the ideal design for evaluative research in penology.

It has emerged recently, however, that there are a great many difficulties involved in the use of controlled trials in the field of corrections. The nature of those difficulties has been described in a British Home Office research study by R. V. Clarke and D. B. Cornish. This is a study of a controlled trial of an experimental regime in an English approved school. Such schools are not penal institutions in the ordinary sense, for the population is not composed exclusively of offenders, but there is no reason to believe that the findings of the study would not be relevant to the conduct of controlled trials in penal institutions.

One of the problems referred to in the study is that which I have just mentioned—the fact that the complexity of the treatments under study makes it difficult to interpret results. As the authors of the study put it:

> . . .[T]hinking of institutional treatments as "molar" variables may lead to serious confusion when it comes to interpreting the results of a controlled trial. . . . Because there has usually been little systematic attempt to study or monitor the "black-box" of treatment it has been easy to conceive of treatment as a single unitary factor and the label it is given is invoked to account for the results. It is only when the attempt is made to reach a better understanding of the treatment process, as was done in the present research, that its complexity is revealed and the inappropriateness of the experimental design is fully appreciated.

Another problem which arises relates to "the practitioner's genuine ethical reservations about exposing his charges to the possibility of getting the 'wrong' treatment." These reservations, together with such factors as the practitioner's fear of losing prestige, power, or responsibility, or of being found inefficient, may lead practitioners to withdraw their cooperation from a research project or alternatively may result in anxieties and tensions which disrupt the cohesion and stability of the institution.

These and other difficulties discussed by Clarke and Cornish lead them to conclude that "the controlled trial would seem to have a more limited function in penal research than has sometimes been ascribed to it in the past and certainly much more limited than it has in medicine." They are, in fact, doubtful whether in the present state of knowledge the controlled trial could often be used effectively in this field and think it highly improbable that its widespread use "would significantly advance knowledge about institutional treatment in ways that could not otherwise be achieved" (1972, p. 21).

Yet the truth is that the authors' conclusion (the controlled trial should not be regarded as a paradigm and its use in penology involves many pitfalls) itself represents a significant advance in knowledge. In the first place their careful analysis throws considerable doubt on the conclusions drawn by those reporting previous trials of this nature and points to unrecognized possibilities of error. In the second place it provides an admirable guide to those who will use this method in the future. Lastly it will serve to direct attention to alternative strategies for research in corrections which might otherwise have been neglected.

Conclusion

Despite all the difficulties enumerated here, the case for evaluative research in corrections is overwhelming. Indeed as the *Report on Corrections* states: "To fail to propound and to achieve ambitious research and data gathering goals is to condemn corrections to the perpetual continuance of its present ineptitude" (1973, p. 14). Of all the impediments to change discussed in this chapter none is more fundamentally disabling than our lack of knowledge. By way of conclusion on this subject two further points may be made.

First, though planners and policymakers frequently preach the virtues of evaluative research, it is unfortunately the case that they tend to believe that it can be done cheaply. There is a tendency to add a small sum and a sparse staff to any new project as its research component. Bad research is peculiarly unhelpful. Good research is expensive. Rules of thumb are, by definition, imprecise, but for the evaluation of the first year of a new program in the penal system administrators should think in terms of 24 to 33 percent of the total budget being allocated to research. Baseline data and outcome data do not collect themselves. Research must start before the program starts. And it must start with an adequate staff, adequate resources, and a well-defined research plan.

Second, evaluative research is necessary for effective planning in the correctional field for one other reason. It seems to be the case that only those agencies in the field of corrections that are themselves involved in evaluative research know about the research work (including evaluative research) of other agencies. Agencies with a well-developed research potential and a sophisticated approach to evaluation are also the agencies which are well informed on correctional programs generally. Their research branches reach out to the developing knowledge and improving practice elsewhere in a way that only research units can achieve. Correctional administrators with strong research assistance gain greatly thereby, not only in evaluating their own programs but in knowing about, learning from, and building on the experience of others.

Selected Reading and References

Abt Associates. *An Evaluation of the Training Provided in Correctional Institutions Under the Manpower Development Act, Section 251, Final Summary Report.* Cambridge, Mass.: Abt Associates, 1971.

American Assembly, Columbia University. *Prisoners in America.* Edited by Lloyd E. Ohlin. Englewood Cliffs, N.J.: Prentice-Hall, 1973.

American Correctional Association. *Correction Officers' Training Guide.* College Park, Md.: American Correctional Association, 1959.

American Friends Service Committee. *Struggle for Justice: A Report on Crime and Punishment in America.* New York: Hill and Wang, 1971.

American Medical Association. "1952 House of Delegates Resolution on Disapproval of Participation in Scientific Experiments by Inmates of Penal Institutions." In *Digest of Official Action: 1846-1958.* American Medical Association, 1959, pp. 617–18.

———. "Principles of Medical Ethics." In *Opinions and Reports of the Judicial Council.* Chicago: American Medical Association, 1969.

Annual Report of the Commissioners of Prisons and Directors of

Convict Prisons 1911-12. London: H. M. Stationery Office, 1912.

Atchley, Robert, and McCabe, M. Patrick. "Socialization in Correctional Communities: A Replication." *American Sociological Review* 33 (1968): 774-85.

Attica: The Official Report of the New York State Special Commission on Attica. New York: Bantam Books, 1972.

Badillo, Herman, and Haynes, Milton. *A Bill of No Rights: Attica and the American Prison System.* New York: Outerbridge & Lazard, 1972.

Bailey, W. C. "Correctional Outcome: An Evaluation of 100 Reports." *Journal of Criminal Law, Criminology and Police Science* 57 (1966): 153-60.

Barkin, Eugene N. "The Emergence of Correctional Law and Awareness of the Rights of the Convicted." *Nebraska Law Review* 45 (1966): 669-89.

Barnes, Harry E., and Teeters, Negley K. *New Horizons in Criminology.* New York: Prentice-Hall, 1943.

Bass, Stanley A. "Correcting the Correctional System." *Clearinghouse Review* 5 (1971): 125-51.

Beaumont, Gustave de, and Tocqueville, Alexis de. *On the Penitentiary System in the United States and Its Application in France.* Translated by Francis Lieber. Introduction by Thorsten Sellin. Perspectives in Sociology Series, edited by Herman R. Lantz. Carbondale, Ill.: Southern Illinois University Press, 1964. First published in Philadelphia by Carey, Lea & Blanchard, 1833.

Bell, Daniel, ed. *Toward the Year 2000.* Boston: Houghton Mifflin, 1968.

Bennett, James V. "The Selection and Training of Correctional Personnel with Special Reference to the Federal Prison System of the United States of America." In James V. Bennett, *Of Prisons and Justice.* Prepared for the Subcommittee on National Penitentiaries of the Committee on the Judiciary, United States Senate. Washington, D.C.: U.S. Government Printing Office, 1964.

Bentham, Jeremy. *Theory of Legislation.* Translated by R. Hildbreth. London: Trubner & Co., 1864.

Bergesen, B. E., III. "California Prisoners: Rights Without Remedies." *Stanford Law Review* 25 (1972): 1-50.

Berk, Bernard B. "Organizational Goals and Inmate Organization." *American Journal of Sociology* 71 (1966): 522-34.

Blumstein, Alfred, and Cohen, Jacqueline. "A Theory of the Stability of Punishment." *Journal of Criminal Law and Criminology* 64 (1973): 198-207.

Boorstin, Daniel J. *The Americans: The Democratic Experience.* New York: Random House, 1973.

Breitel, Charles D. "Controls in Criminal Law Enforcement." *University of Chicago Law Review* 27 (1960): 427-35.

Buxton, R. J. "The Politics of Criminal Law Reform: England." *American Journal of Comparative Law* 21 (1973): 230-44.

Buxton, Thomas Fowell. *An Inquiry whether Crime and Misery are Produced or Prevented by Our Present System of Prison Discipline.* London: J. M'Creery, Printer, Black-Horse Court, 1818. Printed for John and Arthur Arch, Cornhill; Butterworth and Sons, Fleet Street; and John Hatchard, Piccadilly.

California State Assembly Office of Research. *Report on the Economic Status and Rehabilitative Value of California Correctional Industries.* A staff report prepared for the Assembly Ways and Means Committee. Sacramento: Assembly Office of Research, 1969.

Carlson, Norman. "Attica: A Look at the Causes and Future." *Criminal Law Bulletin* 7 (1971): 832-36.

Cavallin, Hector. "The Case Study: A Clinical Approach to the Training of the Correctional Officer." *American Journal of Correction* 29 (1967): 14-18.

Childs, Harwood L. *Public Opinion: Nature, Formation and Role.* Princeton, N.J.: Van Nostrand, 1965.

Christie, Nils. "Changes in Penal Values." In Nils Christie, ed. *Scandanavian Studies in Criminology: Aspects of Social Control in Welfare States.* 2:161-72. Oslo: Scandanavian University Books, 1968.

Clarke, R. V. G, and Cornish, D. B. *The Controlled Trial in Institutional Research: Paradigm or Pitfall for Penal Evaluators?* Home Office Research Studies, No. 15. London: H. M. Stationery Office, 1972.

Clemmer, Donald. "Observations on Imprisonment as a Source of Criminality." *Journal of Criminal Law and Criminology* 41 (1950-51): 311-19.

―――. *The Prison Community.* New York: Rinehart & Co., 1940.

Cline, Hugh F., and Wheeler, Stanton. "The Determinants of Normative Patterns in Correctional Institutions." In Nils Christie, ed. *Scandanavian Studies in Criminology: Aspects of*

Social Control in Welfare States. 2:173–84. Oslo: Scandanavian University Books, 1968.

Cloward, Richard A., et al. *Theoretical Studies in Social Organization of the Prison.* Social Science Research Council, 1960.

Cohen, Fred. "The Discovery of Prison Reform." *Buffalo Law Review* 21 (1972): 855–87.

———. *The Legal Challenge to Corrections.* Washington, D.C.: Joint Commission on Correctional Manpower and Training, 1969.

Cohen, Morten. "The Rights of the Civilly and Criminally Incarcerated." *Clearinghouse Review* 4 (1971): 399–435.

Coke, Edward. *Institutes of the Laws of England.* Vol. 2. London: E. and R. Brooke, 1797.

Conrad, John P. "Corrections and Simple Justice." *Journal of Criminal Law and Criminology* 64 (1973): 208–17.

Council of Europe, European Committee on Crime Problems. *The Effectiveness of Punishment and Other Measures of Treatment.* Strasbourg: Council of Europe, 1967.

———. *The Status, Selection and Training of Prison Staff: First Report of Subcommittee of the European Committee on Crime Problems.* Strasbourg: Council of Europe, 1963.

Cozart, Reed. "The Benefits of Executive Clemency." *Federal Probation* 32 (1968): 33–35.

Cressey, Donald R. "Adult Felons in Prison." In American Assembly, Columbia University. *Prisoners in America.* Edited by Lloyd E. Ohlin. Englewood Cliffs, N. J.: Prentice-Hall, 1973.

———. "Contradictory Directives in Complex Organizations: The Case of the Prison." *Administrative Science Quarterly* 4 (1959): 1–19.

———. "Limitations on Organization and Treatment in the Modern Prison." In Richard A. Cloward, et al. *Theoretical Studies in Social Organization of the Prison.* Social Science Research Council, 1960.

———. "The Nature and Effectiveness of Correctional Techniques." *Law and Contemporary Problems* 23 (1958): 754–71.

———. *The Prison: Studies in Institutional Organization and Change.* New York: Holt, Rinehart & Winston, 1961.

Cronin, Harley. *The Screw Turns.* London: Long, 1967.

Cross, A. R. N. *Punishment, Prison and the Public: An Assessment of Penal Reform in Twentieth Century England by an Armchair Penologist.* London: Stevens & Sons, 1971.

Darrow, Clarence S. *Crime and Criminals.* Chicago: Charles H. Kerr, 1902. Reprinted in Arthur Weinberg, ed. *Attorney for the Damned.* New York: Simon and Schuster, 1957, pp. 3-15.

Davis, Angela Y. "Lessons: From Attica to Soledad." *New York Times.* October 8, 1971, p. 43.

Department of Health, Education and Welfare. *The Institutional Guide to DHEW Policy on Protection of Human Subjects.* Washington, D.C.: U.S. Government Printing Office, 1971.

Departmental Committee on the Employment of Prisoners. *Departmental Committee on the Employment of Prisoners Report.* Part I (1933); Part II (1935). Command no. 4462. London: H. M. Stationery Office, 1933, 1935.

Downey, Richard N., and Signori, E. I. "The Selection of Prison Guards." *Journal of Criminal Law, Criminology and Police Science* 49 (1958): 234-36.

Dreher, Robert H., and Kammler, Linda. *Criminal Registration Statutes and Ordinances in the United States: A Compilation.* Carbondale, Ill.: Center for the Study of Crime, Delinquency and Corrections, Southern Illinois University, 1969.

Du Cane, Edmund F. *The Punishment and Prevention of Crime.* London: Macmillan & Co., 1885.

Duffee, David. "The Correction Officer Subculture and Organizational Change." *Journal of Research in Crime and Delinquency* 11 (1974): 155-72.

————. *Using Correctional Officers in Planned Change.* Washington, D.C.: National Institute of Law Enforcement, National Technical Information Service, 1972.

Dunne, John. "Attica: A Look at the Causes and the Future." *Criminal Law Bulletin* 7 (1971): 824-28.

Emery, Fred E. *Freedom and Justice Within Walls: The Bristol Prison Experiment.* London: Tavistock Publications, 1970.

England, Ralph W. "New Departures in Prison Labor." *The Prison Journal* 41 (1961): 21-26.

"Ethical Aspects of Experimentation with Human Subjects." Symposium. *Daedalus* 98 (1969): 219-597.

Evans, A. A. "Correctional Institution Personnel: Amateurs or Professionals?" *Annals of the American Academy of Political and Social Science* 293 (1954): 70-78.

Federal Probation Officers' Association. *A Compilation of State and Federal Statutes Relating to Civil Rights of Persons Convicted of Crime.* East St. Louis, Ill.: Federal Probation Officers' Association, 1960.

Flew, Antony. *Crime or Disease?* London: Macmillan, 1973.

Forster, E. M. *Abinger Harvest.* New York: Harcourt, Brace, 1936.

Fox, Lionel W. *The English Prison and Borstal Systems.* London: Routledge and Kegan Paul, 1952.

Freedman, Marcia, and Pappas, Nick. *The Training and Employment of Offenders.* Reference Document. Washington, D.C.: President's Commission on Law Enforcement and Administration of Justice, 1967.

Friend, Charles E. "Judicial Intervention in Prison Administration." *William and Mary Law Review* 9 (1967): 178-92.

Fry, Margery. *Arms of the Law.* London: Gollancz, 1951.

Galvin, John J., and Karacki, Loren. *Manpower and Training in Correctional Institutions.* Staff Report of the Joint Commission on Correctional Manpower and Training. Lebanon, Pa.: Sowers Printing Co., 1969. Available from American Correctional Association, College Park, Maryland.

Garabedian, Peter G. "Social Roles and Processes of Socialization in the Prison Community." *Social Problems* 11 (1963): 139-52.

Garrity, Donald. "The Prison as a Rehabilitation Agency." In Donald R. Cressey, ed. *The Prison: Studies in Institutional Organization and Change.* New York: Holt, Rinehart & Winston, 1961.

Gellhorn, Walter. *Ombudsmen and Others: Citizens' Protectors in Nine Countries.* Cambridge, Mass.: Harvard University Press, 1966.

———. *When Americans Complain: Governmental Grievance Procedures.* Cambridge, Mass.: Harvard University Press, 1966.

Giallombardo, Rose. *Society of Women: A Study of a Women's Prison.* New York: John Wiley & Sons, 1966.

Gibbons, Donald C. *Changing the Lawbreaker.* Englewood Cliffs, N.J.: Prentice-Hall, 1965.

Glaser, Daniel. "Criminality Theories and Behavioral Images." *American Journal of Sociology* 61 (1956): 433-44.

———. *The Effectiveness of a Prison and Parole System.* New York: Bobbs-Merrill, 1964.

———. *Routinizing Evaluation: Getting Feedback on Effectiveness of Crime and Delinquency Programs.* Crime and Delinquency Issues, A Monograph Series. Rockville, Md.: National Institute of Mental Health, Center for Studies of Crime and Delinquency, 1973.

———, and Stratton, John. "Measuring Inmate Change in Prison." In Donald R. Cressey, ed. *The Prison: Studies in Institutional Organization and Change.* New York: Holt, Rinehart & Winston, 1961.

Goldfarb, Ronald L., and Singer, Linda R. *After Conviction.*
New York: Simon & Schuster, 1973.

Gough, Aidam R. "The Expungement of Adjudication Records
of Juvenile and Adult Offenders: A Problem of Status."
Washington University Law Quarterly 1966: 147-90.

Greenberg, David F., and Stender, Fay. "The Prison as a Lawless
Agency." *Buffalo Law Review* 21 (1972): 799-838.

Grob, Gerald N. "Welfare and Poverty in American History. . . ."
Reviews in American History 1 (1973): 43-52.

Grünhut, Max. *Penal Reform: A Comparative Study.* Oxford:
Clarendon Press, 1948.

Grusky, Oscar. "Organizational Goals and the Behavior of
Informal Leaders." *American Journal of Sociology* 65 (1959):
59-67.

Haft, Marilyn G., and Hermann, Michelle, eds. *Prisoners' Rights.*
Vols. 1 and 2. New York: Practicing Law Institute, 1972.

Hardesty, Don. *Kansas Correctional Officer Selection Study:
Final Report.* Topeka, Kansas: Consulting for Business,
Industry and Government, 1970.

————. *A One Year Personnel Study of the Correctional Officer
and His Work in the Kansas Penal System.* Topeka, Kansas:
Consulting for Business, Industry and Government, 1969.

Harris, Louis, and Associates. *Corrections 1968: A Climate for
Change.* Washington, D.C.: Joint Commission on Correctional
Manpower and Training, August 1968.

————. *The Public Looks at Crime and Corrections.* Washington, D.C.: Joint Commission on Correctional Manpower and
Training, February 1968.

Hart, H. L. A. *Punishment and Responsibility.* New York:
Oxford University Press, 1968.

Harvard Center for Criminal Justice. "Judicial Intervention in
Prison Discipline." *Journal of Criminal Law, Criminology
and Police Science* 63 (1972): 200-28.

Heinz, John P.; Gettleman, Robert W.; and Seeskin, Morris A.
"Legislative Politics and the Criminal Law." *Northwestern
University Law Review* 64 (1969): 277-358.

Hirschkop, Philip J., and Millemann, Michael A. "The Unconstitutionality of Prison Life." *Virginia Law Review* 55 (1969):
795-839.

Hobhouse, Stephen, and Brockway, A. Fenner. *English Prisons
Today.* London: Longmans Green & Co., 1922.

Hoover, J. Edgar. "Patriotism and the War Against Crime." An
address to the annual convention of the Daughters of the

American Revolution, Washington, D.C., April 23, 1936. Quoted in Sutherland and Cressey, 1970, p. 347.

Howard, John. *The State of the Prisons.* Everyman's Library Edition. London: J. M. Dent, 1929. First published in 1777.

Hyman, Herbert H., and Sheatsley, Paul B. "Attitudes Toward Desegregation." *Scientific American* 211 (1964), No. 1: 16–23.

Irwin, John. *The Felon.* Englewood Cliffs, N.J.: Prentice-Hall, 1970.

Irwin, John, and Cressey, Donald R. "Thieves, Convicts and the Inmate Culture." *Social Problems* 10 (1962): 142–55.

Jackson, Bruce. *A Thief's Primer: The Life and Times of an American Character, a Safe-Cracker and Check-Passer, "Who Makes His Living Completely Outside the Law But Has Some Principles About It."* Toronto: Collier-Macmillan Canada Ltd., 1969.

Jacob, Bruce R. "Prison Discipline and Inmate Rights." *Harvard Civil Rights—Civil Liberties Law Review* 5 (1970): 227–77.

Jacobs, James. "Street Gangs Behind Bars." *Social Problems* 21 (1974): 395–409.

———, and Retsky, Harold. "Prison Guard." *Urban Life* 4 (1975): 5–29.

Jebb, Sir Joshua. *Report of the Surveyor-General of Prisons on the Construction, Ventilation and Details of Pentonville Prison.* London: W. Clowes & Sons, 1844.

Joint Commission on Correctional Manpower and Training. *Offenders as a Correctional Manpower Resource.* Washington, D.C.: Joint Commission on Correctional Manpower and Training, 1968.

———. *Perspectives on Correctional Manpower and Training.* Staff Report. Washington, D.C.: Joint Commission on Correctional Manpower and Training, 1970.

———. *A Time to Act.* Washington, D.C.: Joint Commission on Correctional Manpower and Training, 1969.

Jordan, Samuel. "Prison Reform: In Whose Interest?" *Criminal Law Bulletin* 7 (1971): 779–87.

Kassebaum, Gene; Ward, David; and Wilner, Daniel. *Prison Treatment and Parole Survival: An Empirical Assessment.* New York: John Wiley & Sons, 1971, chapter 2, "Doing Time in a Pastel Prison."

Katz, Jay, et al. *Experimentation with Human Beings.* New York: Russell Sage Foundation, 1972.

Kimball, Edward L., and Newman, Donald J. "Judicial Inter-

vention in Correctional Decisions: Threat and Response."
Crime and Delinquency 14 (1968): 1-13.

Kirby, Bernard C. "Measuring Effects of Treatment of Criminals and Delinquents." *Sociology and Social Research* 38 (1954): 368-74.

Korn, Richard R., and McCorkle, Lloyd W. *Criminology and Penology.* New York: Holt, Rinehart & Winston, 1959.

Kropotkin, Peter. *In Russian and French Prisons.* London: Ward and Downey, 1887.

————. *Memoirs of a Revolutionist.* (1899) Boston and New York: Houghton Mifflin, 1930.

———— Paroles d'un révolte. 1885. Cited in Webb and Webb, 1922, p. 243.

Kutak, Robert J. "From the Outside Looking In: Grim Fairy Tales for Prison Administrators." In *Outside Looking In: A Series of Monographs Assessing the Effectiveness of Corrections.* Washington, D.C.: Law Enforcement Assistance Administration, 1970.

Leopold, Nathan F., Jr. *Life Plus 99 Years.* New York: Doubleday & Co., 1958.

Lerman, P. *Community Treatment and Social Control.* Crime and Justice Series. Chicago: University of Chicago Press, 1975.

Lewis, J. W., and Smith, G. Rand. "The Corrections Ombudsman: A Legislative Note on the Ohio Plan." *Capital University Law Review* 3 (1974): 77-104.

Lundberg, D. E. "Methods of Selecting Prison Personnel." *Journal of Criminal Law and Criminology* 38 (1947): 14-39.

McCleery, Richard. "Communication Patterns as Bases of Systems of Authority and Power." In Richard A. Cloward et al. *Theoretical Studies in Social Organization of the Prison.* Social Science Research Council, 1960.

McCorkle, Lloyd W., and Korn, Richard R. "Resocialization Within Walls." *Annals of the American Academy of Social and Political Science* 293 (1954): 88-98.

Maddison, J. C. "Justice in Corrections: The Dilemma." *A.N.Z. Journal of Criminology* 5 (1972): 5-14.

Maltz, Michael D. *Evaluation of Crime Control Programs.* Washington, D.C.: National Institute of Law Enforcement and Criminal Justice, 1972.

Mann, Floyd. "Studying and Creating Change." In Bennis, W.; Benne, K.; and Chin, R. *The Planning of Change.* New York: Holt, Rinehart and Winston, 1961.

Martin, John Bartlow. *Break Down the Walls.* New York: Ballantine Books, 1954.

Martinson, Robert. "What Works?: Questions and Answers about Prison Reform." *The Public Interest,* no. 35 (1974): 22-54.

Matthiesen, Thomas. *The Defences of the Weak.* London: Tavistock Publications, 1965.

Mattick, Hans W. *The Prosaic Sources of Prison Violence.* Occasional Paper Series. Chicago: University of Chicago Law School, 1972.

———. "Reflections of a Former Prison Warden." In James F. Short, ed., *Delinquency, Crime, and Society.* Chicago: University of Chicago Press, 1976.

———, and Sweet, Ronald P. *Illinois Jails: Challenge and Opportunity for the 1970's.* Chicago: Center for Studies in Criminal Justice, University of Chicago Law School, 1969, Appendix D, "The Pessimistic Hypothesis." See also Hans W. Mattick, "The Pessimistic Hypothesis and an Immodest Proposal." *Public Welfare* 31 (1973): 2-5.

Messinger, Sheldon. "Issues in the Study of the Social System of Prison Inmates." *Issues in Criminology* 4 (1969): 133-41.

Michigan Department of Corrections. *The Use of Correctional Trade Training.* Lansing: Michigan Department of Corrections, 1969.

Millemann, Michael A. "Prison Disciplinary Hearings and Procedural Due Process: The Requirement of a Full Administrative Hearing." *Maryland Law Review* 31 (1971): 27-59.

Miller, Neal, and Jeñsen, Walter, Jr. "Reform of Federal Prison Industries: New Opportunities for Public Offenders." *Justice System Journal* 1 (1974): 1-27.

Minogue, Kenneth R. *The Concept of a University.* Berkeley and Los Angeles: University of California Press, 1973.

Mitford, Jessica. "Experiments Behind Bars." *Atlantic Monthly,* January 1973, pp. 64-73.

———. *Kind and Usual Punishment: The Prison Business.* New York: Alfred A. Knopf, 1973.

Morris, Norval. *The Future of Imprisonment.* Chicago: University of Chicago Press, 1974.

———, and Hawkins, Gordon. *The Honest Politician's Guide to Crime Control.* Chicago: University of Chicago Press, 1970.

———, and Mills, Michael. "Prisoners as Laboratory Animals." *Society* 2, no. 5 (July-August 1974).

————, and Zimring, Franklin E. "Deterrence and Corrections." *Annals of the American Academy of Political and Social Science* 381 (1969): 137–46.

Morris, Terence, and Morris, Pauline. *Pentonville: A Sociological Study of an English Prison.* London: Routledge & Kegan Paul, 1963.

Motivans, J. "Occupational Socialization and Personality: A Study of the Prison Guard." *Proceedings of the American Correctional Association* (1963): 186–96.

Mueller, Gerhard O. W. "Punishment, Corrections and the Law." *Nebraska Law Review* 45 (1966): 58–98.

Nagel, William G. "An American Archipelago: The Federal Bureau of Prisons." Address to the National Institute on Crime and Delinquency, Boston, June 25, 1974.

————. *The New Red Barn: A Critical Look at the Modern American Prison.* New York: Walker, 1973.

National Advisory Commission on Criminal Justice Standards and Goals. *Task Force Report on Corrections.* Washington, D.C.: U.S. Government Printing Office, 1973.

National Council on Crime and Delinquency. *Model Act for the Protection of Rights of Prisoners.* Washington, D.C.: National Council on Crime and Delinquency, 1972.

————. *Standard Act for State Correctional Services.* Washington, D.C.: National Council on Crime and Delinquency, 1966.

National Institute of Law Enforcement and Criminal Justice. *The Role of Correctional Industries: A Summary Report.* Washington, D.C.: U.S. Government Printing Office, 1972.

National Probation and Parole Association. *Parole in Principle and Practice: A Manual and Report.* Edited by Marjorie Bell. N.Y.: National Probation and Parole Association, 1957.

Norman, Frank. *Bang to Rights.* London: Secker and Warburg, 1958.

O'Leary, Vincent, and Duffee, David. "Correctional Policy: A Classification of Goals Designed for Change." *Crime and Delinquency* 17 (1971): 373–86.

"The Ombudsman or Citizen's Defender: A Modern Institution." *Annals of the American Academy of Political and Social Science* 377 (1968). Roy V. Peel, special editor of this volume.

Osborne, Thomas Mott. *Prisons and Common Sense.* Philadelphia: J. B. Lippincott, 1924.

Oswald, Russel G. *Attica: My Story.* New York: Doubleday & Co., 1972.

Pacific Law Journal, Comment. "The Penal Ombudsman: Step Toward Penal Reform." *Pacific Law Journal* 3 (1972): 166-89.

Paterson, Sir Alexander. "Recruitment and Training of Prison Staff." In S. K. Ruck, ed. *Paterson on Prisons: Being the Collected Papers of Sir Alexander Paterson.* London: Frederick Muller Ltd., 1951.

Paul, Benjamin. "Social Science in Public Health." *American Journal of Public Health* 46 (1956): 1390-96.

Perdue, William C. "Screening of Applicants for Custodial Work by Means of a Temperament Test." *American Journal of Corrections* 26 (1964): 14-19.

————. "The Temperaments of Custodial Workers." *American Journal of Corrections* 28, no. 2 (March-April 1966): 16-19.

Playfair, Giles, and Sington, Derrick. *Crime, Punishment and Cure.* London: Secker and Warburg, 1965.

Popper, Karl. *The Poverty of Historicism.* 2d ed. London: Routledge and Kegan Paul, 1960.

Pound, Roscoe. *Criminal Justice in America.* New York: Henry Holt & Co., 1930.

President's Commission on Law Enforcement and Administration of Justice. *Task Force Report: Corrections.* Washington, D.C.: U.S. Government Printing Office, 1967.

President's Task Force on Prisoner Rehabilitation. *The Criminal Offender: What Should Be Done.* Washington, D.C.: U.S. Government Printing Office, 1970.

Prison Officers' Association. "The Role of the Modern Prison Officer." *Prison Officers' Magazine,* November 1963, pp. 1-3.

Quality of Health Care: Human Experimentation. Hearings before the Subcommittee on Health of the U.S. Senate Committee on Labor and Public Welfare, 93d Cong., 1st Sess. (1973).

Ranulf, Svend. *Moral Indignation and Middle Class Psychology.* Copenhagen: Levin and Munksgaard, 1938.

Reckless, Walter C. "Training of the Correctional Worker." In Paul W. Tappan, ed. *Contemporary Correction.* New York: McGraw Hill, 1951.

Reimer, Hans. "Socialization in the Prison Community." *Proceedings of the Sixty-Seventh Annual Congress of the American Prison Association* (1937): 151-55.

Renton, A. Wood. Review of Havelock Ellis's *The Criminal. Law Quarterly Review* 6 (1890): 338-39.

Robinson, Louis. *Should Prisoners Work? A Study of the Prison*

Labor Problem in the United States. Philadelphia: John C. Winston, 1931.

Roebuck, Julian. "A Critique of 'Thieves, Convicts and the Inmate Culture'." *Social Problems* 11 (1963-64): 193-200. See Irwin and Cressey.

Rothman, David J. *The Discovery of the Asylum.* Boston and Toronto: Little, Brown, 1971.

Roucek, Joseph. "Sociology of the Prison Guard." *Sociology and Social Research* 20 (1935): 145-51.

Ruck, S. K., ed. *Paterson on Prisons: Being the Collected Papers of Sir Alexander Paterson.* London: Frederick Muller Ltd., 1951.

Ruggles-Brise, Evelyn. *The English Prison System.* London: Macmillan, 1921.

Schrag, Clarence. "Some Foundations for a Theory of Correction." In Donald R. Cressey, ed. *The Prison: Studies in Institutional Organization and Change.* New York: Holt, Rinehart & Winston, 1961.

Schumpeter, Joseph. *History of Economic Analysis.* New York: Oxford University Press, 1954, pp. 34-43.

Schwartz, Barry. "Pre-Institutional vs. Situational Influence in a Correctional Community." *Journal of Criminal Law, Criminology and Police Science* 62 (1971): 532-42.

Schwartz, Herman. "Attica: A Look at the Causes and the Future." *Criminal Law Bulletin* 7 (1971): 819-24.

———. "Prisoners' Rights: Some Hopes and Realities." In *A Program for Prison Reform: Final Report of the Annual Chief Justice Earl Warren Conference on Advocacy in the United States.* Cambridge, Mass.: The Roscoe Pound-American Trial Lawyers Foundation, 1972.

Sellin, Thorsten. Foreword. *Annals of the American Academy of Political and Social Science* 293 (1954): vii.

———. "Historical Glimpses of Training for Prison Service." *Journal of Criminal Law and Criminology* 25 (1934): 594-600.

———. "A Look at Prison History." *Federal Probation* 31 no. 3 (September 1967): 18-23.

Shaw, George Bernard. *The Crime of Imprisonment.* New York: Philosophical Library, 1946.

———. "Maxims for Revolutionists." In *Man and Superman: A Comedy and a Philosophy.* Westminster: A. Constable, 1903, pp. 225-44.

Sherry, Arthur H. "The Politics of Criminal Law Reform: The

United States." *American Journal of Comparative Law* 21 (1973): 201-29.

Singer, Linda R. "Attica: A Look at the Causes and the Future." *Criminal Law Bulletin* 7 (1971): 838-43.

————, and Keating, J. Michael. "The Courts and Prisons: A Crisis of Confrontation." *Criminal Law Bulletin* 9 (1973): 337-57.

Singer, Neil M. "Incentives and the Use of Prison Labor." *Crime and Delinquency* 19 (1973a): 200-11.

————. *The Value of Adult Inmate Manpower.* Correctional Economic Analysis Series. Washington, D.C.: American Bar Association Commission on Correctional Facilities and Services, 1973b.

Skoler, Daniel L. "Correctional Measures and Institutions." In American Bar Association Commission on a National Institute of Justice. *Quest for Justice.* Washington, D. C.: American Bar Association, 1973.

Stone, Brenda. "Malaria Tests Vital, 'But Just Not for Prisons'." *Chicago Tribune,* June 9, 1974.

Street, David. "The Inmate Group in Custodial and Treatment Settings." *American Sociological Review* 30 (1965): 40-55.

————; Vinter, Robert D.; and Perrow, Charles. *Organization for Treatment: A Comparative Study of Institutions for Delinquents.* New York: The Free Press, 1966.

Suchman, Edward A. *Evaluative Research.* New York: Russell Sage Foundation, 1967.

Sullivan, Clyde E., and Mandell, Wallace. *Restoration of Youth Through Training.* Staten Island, New York: Wakoff Research Center, 1967.

Sutherland, Edwin H., and Cressey, Donald R. *Principles of Criminology.* 5th ed. Philadelphia: J. B. Lippincott, 1955.

————. *Criminology.* 8th ed. Philadelphia: J. B. Lippincott, 1970.

Sykes, Gresham M. *Crime and Society.* New York: Random House, 1956.

————. *The Society of Captives.* Princeton, N.J.: Princeton University Press, 1958.

————, and Messinger, Sheldon L. "The Inmate Social System." In Richard A. Cloward et al. *Theoretical Studies in Social Organization of the Prison.* New York: Social Science Research Council, 1960.

Tannenbaum, Frank. *Wall Shadows: A Study in American Prisons.* New York: G. P. Putnam's Sons, 1922.

Tappan, Paul W. *Crime, Justice and Correction.* New York: McGraw Hill, 1960.

Thomas, J. E. *The English Prison Officer Since 1850: A Study in Conflict.* London and Boston: Routledge and Kegan Paul, 1972.

————. "Training Schemes for Prison Staff." *A.N.Z. Journal of Criminology* 5 (1972): 199-205.

Tibbles, Lance. "The Ombudsman: Who Needs Him?" *Journal of Urban Law* 47 (1969): 1-67.

————. "Ombudsmen for American Prisons." *North Dakota Law Review* 48 (1972): 383-441.

Tittle, Charles. "Inmate Organization: Sex Differentiation and the Influence of Criminal Subcultures." *American Sociological Review* 34 (1969): 492-505.

————, and Tittle, Drollene. "Social Organization of Prisoners: An Empirical Test." *Social Forces* 43 (1964): 216-21.

Turner, William Bennett. "Establishing the Rule of Law in Prisons." *Stanford Law Review* 23 (1971): 473-518.

————, and Daniel, Alice. "*Miranda* in Prison: The Dilemma of Prison Discipline and Intramural Crime." *Buffalo Law Review* 21 (1972): 759-73.

United Nations Department of Economic and Social Affairs. *Prison Labour.* New York: United Nations, 1955.

————. "Standard Minimum Rules for the Treatment of Prisoners." In *First United Nations Congress on the Prevention of Crime and the Treatment of Offenders, Geneva, 22 August-3 September 1955.* New York: United Nations, 1956.

UCLA Program in Corrections Law. "Judicial Intervention in Corrections: The California Experience—An Empirical Study." *UCLA Law Review* 20 (1973): 452-580.

University of Pennsylvania Law Review, Comment. "Constitutional Rights of Prisoners: The Developing Law." *University of Pennsylvania Law Review* 110 (1962): 985-1008.

Vanderbilt Law Review, Note. "Special Project: The Collateral Consequences of a Criminal Conviction." *Vanderbilt Law Review* 23 (1970): 929-1241.

Virginia Law Review, Note. "Civil Disabilities of Felons." *Virginia Law Review* 53 (1967): 403-23.

Vold, George B. *Theoretical Criminology.* New York: Oxford University Press, 1958.

Vorenberg, J. "The War on Crime: The First Five Years." *Atlantic Monthly,* May 1972, pp. 63-69.

Wallack, Walter M. "Some Suggestions for Basic Reforms in Prison Industries for Improved Production and Vocational Training." In *Proceedings of the Seventy-Seventh Annual Congress of Correction of the American Prison Association [American Correctional Association], Long Beach, California, September 12-16, 1947*. New York: American Prison Association [American Correctional Association], 1947.

"War at Attica." *Time*, September 27, 1971.

Webb, Sydney, and Webb, Beatrice. *English Prisons Under Local Government*. London: Longmans Green, 1922.

Wellford, Charles. "Factors Associated with Adoption of the Inmate Code: A Study of Normative Socialization." *Journal of Criminal Law, Criminology and Police Science* 58 (1967): 197-203.

West, Jude P., and Stratton, John R., eds. *The Role of Correctional Industries*. Iowa City: Center for Labor and Management, College of Business Administration, University of Iowa, 1971.

Wheeler, Stanton. "Legal Justice and Mental Health in the Care and Treatment of Deviants." In Morton Levitt and Ben Rubenstein, eds. *Orthopsychiatry and the Law*. Detroit: Wayne State University Press, 1968.

———. "Role Conflict in Correctional Communities." In Donald R. Cressey, ed. *The Prison: Studies in Institutional Organization and Change*. New York: Holt, Rinehart & Winston, 1961.

———. "Socialization in Correctional Communities." *American Sociological Review* 26 (1961): 697-712.

Wickersham Commission. *Report on Penal Institutions, Probation and Parole*. Washington, D.C.: U.S. Government Printing Office, 1931.

Wilkins, Leslie T. "Directions for Corrections." *Proceedings of the American Philosophical Society* 118 (1974): 235-47.

———. *Evaluation of Penal Measures*. New York: Random House, 1969.

Willcock, H. D., and Stokes, J. *Deterrents and Incentives to Crime among Youths Ages 15-21*. London: H. M. Stationery Office, 1968.

Wilson, John M., and Snodgrass, Jon D. "The Prison Code in a Therapeutic Community." *Journal of Criminal Law, Criminology and Police Science* 60 (1969): 472-78.

Wittgenstein, Ludwig. *Lectures and Conversations on Aesthetics, Psychology and Religious Belief*. Edited by C. Barrett. Berkeley: University of California Press, 1966.

Woodcock, George. *The Anarchist Prince*. London and New York: T. V. Boardman, 1950.

Yale Law Journal, Note. "Beyond the Ken of the Courts: A Critique of Judicial Refusal to Review the Complaints of Convicts." *Yale Law Journal* 72 (1963): 506–58.

Zimring, Franklin E., and Hawkins, Gordon. *Deterrence: The Legal Threat in Crime Control*. Studies in Crime and Justice. Chicago: University of Chicago Press, 1973.

INDEX

Abolitionism, 5–12, 15, 36; avoidance by, of remedial measures, 11; contrasted with reductivism, 27; criticism of, 11, 15, 34, 54; mischaracterized as reformism, 6–7; obstacles to, 39–40; penologists' view of, 11; practical implications of, 10, 12; prospects for, 30, 44, 45, 52–54; relativity of, 39; similarity to rigorism, 15; supported by reformists, 39, 44. *See also* Criticism of prisons; Necessity of prisons; Social reorganization, as requisite to prison abolition

Abt Associates, 117

Abuse of power, 52, 55, 82, 135, 138, 153, 154, 161. *See also* Staff of prisons, guards

Administrators of prisons, 14, 16, 18, 19, 26, 28, 29, 31, 37, 42, 43, 50, 51, 76, 77, 79, 83–87, 91, 96, 97, 99, 101, 104, 106, 110, 112, 115, 120, 125, 128, 135, 139, 142–44, 146–50, 161, 165–67, 169, 178, 180, 185; agreement of, with outside observers, 18, 51, 112; corruption among, 49; criticism of, by guards, 82; discretion of, 133–37, 139–41, 153, 154; hypocrisy of, 18–19. *See also* Staff of prisons

Alternatives to prisons, 38, 40, 45, 51. *See also* Noninstitutional corrections

American Bar Association, 134, 165

American Correctional Association, 42, 102, 134

American Friends Service Committee, 10, 14, 18, 19, 24–26, 54, 76; as example of reductivism, 21–29; criticism of, 19, 28

Annual Report of the Commissioners of Prisons and Directors of Convict Prisons 1911-12, 13–14

Arbon v. Anderson, 143

Argot of prisoners, 62, 81. *See also*